The Telephone Patent Conspiracy of 1876

The Telephone Patent Conspiracy of 1876

The Elisha Gray–Alexander Bell Controversy and Its Many Players

by A. Edward Evenson

McFarland & Company, Inc., Publishers
Jefferson, North Carolina, and London

Library of Congress Cataloguing-in-Publication Data

Evenson, A. Edward 1928–
The telephone patent conspiracy of 1876: the Elisha Gray–Alexander Bell controversy and its many players / by A. Edward Evenson.
p. cm.
Includes bibliographical references and index.
ISBN 0-7864-0883-9 (softcover : 50# alkaline paper) ∞
1. Bell, Alexander Graham, 1847–1922. 2. Gray, Elisha, 1835–1901. 3. Telephone—United States. 4. Telephone—Patents. I. Title.
TK6018.B4 E94 2001
384.6'0973—dc21 00-48979

British Library Cataloguing data are available

Front cover: Elisha Gray *(left)* and Alexander Graham Bell
Back cover: Early telephone. *All images © 2000 Art Today*

Manufactured in the United States of America

McFarland & Company, Inc., Publishers
Box 611, Jefferson, North Carolina 28640
www.mcfarlandpub.com

To my wife, Barbara,
for her unwavering support and help

Acknowledgments

Those who choose to write on historical topics are dependent on so many people that there is always the risk of overlooking the help of a valuable contributor. Among the many who have helped me so much on this project, I wish to thank Stephen Mican, intellectual property attorney, for his valuable comments and insight on patent matters and procedures; Ellsworth Mills, managing director of the Highland Park Historical Society, and his staff, for making available their files on Elisha Gray; Elliot Sivowitch, museum specialist for the National Museum of American History (Smithsonian Institution, Washington, D.C.), for his unique knowledge of early telephone history, and to the staff of the Archive Center of that same institution for their help with the museum's Elisha Gray collection.

In addition, I wish to thank Arlene Sergot of the Rolling Meadows Public Library for her never-failing ability to track down and obtain the most obscure of out-of-print reference books. Among the various other libraries and repositories involved were the Center for Research Libraries of Chicago, Illinois; the National Archive Center of Suitland, Maryland; and the Reading Room of the Library of Congress, where my wife and I spent many days exploring the extensive collection of Alexander Bell letters and documents. All of the reproduced Bell letters are from this source.

Contents

Prologue

Monday morning, February 14, 1876, began with a light, easterly breeze that brought just enough rain to dampen the alphanumeric streets of Washington, D.C. The temperature had already pushed past an unseasonable 55 degrees, suggesting that spring might not be too far behind. Nevertheless, historians would later describe this otherwise pleasant morning as "stormy and threatening," a portent of the fateful events to follow.

It was Valentine's Day, and a tall, bearded young man, an envelope clutched firmly in his hand, hurried along F Street towards 8th Street. This was the day to deliver envelopes, but this one contained no crimson heart nor sugary sentiment. It held instead a caveat, a confidential document being hand delivered to the United States Patent Office.

A caveat was a prelude to a patent application. It was a formal notice to the Patent Office that an invention was being worked on, but one that was not quite ready for a patent application. Its purpose was to establish priority of conception, a point of paramount importance should a conflicting patent application also be filed, known in Patent Office terminology as an *interference*. Until discontinued by the Patent Act of 1909, the caveat system was a popular and affordable way for inventors to lock in their inventions. Nearly a third of the documents received at the Patent Office were caveats. According to patent law, a caveat had the same rights and was treated in the same confidential manner as a regular patent application. It contained privileged information known only to the inventor, his attorney, and the patent examiner.

As he approached the 8th Street entrance to the Patent Office, 40-year-old Elisha Gray reflected—dreamed, perhaps—on the possibilities of his caveat. He knew that it contained the seed of a great idea, but like Jack and his beanstalk, he had no clue as to how that seed would grow. Little did he know that its fruit would soon spark a decade of bitter patent battles, that it would challenge the integrity of the U.S. Patent Office, that it would be embroiled in a full-scale congressional investigation, and that it would ultimately lead to a Supreme Court decision. Who would have believed that so much could fit into one small envelope?

Gray was no stranger to the Patent Office. In the past year alone he had received no fewer than seven patents. As the former chief engineer and now board member of the recently reorganized Western Electric Manufacturing Company, invention was his business.

He entered the imposing Greek revival structure with its towering Doric columns and went directly to the Department of Electricity. After receiving the $10 registration fee, the clerk accepted Gray's caveat, tossed it in the in basket, and handed him the usual receipt. It was not Patent Office practice to record the time of day of a filing—a fact that would forever haunt Gray and that would forever change the course of history. From here his caveat would wend its way through the normal office channels and arrive sometime the next day in Room 118, at the desk of the principal patent examiner, the government official in charge of evaluating all telegraph-related inventions.

And so the design for what many have claimed to be the first working telephone was officially registered at the U.S. Patent Office. It bore the title "Instruments for Transmitting and Receiving Vocal Sounds." Although the now-common term *telephone* was yet to come, the illustration in Gray's caveat, of two people conversing through an electrical device, left little doubt as to what he was intending to patent. The opening paragraph claimed:

> It is the object of my invention to transmit the tones of the human voice through a telegraphic circuit, and reproduce them at the receiving end of the line, so that actual conversations can be carried on by persons at long distances apart.

Shortly before noon on that same Valentine's Day, by a strange coincidence, a patent application for a multiple-message telegraph device was also filed in the Department of Electricity. It, too, claimed, among other things, to transmit "vocal or other sounds." Curiously, the person filing the application made a most unusual and unorthodox request. He insisted, over the objections of the clerk, that it bypass the normal office channels and be hand delivered immediately to the principal patent examiner in Room 118. There was something about the man's manner and bearing—

perhaps he was a retired army officer—that said he expected his orders to be obeyed. Rather than argue, the clerk picked up the application, made a notation in the daily log, and headed for Room 118. That application, signed by 28-year-old Alexander Graham Bell, was now on a collision course with Elisha Gray's caveat.

The stage was set for the greatest patent drama in the history of technology. From that fateful Valentine's Day in 1876, it would take ten litigious years for the full story to unfold—in particular, for two extraordinary documents to materialize. One, a sworn affidavit by a former government official, would detail acts of bribery and conspiracy in the Patent Office; the other would lead to charges of patent fraud.

Before that turbulent decade ended, however, a subtle yet significant change had taken place. The principal player, the American Bell Telephone Company, was no longer the cash-poor, debt-ridden, start-up fighting to keep its only true asset—a vague but valuable patent. It was now a prosperous, nationwide-expanding industry determined to preserve its patent-based monopoly against all comers and at all costs. And preserve it the Bell company did. Through a dozen court battles, it never lost a case; all that challenged the Bell patent failed in their attempt. So broadly did the courts interpret the Bell patent that everyone else was prohibited, under threat of patent infringement, from manufacturing any telephone that utilized electricity. Not surprisingly, manufacturers of non-electric—or "string-type"—telephones enjoyed a limited but profitable market making commercial versions of that popular children's toy.

ELISHA GRAY'S LIFE IS OVER

Inventor of the Telephone Dies Suddenly of Heart Trouble

WAS SIXTY-FIVE YEARS OLD

Newton, Mass., Jan. 21.—Professor Elisha Gray, the inventor of the telephone, died suddenly in Newtonville shortly after midnight.

Mr. Gray was walking in Walnut street

Until the end of the nineteenth century, and despite the American Bell Telephone Company's court victories, the vast majority of the people, as well as the press, believed that Elisha Gray was the true inventor of the telephone. Although the courts repeatedly sustained Bell's patent claims, the public was convinced that this was somehow a legal technicality to perpetuate the unpopular Bell Company and its monopolistic pricing. Reinforcing the public's jaundiced view were revelations that more than one judge involved in those court cases had a financial interest in the Bell company. However, all this changed with Gray's passing, just as the twentieth century began to unfold.

Shortly before his death on January 21, 1901, Elisha Gray had completed a three-volume work on science entitled *Nature's Miracles*. On a scrap of paper tucked away among his writings was found the following note:

> The history of the telephone will never be fully written. It is partly hidden away in 20 or 30 thousand pages of testimony and partly lying on the hearts and consciences of a few whose lips are Sealed—Some in death and others by a golden clasp whose grip is even tighter [From private collection of Lloyd W. Taylor, former professor of physics, Oberlin College].

Gray's obituary in the *Scientific American* for February 2, 1901, page 72, said: "He was a man of marvelous talent and ingenuity, and in the opinion of many who have calmly weighed all the evidence, it is likely that he will receive justice at the hands of future historians by being immortalized as the inventor of the speaking telephone."

The question of who deserves credit for inventing the telephone is no longer the acrimonious subject it once was, and the former voices of dissent have been muted by a century of popular history. Yet the question remains. Historians never did immortalize Gray as "the inventor of the speaking telephone." But then, neither did they venture to explore the more fascinating parts of this story—the sometimes tortuous and darker passages. What follows is a chronicle of the telephone's birth from another perspective.

Chapter 1

Profiles

Alexander Graham Bell and Elisha Gray

The little Skye terrier had no idea what he was saying. Yet, when prompted, he would solicitously inquire: "How are you, Grandmama?" Well, almost—if you listened with a noncritical ear and used your imagination. Like most talking dogs, he needed a lot of assistance, which a young Alexander Bell provided by carefully manipulating the dog's throat as it let out a little growl.[1] But making a dog talk was just a playful diversion for the son of a speech teacher. Little did he know that a decade later he would make a piece of iron talk.

Alexander Graham Bell, the second of three sons of the illustrious Alexander Melville Bell, was born in Edinburgh, Scotland, on March 3, 1847. His father, a well-known authority in the correction of speech disorders, particularly stammering, specialized in teaching the deaf to speak. This latter area would bring Melville Bell considerable fame not only in Great Britain, but in Europe and America as well. Alexander's mother, Eliza Bell, who lost her hearing later in life, was some ten years older than her husband. She was well-educated and an accomplished artist and musician.[2] No doubt, Alexander inherited his musical talent from his mother. Although his mother gradually lost her hearing over time, Alexander would marry a woman who had been deaf since the age of five. Deafness was quite prevalent in the nineteenth century, particularly among children, much of it the result of scarlet fever and other infectious diseases. The affliction was common enough to support dedicated newspapers, such as the Washington, D.C., biweekly, *Silent World*.

Alexander's two brothers, Melly (Melville James) and Ted (Edward Charles), died of tuberculosis, first Ted at 18 and then Melly at 25. Tuberculosis, or the "white plague" as it was sometimes called, was another relatively common disease. It was not then accepted that it was caused by a germ, or even that it was contagious, being generally blamed on a bad climate, the consequences of "the night air," or even heredity. Melville Bell, fearful that Alexander might succumb to the same peril, concluded that perhaps England was not the best environment for his remaining son, a conclusion reinforced when he was told by a local doctor that Alexander seemed prone to the same disease.

Earlier, in 1868, Alexander's father had made a trip to Canada and the United States for a series of lectures promoting his recently announced Visible Speech method. Remembering the pristine country and its bracing climate, he concluded that either Canada or America would be an ideal place for Alexander. He even went so far as to look towards his son's employment opportunities, and, on this visit, laid the groundwork for a possible future teaching position for Alexander. The father's decision to emigrate fell close upon Melly's death on May 28, 1870. On July 21, 1870, Melville and Eliza Bell, along with Alexander and Melly's widow, Carrie, sailed for Canada.[3]

Alexander Bell's Early Years

Alexander grew up in a world of speech therapy, elocution, and profound dedication to helping the deaf learn to speak. Alexander's paternal grandfather, the first Alexander Bell, was a well-known London actor and, in a small way, a successful playwright. In addition to his theatrical work, he ran a small school specializing in elocution and the correction of such defects as stammering, and he was a highly respected teacher of speech. He also achieved a measure of fame with several publications: *The Practical Elocutionist* and *Stammering, and Other Impediments of Speech*.

Young Alexander spent a year in London with his grandfather, a period that he later said transformed him from a boy to a man. During this time, he discovered that people who had achieved a certain level of recognition, as had his father and grandfather, enjoyed a satisfying measure of prestige and respect. He learned from his grandfather, who saw to his social and intellectual development, the importance of being important.

Throughout his early life, Alexander's whole environment, under the influence of his father and grandfather, centered around the concept of speech—studying it, analyzing it, correcting it, and teaching it. Under the tutelage of his father, he mastered the art of impressive speech, a skill that would later set him apart from less articulate men. It was a skill that would lend an aura of conviction and authority to his statements. Later, these oratorical talents would benefit him during his telephone promotion tours in late 1876 and early 1877 and then during his depositions and court testimony sessions.

His exceptional speaking ability along with his command of the language made Alexander seem older than he really was. In addition, his experience working professionally as a speech teacher while still in his late teens gave him a sophistication beyond his years. Even as early as 16, he had a job as a pupil-teacher of elocution and music.[4] Because he began teaching at such an early age, he cultivated a veneer of maturity to mask his youth. Years later, when he first expressed a romantic interest in his 17-year-old wife-to-be, her parents became quite alarmed; they had assumed that he was considerably older than he was. Actually, they were only ten years apart.

Although largely home taught by their mother during their early years, Alexander and his brothers did receive formal training at James Maclaren's Hamilton Place Academy and at the Royal High School, for a total of perhaps five years. He was only 13 when he graduated from high school. Typical of that era, his schooling was along classical lines. Bell's biographers are a little uncertain as to the extent of his higher education, but he did spend a year at the University of Edinburgh. Later, while living in London, he attended University College for at least a year and probably longer, studying anatomy and physiology.[5]

Figure 1-1. Alexander Graham Bell, c. 1876. From Library of Congress, Bell Family Collection.

Just how much formal training Bell had in electricity is unknown, but it was probably slight at best. Given his academic background, there is no doubt that he would have been exposed to basic electrical concepts. However, in the 1860s, the academic treatment of electricity was minimal. Most of the textbooks of that era that dealt with electricity focused largely on static electricity, which was virtually useless for any practical application. In a typical 400-page volume of natural philosophy (physics), perhaps no more than a scant ten pages would be devoted to the emerging science of voltaic electricity and electromagnetism. Even this treatment consisted of little more than laboratory demonstrations. The only practical application of electricity at this time (1850–1860) was in the field of telegraphy, which embraced burglar and fire alarms, and in the emerging art of electrometallurgy, or electroplating, as we call it now. All of the electricity of that era came from batteries; generators and dynamos were yet to come.

We do know that early in 1875, when he discussed his voice-transmitting ideas with Joseph Henry, the aging director of the Smithsonian Institution, Bell complained that he lacked the electrical knowledge needed to develop those ideas. Henry's quick and brusque reply made a deep impression on Bell and no doubt inspired a course of self-instruction in electricity. In a letter to his parents describing his meeting with Henry, he wrote:

> I felt so much encouraged by his interest, that I determined to ask his advice about the apparatus I have designed [the multireed harp receiver] for the transmission of the human voice by telegraph. I explained the idea and said "What would you advise me to do—publish it and let others work it out—or attempt to solve the problem myself."
>
> He said he thought it was "the germ of a great invention" and advised me to work at it myself instead of publishing.
>
> I said that I recognized the fact that there were mechanical difficulties in the way that rendered the plan impractical at the present time. I added that I felt that I had not the electrical knowledge necessary to overcome the difficulties. His laconic answer was "Get it!" I cannot tell you how much those two words have encouraged me.[6]

Henry, remembering the invaluable assistance he had rendered to Samuel Morse during the early development of the telegraph, for which he received little in return, had bitter memories of letting "others work it out." It's no wonder he advised Bell to work at it himself. Just how much Henry was impressed by Bell's multireed device for voice transmission we don't know; it was a concept that never materialized. However, we should point out that the idea of transmitting the human voice by electricity was not original with Bell. A number of inquisitive minds, some of whom we will meet later, had been pondering that same thought.

The ancient adages "The acorn never falls far from the tree" and "Like father, like son" define Alexander's relationship to his father. The achievements and attitudes of his father and grandfather molded young Alexander's future plans. Alexander and his father had a close relationship because of their common interest in the physiology of speech. Before he was 20, Alexander was already his father's full-time professional associate. His father's only wish was for Alexander to establish himself as a teacher of speech, perhaps at some university, and carry on the family tradition of promoting Visible Speech. But the family tradition that young Bell wanted to follow was to achieve his own measure of fame, or at least some ration of recognition. More than anything, he wanted to escape from the shadow of his famous father and make a name for himself in his own right; he did not want to be known forever simply as Melville Bell's son. But it would not be an easy task. To understand better this challenge, we must look briefly at the accomplishments of the father.

Alexander's Father

Alexander Melville Bell had also been influenced by his father and had followed in the latter's footsteps. Melville Bell, too, specialized in the teaching of elocution and the correction of speech defects. His primary interest, though, was in teaching the deaf to speak, especially those who had been deaf since birth or from an early age. This was a formidable task, since how does one teach someone to speak, especially a child, who has never heard or who does not remember actual speech? Few in the field of speech therapy had ever attempted such a challenge. Sign language, in the opinion of the experts of the day, was the only viable option available.

However, after many years of study, Melville Bell conceived of a method he labeled Visible Speech, a system of symbols that depicted which parts of a person's voice-producing organs were used to create the various vowel and consonant sounds. Visible Speech would make him famous. It was a complex system, in essence a symbolic language, and its mastery required considerable work and dedication. It was not a system for everyone. But for those with the intelligence and determination to master it, it worked.[7] As a demonstration, Melville Bell would have someone speak a sentence in some foreign language, which would be recorded in the symbolic format of Visible Speech. Alexander, who had not heard the original speaker, would look at the symbols and then repeat the original sentence almost exactly as it had been spoken, even though he knew nothing of the original language. It was a very impressive demonstration.[8]

Even apart from his highly regarded work on Visible Speech, Melville Bell's literary output alone would have secured for him a respected position as an authority on elocution and speech training. Although the first book describing Visible Speech, *The Science of Universal Alphabetics*, didn't appear until 1867, he had been publishing for many years. In 1849 his *A New Elucidation of the Principles of Speech and Elocution* was published in Edinburgh. In 1852 he came out with *Steno-Phonography,* a system of sound writing, or shorthand, as we now call it. This was followed in 1858 with *Letters and Sound*, in 1860 with *The Standard Elocutionist*, in 1863 with *Principles of Speech* and *Dictionary Sounds* and, in 1867, with the abovementioned work of Visible Speech. He went on to write another half dozen books before he died in 1905.[9] Melville Bell achieved fame and professional recognition through his system of Visible Speech on an international scale, particularly in the United States and Canada.[10]

Clearly, young Alexander Graham Bell had some impressive footsteps to follow—those from a well-known grandfather as well as those from an even better known father. However, there was no apparent pressure from his father for him to go out and make a name for himself. If anything, the father was both devoted and indulgent towards the son. Shortly after the family moved to Brantford, Canada, Alexander decided to break away from rural Canadian life and seek his calling in a more academic environment. In April 1871, he visited Boston to deliver a series of lectures. Apparently, the city met his cultural needs, and in October 1872 he chose Boston as his permanent residence. Its various universities and other cultural benefits were well-suited to his plans.[11]

Alexander Bell, Teacher

The plan was for Alexander to work with one of the schools for the deaf and to take on some private pupils for extra income. Perhaps he could even secure a teaching position, specializing in speech therapy, at one of the universities. Alexander was expected to pay his own way as he sought to establish himself. But to relieve him of the stress of finding immediate and profitable employment, his father provided him with a $1,000 nest egg—just in case. Considering that a Boston school teacher at the time earned no more than $800 a year, Bell's nest egg was quite generous. He wasn't supposed to tap into it except in the most dire emergency, and then only frugally. Sometime later, suspecting that Alexander might have been borrowing from his nest egg to further his experiments in multiple telegraphy, a subject that had been absorbing much of his time, his father wrote to ask:

> you told me ... that the $1,000 with which you started in Boston was still intact ... but I fear from the tenor of your last letter, that you no longer possess this nestegg! Is it so?[12]

Bell's father, in paternal fashion, worried that Alexander was spending too much time, and possibly too much money, on nonprofessional pursuits, such as his telegraph studies. He feared that his son was subordinating his true calling. In short, he didn't think Alexander was attending to business. The father had no objection to his son's electrical experiments, but they should be placed in proper perspective and indulged in only when other duties permitted. Melville Bell still held to his wish that his son would establish himself as a teacher of speech at some university and continue promoting the family business of Visible Speech.

Although Alexander would have been happy to achieve such a position, he dreamed of much more. In a short time he would meet the two men in America, perhaps the only two, Gardiner Greene Hubbard and Thomas Sanders, who could make those dreams come true.[13] Although initially unknown to each other, these two men shared a common bond: they each had a child who suffered total hearing loss. Georgie Sanders was the deaf-since-birth son of Thomas Sanders and was one of Bell's first private students. Mabel Hubbard, also a Bell pupil, had been deaf since the age of five.[14] These three men, Bell, Hubbard, and Sanders, would soon form a pact (the Bell Patent Association) that would eventually evolve into one of the world's largest corporations.

Bell's involvement in the business that bore his name was relatively brief, spanning less than five years. Yet the financial rewards he received from it allowed him to enjoy a long life of scientific inquiry in many fields. His mind never took a holiday. Even as he waited to testify in one of the telephone trials, he wrote to his wife of a new idea that had just occurred to him:

> Another idea which is of more practical value is a new method of deep sea sounding ... a *submarine* Fog-horn.... There must be *echoes* in water as well as in air ... and if a sound were made in the water a short distance from the surface—the sound would travel to the bottom—be reflected up—and reach the submerged ear (or apparatus) after a longer or shorter time as an *echo*.... The computation of the depth would be easy once the velocity of sound in water is known.[15]

Bell spent more years investigating the mysteries of powered flight, among many other interests, than he did in his work with the telephone, yet few associate his name with early aviation. Like Elisha Gray, Bell enjoyed a long and productive life. He died at his summer home in Nova Scotia on August 2, 1922.[16]

Elisha Gray

Elisha Gray was born on August 2, 1835, on a farm just outside of Barnesville, Ohio, the son of Quakers David and Christina Gray.[17] Little is known of his early childhood, except that he seemed destined to a life of creating and building things, particularly things of a technical nature. Given his natural proclivities, it was perhaps inevitable that he would become an engineer, although he certainly hadn't planned on it. As far back as he could remember he had been building things.

He was probably no more than ten or eleven when he built a working model of a telegraph station, an invention not much older than he was. Through boyish persuasion he got the local blacksmith to forge the U-shaped iron core for the electromagnets. The insulated wire needed for the windings was unavailable, so he made his own from brass wire laboriously hand wrapped with linen tape. From discarded candy jars he fashioned the necessary wet-cell batteries. In the end, mostly through ingenuity and improvisation, he had created a fully functional telegraph—and an engineer was born.[18]

In Barnesville, Elisha received his elementary education until the death of his father. He was only 12 at the time and, in the hope of learning a trade by which to support himself, he became a blacksmith's apprentice. Although he learned the trade of blacksmithing, the rigors of the profession were too much for him, and he was forced to find other employment. He turned to boat building, and after a three-and-a-half-year apprenticeship learned the trade of ship joiner. The skills he acquired in these trades were to serve him well in the years to come.

Elisha soon realized, however, that he would need more than just manual skills to do the things he truly wanted to do. While serving his apprenticeship as a ship joiner he became friends with a student from Oberlin College, H. S. Bennett (later a professor at Fisk University), who told him of the exceptional educational opportunities available at that institution. Bennett told Elisha that he would be allowed to work his way through college, a rather novel concept in those days.[19] As soon as he finished his apprenticeship, Elisha began, at the age of 22, a five-year program of preparatory school and college, concentrating on the physical sciences, especially electricity. During this period he supported himself through carpentry jobs and the making of specialized laboratory equipment for the science departments. The experience gained in this last area would mold his career for the rest of his life, although at the time he was not aware of it.

The work load he carried at Oberlin, both physically and academically, overtaxed Elisha's health and he was plagued with periodic illness for the next five years. However, it wasn't all work and study. While at Oberlin he met and courted Delia Shepard, whom he married in 1862 after completing his studies. Now, with his education behind him and a wife to support, it was time to choose a career, something befitting his training and natural proclivities. For some time he had been seriously considering entering the ministry, apparently a reflection of his Quaker upbringing (he later became a "devout Presbyterian").[20] But it was his future mother-in-law who saw his true abilities and who was able to point him in the right direction. As Gray related many years later, Delia's mother made the comment, "It would be a pity to spoil a good mechanic to make a poor minister!"[21] Gray took the hint.

Gray's lifelong career of invention began in 1867 with a string of designs: a self-adjusting telegraphic relay, a telegraph switch, an annunciator for hotels, a telegraph printer, and a telegraphic repeater. Not all of these devices brought in rich rewards, but they did bring him recognition in the telegraphic field as a serious inventor. Especially impressed with Gray's creativity and ingenuity was General Anson Stager, general superintendent of the Western Union Telegraph Company. (It was a common affectation in the post–Civil War era for high-ranking former army officers to retain their wartime honorifics even in civilian positions.)

Around 1870, Gray formed a partnership with Enos M. Barton, a former telegraph operator, and started the Cleveland manufacturing firm of Gray and Barton. Although they manufactured a wide range of electrical devices, their main product line was telegraphic equipment. America's westward expansion ensured a steady market for such products. Gray served as chief engineer, or electrician, as the position was then called, and was in charge of design and development, while Barton served as production manager. Business was good, and they employed many people. Also around 1870, Anson Stager invested a large sum in the company and became an active partner. They moved the operation to Chicago where, in 1872, it was renamed the Western Electric Manufacturing Company.[22] At this time they were still an independent company and served many customers, including the giant Western Union Telegraph Company and later the fledgling Bell Telephone Company. Gray became one of the pioneer residents of Highland Park, Illinois, and built a large home that included a laboratory for his personal use. Eventually, Western Electric would be bought by the Bell Telephone System and would become its exclusive manufacturing wing.

Shortly after the move to Chicago, Gray gave up his corporate position as chief engineer, although he remained on the board of directors, to

Figure 1–2. Elisha Gray, c. 1878. **Banquet to Elisha Gray, Ph.D.,** *November 15, 1878, Highland Park Historical Society.*

devote himself full time to invention. In this endeavor, he had a financial backer, Dr. Samuel S. White of Philadelphia, who supplied the necessary funds and shared in the profits from Gray's inventions. White had made a tidy fortune from his own invention for making porcelain teeth.[23] This was the best of both worlds for Gray, an engineer's dream. Unfettered by the demands of daily business details and with someone else to supply the funds, he was now free to do what he did best—create and develop new products. Gray was indebted to White for the faith he showed in Gray's inventive genius, and he later acknowledged "the man who had the foresight to see the oak when it was even less than an acorn. I owe much, very much to him as a patron."[24] He still maintained his relationship with the company he helped found and would make frequent use of its facilities in the course of his development work.

In his later years, Gray taught at his alma mater, Oberlin College, and received several honorary degrees from various institutions as well as the French Legion of Honor medal. Along the way he found time to write several books, *Experimental Researches in Electro-Harmonic Telegraphy* (1878), *Telegraphy and Telephony* (1878), and *Electricity and Magnetism* (1900), in addition to the previously mentioned *Nature's Miracles* (1900).[25] This last work was a nontechnical discussion written for the general public, covering a variety of scientific topics such as weather, geology, and, of course, electricity. In it he also described some of the lesser-known works of other scientists and inventors, such as Thomas Edison's wireless scheme for telegraphing from moving trains and Bell's photoelectric device for talking over a light beam, the precursor of modern infrared data transfer. Always on the forefront of technology, he gave what is perhaps one of the first descriptions of a closed-circuit television system, a device he referred to as a "telephote":

> It is an apparatus by which an illuminated picture at one end of a line of many wires is reproduced upon a screen at the other end. The light is not actually transmitted, but only its effects. Suppose a picture is laid off into small squares and there is a selenium cell corresponding to each square and for each selenium cell there is a wire that runs to a distant station in which circuit there is a battery. At the distant station there are little shutters, one for each wire, that are controlled by the electric current and so adjusted that when the cell at the transmitting end is in the dark the shutter will be closed.[26]

The intended operating mode is quite apparent, but even Gray admitted that the idea was still in the embryo stage. To what extent, if any, he was involved in the development of the telephote is unknown. It would be another 30 years or so before television (or visual radio, as it was once called) became a commercial reality. There are few inventions of any note that were not anticipated or conceived of, in one form or another, long before the "real" invention was patented.

One of Gray's true, commercial successes in the early days of facsimile transmission was a device that he named the "telautograph." He designed his instrument to work, not through telegraph wires as the earlier inventors had tried, but through the phone lines, which made it much more available to businesses. Unlike the earlier facsimile transmissions, which attempted to transmit a graphic reproduction of the message, Gray simply transmitted the *motions* one used to create a message. As a result, the resolution of Gray's telautograph was extremely high. The received message was almost a virtual copy of the transmitted message.

The transmitter, or sending unit, incorporated a special pencil to which two light cords were attached. As the sender wrote his message on the supplied paper, the movement of the pencil changed the length and angle of the attached cords. These relative motions of the cords were picked up by an electrical device, essentially a sophisticated rheostat, that converted them to a varying electrical current. The receiving station picked up these currents and, through another electromechanical device, recreated the motions of the original writer.[27] Thus, the sender could write, print, draw, scribble, or doodle, and the results would be reproduced in virtually identical form at the receiving station. In addition, the receiving pencil would lift up when the sender lifted his pencil so that discrete lines could be reproduced.

Another legacy that Gray left to the modern engineering world was the invention of the Gray Code, a modified binary coding scheme for such applications as shaft encoding, which is used in industrial control systems.[28]

In one sense, Gray's telautograph was even faster than today's fax machines; transmission was instantaneous. The message was completed and delivered the instant the writer stopped writing. Gray developed his instrument during the late 1880s and early 1890s and displayed it in 1893 at the Chicago World's Fair, where it created quite a sensation. Gray sold his interest in the telautograph shortly thereafter to a group of investors who later put it into commercial production. Even though the instruments were expensive, they found widespread use in banks and other institutions where signatures were frequently required. Factories and train stations were big users for internal message transmission since the recipient could retrieve his written messages at leisure. The Telautograph Corporation enjoyed a century of production, existing under its own name until 1994, when it merged with a company that produces—what else?—fax machines. You might say that Gray, through his remarkable Telautograph, anticipated the modern answering machine and e-mail.

Gray was the chairman of the International Congress of Electricians at the World's Columbian Exposition of 1893.[29] He remained an active engineer and inventor, with over 50 patents to his name, until the very day of his death. At the time, he was staying in Newton, Massachusetts, conducting research on an underwater warning system for ships navigating in shallow water. On a Sunday afternoon, January 20, 1901, feeling somewhat ill, he consulted a local doctor, who reassured him that his problem was merely "a slight acidity of the stomach." Shortly after 10 o'clock that evening, Gray collapsed on the street and died a few hours later. The cause of death was listed as "neuralgia of the heart." He was 65.[30]

Notes

1. Thomas B. Costain, *The Cord of Steel: The Story of the Invention of the Telephone*, Doubleday, New York, 1960, p. 43.
2. *Dictionary of American Biography*, 1961, vol. 1, p. 148.
3. *American National Biography*, 1999, vol. 2, p. 497.
4. *Dictionary of American Biography*, 1961, vol. 1, p. 149.
5. American Bell Telephone Company, *Deposition of Alexander Graham Bell*, 1908, p. 1.
6. AGB to parents, March 18, 1875.
7. *Dictionary of American Biography*, 1961, vol. 1, pp. 148–152.

8. Robert V. Bruce, *Alexander Graham Bell and the Conquest of Solitude*, Cornell University Press, Ithaca and London, 1990, p. 174.
9. *Encyclopædia Britannica*, 14th ed., vol. 3, p. 370.
10. *Dictionary of American Biography*, 1961, vol. 1, p. 149.
11. Ibid.
12. AMB to AGB, March 28, 1875.
13. *Dictionary of American Biography*, 1961, vol. 1, p. 149.
14. Ibid.
15. AGB to Mabel Bell, April 5, 1879.
16. *Dictionary of American Biography*, 1961, vol. 1, p. 152.
17. Ibid., vol. 4, p. 514.
18. George B. Prescott, "Sketch of Elisha Gray," *Popular Science Monthly*, February 1879, p. 523.
19. *Biographical Dictionary and Portrait Gallery of the Representative Men of the United States*, 1896, Illinois volume, p. 143–146.
20. Perry R. Duis, "Yesterday's City," *Chicago History*, Spring 1987, p. 67.
21. *Biographical Dictionary and Portrait Gallery of the Representative Men of the United States*, 1896, Illinois volume, p. 143–146. The term *mechanic* was an early designation for engineer, usually mechanical engineer.
22. Duis, p. 67.
23. Bruce, p. 174.
24. *Reception and Banquet to Elisha Gray, Inventor of the Telephone*, Highland Park, November 15, 1878, Highland Park Historical Society.
25. *Encyclopædia Britannica*, 14th ed., vol. 10, p. 669.
26. Elisha Gray, *Nature's Miracles*, Baker & Taylor, New York, 1900, p. 174.
27. *Encyclopædia Britannica*, 14th ed., vol. 21, p. 885.
28. Eric Deeson, *Dictionary of Information Technology*, HarperCollins, 1991, p. 137.
29. *Encyclopædia Britannica*, 14th ed., vol. 10, p. 669.
30. "Prof. Elisha Gray Dead," *New York Times*, January 22, 1901, p. 9.

Chapter 2

THE BEGINNING

The U.S. Postal Telegraph Bill: Nationalizing the Telegraph Industry

In 1862, five-year-old Mabel Hubbard, the daughter of prominent Bostonian Gardiner Greene Hubbard, contracted scarlet fever. Scarlet fever, along with a variety of other debilitating and often deadly diseases afflicting primarily the young, was an ever-present threat in the early nineteenth century. Infant mortality was extremely high, with a newborn's life expectancy being less than 20 years; the heaviest toll occurred before children reached school age.[1] Children who survived their early years were frequently left with the aftermath of these all-too-common diseases. There were no medical cures in those days, only what nature afforded. Nature cured little Mabel of scarlet fever but in the process took away her hearing.

As devastating as this was to a child just beginning to build a vocabulary, Mabel at least had the advantage of knowing *how* to speak. She knew how spoken words sounded, which was more than Georgie Sanders knew. Born in 1867, the son of Thomas Sanders, a wealthy manufacturer of leather products, Georgie had been deaf since birth and, consequently, was devoid of speech. His father could well afford, and was more than willing, to pay anyone who could help his son talk, but so far no one could. Then, almost as if it had been preordained, both children became pupils of Alexander Graham Bell. As such, they played a vital yet unheralded role in the telephone story: they brought together the three main players—Alexander Bell, Gardiner Hubbard, and Thomas Sanders. Had

Mabel Hubbard and Georgie Sanders been normal hearing children, there is little doubt that the Bell Telephone Company would never have happened.

But even without that partnership and without the Bell label, the telephone industry would still have evolved, although under what circumstances and in what form we can only imagine. The development of the telephone, like all notable technological achievements, was inevitable and depended on neither the genius nor luck of any one individual. The history of science and technology offers abundant proof of this and is replete with examples of multiple, independent, and contemporaneous discoveries of virtually the same thing. Unfortunately, popular history obscures this basic fact by singling out and crediting but one in a field of many.

Gardiner Greene Hubbard, Mabel's father, was the quintessential nineteenth-century mover and shaker. Born to a wealthy and socially prominent Boston family, he grew up among the privileged upper class, graduating from Dartmouth College in 1841 and then studying law at Harvard. His choice of the legal profession was no doubt influenced by his father, Samuel Hubbard, a Massachusetts Supreme Court justice. Gardiner settled in Cambridge, joined a Boston law firm, and shortly afterward married Gertrude McCurdy, of the even more wealthy McCurdy family of New York.[2] But the practice of law alone was not enough to satisfy the boundless energy of the visionary Hubbard. He had an almost insatiable need to involve himself in all manner of projects, both civil and commercial.

Hubbard was instrumental in establishing a municipal water works for Cambridge, was a founder of the Cambridge Gas Company, and went on to organize the first intercity Cambridge-to-Boston trolley system. Hubbard entertained no small thoughts nor undertook any trivial projects. Because of the deafness of his daughter, he was involved with a movement that led to the formation of the Clarke School for the Deaf, and served as its president for ten years. Through this institution and his daughter, Mabel, he became acquainted with Alexander Bell, the enthusiastic teacher of Visible Speech and equally ardent telegraph experimenter. They would ultimately discover a common bond—telegraphy—and through that relationship Hubbard would become first Bell's mentor, then his financial backer, and eventually his father-in-law.[3]

With all those public-spirited projects under his belt, the indefatigable Hubbard embarked on his grandest challenge yet. He had made extensive and parallel studies of the government-controlled mail system and the commercially owned telegraph industry. As a result of these investigations, he came to a basic conclusion: telegraph offices were not always readily accessible to the general public and, even more significantly, their rates were much too high for the average citizen. In addition, those rates displayed geographic discrepancies that defied logic. By contrast, the U.S. postal system, being government controlled, offered uniform rates with a relatively efficient delivery system. Based on his analysis of that study, he proposed what he considered a most logical consolidation.[4]

In the late 1860s, Hubbard began lobbying Congress for passage of the U.S. Postal Telegraph Bill, soon to be known as the Hubbard Bill.[5] The purpose of this bill was to authorize Congress to charter a quasi-government corporation identified as the U.S. Postal Telegraph Company,[6] which would operate a nationwide telegraph business under the auspices of the Post Office Department. What this amounted to was a scheme to nationalize America's telegraph industry and effectively incorporate it into the Post Office Department. Others had made similar proposals for a government takeover, but Hubbard's plan was perhaps the most workable and the least draconian. His extensive research on the telegraph industry in general, and in particular on the subject of telegraph rates, earned him a popular following. He was acknowledged as one of America's leading authorities in this area.[7]

In addition to his lobbying efforts, Hubbard wrote various magazine articles on the subject of telegraph service and rates. But strangely enough, his Postal Telegraph Bill received relatively little newspaper coverage. Although difficult to prove with documentary evidence, part of his lack of media attention can be attributed to the unique relationship between the Associated Press and the Western Union Telegraph Company. The Associated Press was the life blood of many newspapers, which relied heavily, almost exclusively, on the AP to supply all of their nonlocal news. The AP, in turn, relied heavily on Western Union to transmit those dispatches.[8]

Because of the sheer volume of business the AP supplied, it received not only special rates, but priority service from Western Union. At a time when an ordinary ten-word telegram might be sent for 50 cents, AP news dispatches could go for as little as a penny a word. As a result, the AP and Western Union had a mutually advantageous relationship. Under this deal, Western Union got all of AP's business, and the AP in turn got good rates. The AP would be understandably reluctant to report on, much less support, a scheme that could change or even destroy that relationship.[9]

Western Union was quick to chastise any newspaper that dared to support or advocate government intervention in the telegraph industry. Newspaper spokespeople, those brave enough to speak out, claimed that it was impossible to establish a newspaper without the consent of the AP and Western Union. Two San Francisco newspapers, the *Herald* and the *Alta California*, learned the hard way what happens to those who have the temerity to suggest reforming the telegraph industry. When the *Herald* violated this canon, it experienced a 250 percent increase in telegraph rates. Under similar circumstances, the *Alta* suffered the loss of all Western Union telegraph dispatches. The excuse Western Union offered for this bully tactic was based on the alleged "difficulty" it had in collecting its bills.[10] Other newspapers, such as the Petersburg, Virginia, *Index*, were told that they would have their AP dispatches withheld if they dared to print articles critical of the telegraph industry. AP dispatches were vital to local newspapers' survival; without them, they might as well close their doors.[11]

> The abuses of this system [the telegraph industry] are growing, and will increase rapidly until the government interferes to perform the duties for which it was constituted—to protect the people until the rates for the press are fixed by law, equal rights and privileges secured to all, with rates so low that all can use the telegraph. Not until then will a free and independent press be assured to the country.[12]

The proposed nationalization of the telegraph industry was not original with Hubbard, neither here nor abroad. There was ample precedence for such a proposal, since in all other countries control of the telegraph business was vested in the government. At that time England had just recently (February 5, 1870) nationalized its telegraph industry. Needless to say, the Hubbard Bill did not sit well with the commercial telegraph interests and especially not with William Orton, president of Western Union. He derisively referred to it as "the Hubbard Scheme."[13] In addition to his Cambridge residence, Hubbard also maintained a home in Washington, D.C., to further his lobbying efforts with Congress. The Hubbard Bill was a high-priority project with the crusading Gardiner Greene Hubbard.

The telegraph companies, of course, were anxious to preserve the system as it was, and toward this end they, too, engaged in lobbying to support their position. One not-so-subtle gimmick to curry favorable congressional support was their issuance of franking cards. Although such a practice would be illegal today, it was one of the industry's tools to maintain the status quo in the face of proposed government interference or takeover. All members of Congress received free telegraph franking cards. A congressman could send as many free telegrams as he wished, to anyone he chose, merely by presenting one of those cards at any sponsoring telegraph office. The implied promise that went along with the cards was that this perk would likely disappear if the industry were nationalized.[14]

Hubbard managed to create an impressive argument for his case. His expressed goal was to make telegraphy more accessible and affordable for the average citizen. As he pointed out, most telegraph offices were located in train stations, a locale not especially convenient for many potential users. A post office, on the other hand, was always readily accessible. Hubbard's plan was to utilize the facilities and personnel of the post office as part of the U.S. Postal Telegraph Company. Because the overhead and labor costs would be shared between the postal business and the telegraph business, operating costs would be at a minimum. And because these costs would be substantially lower than those of the commercial telegraph companies, telegraph rates would be more affordable.[15]

Hubbard was well aware of the price-volume relationship in marketing. Within certain limits, as you lower prices, sales volume goes up. Although the per-telegram profit margin would be less than that of a commercial operation, the increased volume would ensure overall profitability. Or so Hubbard argued. Since the U.S. Postal Telegraph Company would be allowed to string its own lines, generally along postal routes, it would be in direct competition with the commercial telegraph companies. Since this might make it difficult for some of those companies to survive, provision was made to allow a commercial company to sell out to the U.S. Postal Telegraph Company, if it so chose, at an arbitrated price.

Unlike other nationalization proposals, which advocated direct government takeover of the telegraph industry, Hubbard's plan was more along the lines of peaceful coexistence—assuming, of course, that the industry could withstand the federally subsidized competition. In reality, Hubbard's plan would have resulted in the elimination of commercial telegraphy, just as certainly as the other nationalization plans would have. However, from a public relations standpoint, his approach seemed almost benevolent.

Hubbard's most convincing argument centered on the high, and often inexplicably varying, telegraph rates. They often made little or no sense. For example, a ten-word telegram from Washington, D.C., to Boston cost 55 cents. The same message sent from Washington to a town ten miles outside of Boston cost $1.75. These rate anomalies were commonplace. For example, the citizens of Omaha, Nebraska, had an even stranger rate puzzle. If they sent a telegram to Chicago, they paid $3.55. But if they bought a $1.50 round-trip trolley ticket to go across the river to Council Bluffs, Iowa, they could send the same telegram for $1.55, thus saving themselves 50 cents, not an insignificant amount in those days.[16]

To be meaningful, these telegraph rates must be evaluated in light of the era's wage rates. Considering that a skilled craftsman, such as a machinist, earned between $2.50 and $3.00 a day, sending a telegram was not a trivial exercise—at least not for the average worker. One had to have a compelling reason for such rapid communication. Playing as he did to the ordinary citizen, Hubbard's plan enjoyed considerable support.

Hubbard's professed goal was to provide fast, affordable communication for all members of society, not just the well-to-do. He summarized the basic objective of his proposal and the relationship between the *company* (his U.S. Postal Telegraph Company) and the *department* (the U.S. Post Office Department) as follows:

> The Postmaster General has the same means for enforcing the prompt and accurate transmission of this [telegrams] as all other correspondence. No monopoly is conferred, and any company can transmit telegrams if they do so more satisfactorily [than Hubbard's proposed U.S. Postal Telegraph Company] to the public. The rates are fixed at twenty-five cents between offices not over 250 miles apart, fifty cents between 250 and 500 miles, seventy-five cents between 500 and 1500 miles, and a dollar and a half for all greater distances. Letters are generally written after the close of business hours and sent by night mail. To provide for this correspondence the rates for night telegrams are fixed at twenty-five cents for distances under 1,500 miles, and seventy-five cents for greater distances. These rates will be prepaid by telegraphic stamps sold at the post-offices. The department will retain five cents for its service, and pay the rest to the company as full compensation for furnishing and operating the lines.... Every post-office near a telegraph line is made a postal telegraph office, while others are established wherever they now are or may be required by the wants of business.[17]

Hubbard and his associates, including his brother Charles Hubbard and his Washington lawyer, Anthony Pollok, of course, would play key roles in the newly created quasi-government corporation; in this respect, their motives were not totally altruistic. It has also been claimed, although never truly substantiated, that another associate was a young Andrew Carnegie.[18] This is plausible, since Carnegie began his career as a telegraph operator and naturally would have a keen interest in telegraph matters.

Hubbard was not a lone voice in the wilderness. Supporting him and his associates in this proposed bill was Postmaster General Creswell. Historically, advocacy of government control of the telegraph industry dated back to the very origins of the Morse system:

> As early as 1844 and 1845, Post-Master Johnson, under Polk's administration, in his reports for those years referred at length to the telegraph and

> recommended its adoption by the Post Office Department as of vital importance to the interests of the country, and as an invention which ought not to be controlled by private parties. In 1869, under Mr. Johnson's administration, Mr. Randall urged the importance of this measure, and Mr. Creswell three times recommended it to Congress.[19]

Despite his valiant lobbying efforts, passage of the Hubbard Bill never occurred.[20] But at the time he met Bell and until well after the famous patent was issued in 1876, Hubbard maintained high hopes and actively and energetically pursued his lifelong dream. Because of his expertise in post office matters, in 1876 Hubbard was appointed chair of a presidential commission to study the mail transportation system. As he traveled about the country under the auspices of this commission, he made contacts with influential people, who would later prove invaluable when the nascent Bell Telephone Company started to establish franchises in various cities.

It's hard to pinpoint just when Bell became interested in telegraphy and particularly harmonic or multiple-message telegraphy. After traveling about some of the New England states early in 1872, giving lectures on Visible Speech, Bell took up residence in Boston in the fall of that year. There, he conducted a private school for a small group of deaf children. This was also the time when news of the J. B. Stearns duplex telegraph was announced. The news accounts of this breakthrough system spurred him on in his own telegraphic pursuits, as no doubt did reports in 1873 of the exciting Loomis worldwide telegraphic system. An enthusiastic Alexander Bell wrote to his parents:

> A bill has just passed Congress, and now awaits the President's signature incorporating the "Loomis Telegraph Company." The Company has been formed to carry out the project of Dr. Loomis—namely to telegraph to Europe *without a wire and without a battery*!!!
>
> ...The idea, then seems to be that there is a *shell* of electrified air at a considerable height all around the world.
>
> ...He proposes therefore to erect poles supporting apparatus capable of collecting atmospheric electricity upon the highest summits of the Alps and the Rocky Mountains and by burying plates in the earth at either end make a complete circuit as in the ordinary telegraph.[21]

Bell wrote a week later that the president had signed the Loomis Telegraph Bill, although the scheme, of course, would come to nothing. However, things were happening in the field of telegraphy, and Bell now began experimenting in earnest.

Despite Western Union's ability to quash news articles critical of the telegraph industry, it still couldn't hide the fact that Gardiner Hubbard was proposing to nationalize the industry. Fortunately, magazines had little to fear from either Western Union or the Associated Press. It would have been almost impossible for Bell not to know of Hubbard's telegraphic interests. A few months later, Bell wrote to his parents:

> By the bye [sic] I don't know if I told you that the gentleman who has introduced a Bill into Congress for the purchase of all the telegraph lines by the government on the English model is the father of one of my pupils. I know him personally. Would it not be well to write to him about the telegraph scheme? [22]

So, aside from Hubbard's attractive, teenage daughter, there may have been another incentive for Bell to want to become a part of Mabel's world of privilege and high society. Hubbard, even long after he had met Bell, was ignorant of Bell's telegraph interests. Bell had been working up to broaching his telegraphic ideas to Hubbard and on October 20, 1874, wrote to his parents:

> My caveat is now in the hands of my solicitor. I expect it will be filed in the secret archives at Washington.... I have received a note from Mr. Hubbard requesting me to take tea with him, as he wished to see me "immediately" in connection with my telegraphic scheme.[23]

Their mutual interest wouldn't become known until Bell became better acquainted with the Hubbard family—especially Mabel Hubbard.

Through his deaf daughter, Hubbard met the intense and articulate teacher of speech, Alexander Graham Bell. Bell would later reveal to him his multiple message telegraph scheme, which could, as Hubbard saw it, inject needed new life into his flagging U.S. Postal Telegraph Bill. He became absolutely convinced of this when Bell claimed that his yet-to-be-perfected harmonic telegraph system could send up to ten times as many messages over the same wire as any commercial telegraph system, then limited to four messages at a time. But Bell's amazing system would work to the advantage of Hubbard's U.S. Postal Telegraph Company only if Hubbard and his associates controlled the patent or patents on such a system. This facet of the enterprise would be handled by Anthony Pollok, whom we will meet in chapter 4.

Notes

1. *Mathematical and Philosophical Dictionary*, Charles Hutton, London, 1795, pp. 27–28.

2. *Dictionary of American Biography*, 1961, vol. 5, p. 324.
3. Ibid.
4. Ibid.
5. Robert V. Bruce, *Alexander Graham Bell and the Conquest of Solitude*, Cornell University Press, Ithaca and London, 1990, p. 127.
6. Not to be confused with a commercial telegraph company of the same name created later.
7. *Dictionary of American Biography*, 1961, vol. 5, p. 325.
8. Alvin F. Harlow, *Old Wires and New Waves*, D. Appleton-Century, New York, 1936, p. 332.
9. Ibid., p. 333.
10. Gardiner G. Hubbard, "The Proposed Changes in the Telegraph System," *North American Review*, July 1873, p. 98.
11. Ibid, p. 98.
12. Ibid, p. 99.
13. *Argument of William Orton … on the Bill to Establish Postal Telegraph Lines*, Russells' American Steam Printing House, New York, 1870.
14. Harlow, p. 336.
15. *Argument of William Orton.*
16. Harlow, p. 334.
17. Hubbard, p. 106.
18. Harlow, p. 335.
19. "Our Post-Office," Gardiner Hubbard, *Atlantic Monthly*, January 1875, p. 103.
20. Nationalization proposals continued long after Hubbard gave up the fight.
21. AGB to parents, January 1873.
22. AGB to parents, March 1874.
23. AGB to parents, October 20, 1874.

Chapter 3

STATE OF THE ART

A Brief Review of Telegraph Developments to 1874

It wasn't a telephone that Alexander Bell set out to invent but simply an improved form of telegraph, because he had learned that the rewards could be quite generous. He hoped that the emerging field of multiple-message telegraphy would bring him the recognition he so eagerly sought. Indeed, his famous patent is titled "Improvements in Telegraphy" and describes just such a system. How this telegraph patent ultimately turned into a telephone patent will be discussed in the following chapters. But to understand better the motivation behind the quest for faster and better communications, we need to consider briefly the telephone's inspiration: the telegraph.

To most of us, the telegraph seems almost synonymous with artist-turned-inventor Samuel Findley Breese Morse. Yet, he was far from the first to explore the mysteries of long-distance communications. The name itself, the *telegraph*, loosely defined as "far writing," was coined in 1792 by Frenchman Claude Chappe, who, along with his brothers, invented an improved system of long-distance semaphore signaling.[1] Transmission was strictly visual; each station repeated the message from the previous one. Still, it was claimed that it took a "telegram" only 15 minutes to travel 150 miles.[2] While the public readily accepted the word *telegraph*, linguistic purists denounced the barbaric term *telegram* for the transmitted message. The correct expression, they insisted, was *telegraphic dispatch* or *telegraphic communication*.

Over the centuries, pre-electric telegraphy, as contrasted to electric telegraphy, has always taken one of two forms: audible or visual. Audible telegraphy, such as the beating of signal drums, has existed for thousands of years, and even today it still serves a limited purpose in such applications as tornado warning systems. Visual telegraphy—smoke signals, semaphores, and especially light signals—has an equally ancient origin and also still exists. The Greek historian Polybius tells of torches being used for signaling as early as 2 B.C., and certain American Indian cultures employed a highly effective system of smoke signals.[3] Semaphore signaling towers were common during the Middle Ages, with one line of towers extending for 1200 miles from St. Petersburg in Russia to the then-Prussian border. Since each message, before it could be transmitted to the next tower, had to be verified by retransmitting to the originating tower, communication was a bit slow—but accurate.[4]

Solar telegraphy by means of a little-known device called the *heliograph* was highly developed during the nineteenth century, primarily for military communications. Napoleon is said to have used this instrument during his Egyptian campaigns.[5] The heliograph was essentially a sophisticated mirror for reflecting flashes of sunlight in Morse-code fashion. It was especially appropriate for sunny or mountainous regions, such as in Egypt or India, and offered good message security. Because of its narrow, pencil-thin beam, it could be aimed at the message recipient with rifle-like accuracy. Unless one were almost directly in line with the sender and the receiver (e.g., within 50 yards over a six-mile range), it was nearly impossible to "tap into" or eavesdrop on a heliograph.[6] The instrument survives today in the form of the emergency signaling mirror carried by many offshore sailors.

However, the most intriguing instrument of all was the fabulous *sympathetic telegraph.* This mystic device was first described in 1558 by the Italian scientist Gaiambattista della Porta in his book *Magia Naturalis.*[7] It consisted of a dial around which were engraved the letters of the alphabet and a magnetic needle that pivoted in the center. The needle could be rotated to any desired letter. An identical device, which apparently served as both a receiver and a transmitter, could be located *any place in the world.* When the needle of the first device was pointed to a particular letter, the needle of the second device would point—in sympathy—to the corresponding letter on its dial. Unfortunately, della Porta, long suspected by Rome of practicing the black arts, never explained how this incredible telegraph worked, nor did the Jesuit priest Strada, who reported on it almost a century later.[8] Fake that it was, the sympathetic telegraph exemplified society's desire for quick, long-distance communication.

As intriguing as these diverse early telegraphic devices were, it is the electric telegraph that provides us with our point of departure. To gain a better perspective on the technological environment that spawned the telephone, we need to take a quick look at its origins.

Three Generations of Electric Telegraphs

From its earliest beginnings in the mid-eighteenth century, clever and hopeful inventors sought to improve the art of electric telegraphy—a quest that would become the cutting edge of mid-nineteenth-century technology. There have been three distinct types of electric telegraphs.

Static-Electricity Telegraphs

The first recorded attempt to transmit messages electrically occurred in 1747 when Bishop Watson of London sent a spark discharge from a Leyden jar through 10,600 feet of wire. This demonstrated that the "electric fluid," which we now call static electricity, could be transmitted for an appreciable distance,[9] which suggested that a signal, and hence intelligence, could be sent through the wire. Static electricity at that time was well known among natural philosophers, and machines for generating it were fairly common. For the rest of the eighteenth century, various schemes appeared that employed the mysterious electric fluid for message transmission. In 1774, an inventor named Le Sage came up with a fanciful scheme that employed one wire for each letter of the alphabet. Supposedly, one could spell out words by this method.[10] Later, in 1787, an inventor named Bethancourt managed to establish a static-electricity telegraph line in Spain between Madrid and Aranjuez, a distance of 26 miles.[11] Some were more successful than others, but none ever achieved commercial success.

These static-electricity telegraphs were later classed either as *pith ball telegraphs* or as *spark telegraphs*, depending on their operating mode. The first group depended upon the electrical attraction or repulsion of pith balls (from plant stem cores) to detect the received signal. The second group relied on an actual spark discharge for signal detection.

In one system employing pith balls, a dial bearing all the letters of the alphabet was driven by clockwork, making one revolution per minute. The dial was concealed behind a screen or shield so that only one letter at a time could be seen through a small window. The receiving station had a similar screened dial also driven by clockwork in synchronization with the first dial. When the letter to be transmitted appeared in the window, the sender sent a high voltage static charge along the wire to the receiving station, causing the pith balls to deflect. At this instant, the recipient would note and record the exposed letter. The transmission rate was agonizingly slow, but since there were no codes to memorize, anyone could use it. Synchronization was achieved by a prearranged signal.[12]

These static-electricity telegraphs all shared a common problem: static electricity, although easily generated, was quite difficult to control. Electrical leakage was a big problem, especially over a distance. But those early inventors had little choice—it was the only electricity then available.

Dynamic-Electricity, or Chemical, Telegraphs

When dynamic electricity (i.e., electricity produced from batteries) appeared in the early nineteenth century, the chemical telegraph was born. With this breakthrough, telegraphy took a different turn and became commercially viable. Voltaic electricity, as it was more commonly known, was easily generated by chemical action and just as easily controlled. A popular source of this voltaic electricity was the Daniel cell, destined for widespread use in the emerging telegraph industry, although it was just one of many battery cells that appeared.[13] Experimenters soon discovered that when an electric current passed through paper treated with a solution of potassium cyanide and nitric acid, a vivid blue color (Prussian blue) occurred at the point of contact. The message-sending potential was immediately recognized, and various schemes were developed to take advantage of it. Most of them involved drawing a moistened strip of chemically treated paper between two electrodes. Because the paper was fairly conductive, each time a current pulse passed between the electrodes, a mark appeared on the treated paper.

The most popular chemical system was developed by Bain of England. The process was not unlike the thermal printing systems of today, such as those used in various printers and fax machines. Bain's system enjoyed a period of popularity in America and competed successfully with the Morse system.[14] It was one way to circumvent the Morse patent.[15] Even as late as the 1870s, Thomas Edison was still receiving patents on various chemical telegraph designs.

Electromagnetic Telegraph

Electromagnetism, which established the relationship between electricity and magnetism, was discovered in the 1820s, and shortly afterward a third generation of telegraph systems appeared: the electromagnetic telegraph. As with the chemical telegraph, which coexisted for many years with the electromagnetic system, various schemes were developed to exploit its message-sending capabilities. One of the first practical systems, widely used in England, was Wheatstone's needle telegraph.[16] In this system, which went through various stages of development, the magnetic deflection of compasslike needles by current pulses passing through adjacent wire coils was used to spell out a message. Interestingly, the previously mentioned pith ball dial telegraph was "modernized" to utilize electro-magnetic stepping-type relays to drive the dial pointer, which eliminated the need for synchronization.[17] Dial-type telegraphs enjoyed a certain popularity since they did not require much training.

However, the best known telegraph by far was the system developed by the American portrait painter Samuel Morse in the late 1830s. Today, most people associate Morse's system with a telegraph key as the transmitting device and an electromagnetic sounding instrument as the receiving device. Although this was the system that eventually evolved, it started out considerably different.

The original Morse system was fully automatic. The message being sent was first encoded in Morse's code of dots and dashes. The dots and dashes were then mechanically handset on a "port rule" device, much like the way early printers would set type, which was then pulled by clockwork through a switch mechanism. As the handset dots and dashes passed through, the switch would alternately open and close, sending the coded current pulses to the receiving device. The receiver consisted of another clockwork mechanism drawing a strip of paper beneath a pencil activated by an electromagnet. When the electromagnet received a current pulse from the sending device, it caused the pencil to draw a short line across the moving paper, thus leaving a mark. The length of the mark indicated either a dot or a dash. The message recipient would then decode the penciled dots and dashes into words.[18]

However, it was soon discovered that experienced operators were able to ignore the pencil marks and simply listen to the clicking patterns of the electromagnet. From this they learned to

Figure 3–1. A Breguet indicator or dial telegraph.

discern the unique patterns for the individual letters and thus decode the words. It was called "sound reading," and a good operator could write down the message as it was being transmitted without ever having to decode the tape.[19] Once this discovery was made, it soon became obvious that the complex clockwork mechanisms of the port rules and the moving tapes were unnecessary. All that was really needed for a basic system, aside from a battery, was a telegraph key to send the current pulses and an electromagnetic sounder to respond to them.[20]

This marvelously simple system, which, with electromagnetic repeaters, could send a message across the continent, had its limitations. It could transmit or receive only one message at a time. It's little wonder then that when an inventor devised a way to send two messages simultaneously on a single line, he became very rich. This was the J. B. Sterns duplex system, introduced in 1872, which effectively doubled the telegraph's throughput. The Sterns system allowed one message to be transmitted and one message to be received simultaneously on the same wire.[21]

This was followed in 1874 by Edison's quadruplex system, which allowed, on a single wire, four simultaneous messages, two going and two coming.[22] The advantage to the telegraph industry was obvious: each of these inventions doubled the throughput of the telegraph line, and hence its profitability, without incurring the cost of stringing more wire. This was the state of the art when Alexander Bell came upon the scene.

Quest for the "Fax" Machine

Experience has a way of playing tricks on our perception of history. Today, most of us assume that the miracle of the fax machine is a recent outgrowth of modern telephone and computer technology, combined with a host of other technologies. But surprisingly, the perception is backwards. The concept and implementation of the fax machine preceded the development of the telephone by over 20 years.

Many people of the early Victorian era, including some notable scientists, doubted whether anything as complex as the human voice could ever be transmitted electrically. Strangely enough, though, they had no problem believing that a facsimile, or "autographic message," could be sent by telegraph. Ever since the electromagnetic telegraph became a commercial reality, circa 1840, experimenters and inventors had been trying to devise ways of sending graphic images—facsimiles of handwritten messages—over a telegraph wire. Some of the early fax experimenters, such as Blakewell and Caselli,[23] did manage, with varying degrees of success, to accomplish this, although none of those early devices ever became commercially successful in the true sense of the word. Speed of transmission was the big problem, but although those first fax machines were incredibly slow, they did work.

Caselli's fax machine (see fig. 3-2) while giving good results, transmitted at a rate of only one square inch per minute —sending a 5 × 7 inch picture would take over half an hour. However, it could print out either in blue on paper treated with potassium cyanide or in black on tinfoil, after being developed with nitric and pyrogallic acid.[24]

French writer J. Baille, commenting in 1871 on the marvels of the electric telegraph, made the following observation on the fax machine and offered a bold prophecy:

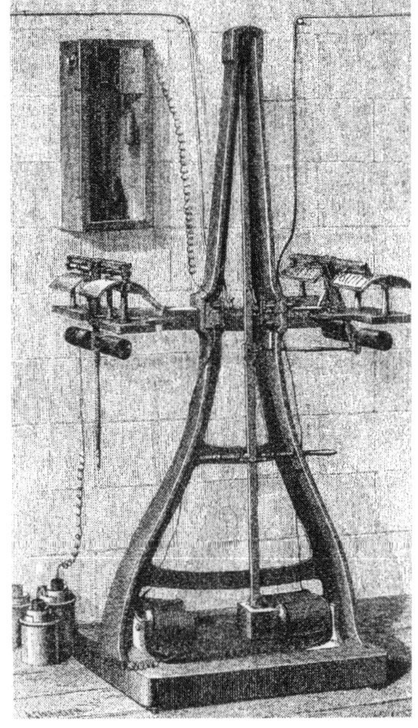

Figure 3-2. Caselli's facsimile telegraph.

> Wonderful as are these achievements, the inventions in telegraphy have gone still further. To be able to transmit thought to a distance is a triumph which was formerly astonishing, but now we are accustomed to it.... To be able to transmit handwriting, and even drawings, appeared to be more difficult, but this problem has also been resolved.... Some years hence, for all we know, we may be able to transmit the vocal message itself, with the very inflection, tone and accent of the speaker.[25]

Baille's prophecy reflects the scientific mind set of the mid-1800s: something as complex as facsimile transmission was a fait accompli, yet something like voice transmission (which would turn out to be incredibly simple) was almost incomprehensible. The only one to achieve a measure of success with a facsimile telegraph in those early days was an engineer named Patrick Delany. By 1885 he was transmitting remarkably good facsimile reproductions of handwriting, drawings, and just about anything else that could be produced on paper with a pen.[26] His machine, it was claimed, would transmit at a fairly respectable 12 square inches per minute. But apparently there were technical and other problems that precluded its commercial exploitation. It would take many years for technology to catch up to the goal of facsimile transmission.

Figure 3–3. Transmitted fax images from the Caselli telegraph on paper (left) and tinfoil.

Bell felt that his version of the harmonic telegraph concept, which is what he was really attempting to patent, could overcome the pokiness of the earlier methods. In Bell's mind, his version would be the ideal mechanism for a facsimile transmission system or, as he referred to it, an "autograph telegraph." He was well aware of the primitive results of previous facsimile schemes. Still, he believed that his approach might hold the elusive secret. Bell's autographic telegraph was straightforward in design. Actually, his patent application was an adaptation or improvement on an existing autographic device. As he explained to his father:

> I have just invented an attachment to the apparatus that more than doubles the value of the idea.... The arrangement consists of a device by means of which a vibrating armature can be made to work "Meyer's Autographic Apparatus"—so as to admit of the simultaneous transmission of written messages or pictures.[27]

According to his patent, an array of perhaps 30 closely spaced inking pens were arranged side by side above a strip of paper moved by clockwork (a practical electric motor was yet to come). Each pen could be individually raised or lowered electromagnetically onto the moving paper in response to a signal, thereby leaving a mark. The signal for each pen would be transmitted at a different frequency, thus each pen would respond to its own frequency. The transmitter required that the document to be transmitted be written on metallic foil with a nonconductive ink. That way, as it passed under an array of electrical contacts (one contact for each pen), the appropriate transmitter would be turned on and off as the contacts passed over the prepared foil. At the receiving end, the appropriate pen would be raised or lowered at the proper time, leaving marks analogous to the original message on the foil.

Figure 3–4. A fax from the Delaney facsimile telegraph.

On April 6, 1875, Bell received a patent, his first for

this device, which was titled "Transmitter and Receiver for Electric Telegraphs." The title obscures the fact that the instrument was intended to transmit facsimiles of handwritten messages. In modern terminology this would have been, in essence, a fax machine. Had the harmonic telegraph concept itself proved viable, a practical fax machine—perhaps even Bell's—might have appeared long before the telephone was perfected.

Notes

1. Lewis Coe, *The Telegraph*, McFarland, Jefferson, NC, 1990, p. 6.
2. *Encyclopædia Britannica*, 11th ed., vol. 5, p. 854.
3. Lewis Coe, *The Telegraph*, McFarland, Jefferson, NC, 1990, p. 2.
4. *Universal Standard Encyclopedia*, vol. 23, p. 8320.
5. *Compton's Picture Encyclopedia*, 1933, vol. 14, p. 30.
6. *Encyclopædia Britannica*, 11th ed., vol. 25, p. 72.
7. *Universal Standard Encyclopedia*, vol. 23, p. 8320.
8. George B. Prescott, *History, Theory and Practice of the Electric Telegraph*, Ticknor and Fields, Boston 1866, p. 6.
9. A. Privat Deschanel, *Elementary Treatise on Natural Philosophy*, D. Appleton, New York, 1878, pt. 3, p. 713.
10. *Encyclopædia Britannica*, 14th ed., vol. 21, p. 880.
11. Alexander Jones, *Historical Sketch of the Electric Telegraph*, Putnam, New York, 1852, p. 8.
12. *Encyclopædia Britannica*, 14th ed., vol. 21, p. 881.
13. Henry S. Carhart, *Primary Batteries*, Allyn and Bacon, Boston, 1891, p. 28–29.
14. Prescott, p. 135.
15. Lewis Coe, *The Telegraph*, McFarland, Jefferson, NC, 1990, p. 17.
16. *Encyclopædia Britannica*, 11th ed., vol. 26, p. 511.
17. E. Atkinson, *Elementary Treatise on Physics*, New York, 1886, p. 834.
18. Mitchell Wilson, *American Science and Invention*, Bonanza, NY, 1960, p. 118–119.
19. Lewis Coe, *The Telegraph*, McFarland, Jefferson, NC, 1990, p. 20.
20. Much later, the telegraph industry would go back to an automated system for fast, high-volume transmission.
21. *Encyclopædia Britannica*, 14th ed., vol. 21, p. 884.
22. Ibid.
23. Deschanel, p. 731–732.
24. Ibid., p. 733.
25. J. Baille, *Les Merveilles de l'Electricite*, Paris, 1871. English tr. *Wonders of Electricity*, Scribner, Armstrong, NY, 172, p. 140.
26. Edwin J. Houston, "Delany's Facsimile Telegraphic Transmission," *Journal of the Franklin Institute*, March 1885, pp. 223–224.
27. AGB to AMB, February 12, 1875.

Chapter 4

Race for Multiple Telegraphy

October 1874–April 1875

The Stearns duplex system in 1872 and, later, Edison's quadruplex system in 1874 showed that it was possible to send more than one message at a time along the same wire. Now the race was on to crowd even more messages onto a wire. Multimessage handling meant more efficient utilization of existing lines, which would translate to lower costs. And lower costs, in turn, meant lower prices, more business, and better profits.

As we discussed previously, the goal of lower prices was at the core of Gardiner Hubbard's U.S. Postal Telegraph Bill. Only a government-run telegraph network, operating under the auspices of the Post Office Department, Hubbard had argued, could offer low, uniform prices to the public. He realized now, after meeting Bell, that if he held a controlling patent on a multimessage telegraph system, he could ensure his goal of low prices to the public. Also, a multimessage system could inject some new life into his flagging Postal Telegraph Bill—enough, perhaps, to ensure congressional passage. This is what drew Hubbard's attention to Bell's as-yet-undeveloped new telegraph scheme.

Hubbard and his Hubbard Bill associates were well aware of the competitive advantage of a controlling patent. And in the fall of 1874, Bell was working on a method for sending not just four but a multitude of messages simultaneously over the same telegraph wire. It wasn't a new idea, and he wasn't alone in this quest. A number of other inventors were also pursuing the same goal. The motivation was money: invent a way to send more messages over a telegraph wire, and you will become rich. Bell wrote enthusiastically to his parents regarding the possible financial rewards for any new telegraphic device:

> But last year a man invented a method of sending *four messages* simultaneously along the same wire, and the Pacific Telegraph Company bought his patent for seven hundred and fifty thousand dollars ($750,000).
>
> The result has been that the Pacific Company has been able to reduce their prices so as to compete successfully with the Western Union.[1]

The method that seemed to hold such great promise was called *harmonic telegraphy* to distinguish it from the current duplex and quadruplex systems. This was the basic approach that was receiving the attention of not only Bell, but men like Gray, Edison, Van Rysselberghe, Mercadier, and La Cour,[2] who was from Denmark but was seeking American patents. It is almost certain that there were others, both here and abroad, who were also working along similar lines, but their efforts received little attention. However, Elisha Gray seemed to be leading the field in the pursuit of a practical harmonic telegraph system.

The idea behind harmonic telegraphy was simple enough: each message would be sent along the same wire, but at a different tone or frequency. It was analogous to modern radio and TV transmission—a different frequency for each station or channel. The electromagnetic receiving device normally used, similar to a modern buzzer, was mechanically "tuned" to a particular frequency and therefore would respond only to messages sent by a similarly tuned transmitter, or so the theory stated. The signals involved were in the audio frequency range merely because these were easily generated by the electromechanical devices then available. Theoretically, a great number of messages could be transmitted simultaneously over the same wire by this method. Bell, basing his projections more on theory than on experimentation, explained to his parents the salient feature of his particular version of the harmonic telegraph:

> Now my invention comes out as a means by which 30 or 40 messages may be sent simultaneously and by which intermediate stations may communicate with each other. If the Western Union take [sic] it up it would enable them to recover lost ground. At all events it is evidently a good time to bring out the invention.[3]

This was the promise that piqued Hubbard's interest. Had Bell's as-yet-unperfected harmonic telegraph lived up to his hopes, it would have dwarfed all previous telegraphic breakthroughs. Yet, even after he filed his second telegraph patent application in February 1876, he had succeeded in sending no more than three simultaneous messages, far short of his hoped-for goal. But unknown to Bell and all the other telegraph hopefuls, harmonic telegraphy was not to be. At the time, neither the necessary technology nor the basic understanding of audio frequency transmission were available to make it a commercial reality.

Elisha Gray came the closest to achieving a workable, commercial system and was eventually able to transmit eight messages over a single wire. And even though a new corporation, the Harmonic Telegraph Company, was formed to exploit his system, there were simply too many problems to overcome. The promise of harmonic telegraphy was much better than the reality. In practice, it just couldn't compete with the existing duplex and quadruplex systems, which would rule the telegraph industry for many years to come.

However, in the mid-1870s, the unfulfilled hope of harmonic telegraphy was too alluring to dampen any enthusiasm. Nobody knew then that it was a theory ahead of its time. They were all searching for the telegraphic equivalent of the philosopher's stone, that elusive element that would transform Morse's single-message instrument into a true multi-message machine.

Bell and the Competition

Bell was well aware that he was not alone in the race to perfect the harmonic telegraph and that he was up against some formidable competition. Competition was something Bell could relate to, especially when it came to spies—those anonymous agents who seek to discover just what it is the inventor is up to, or even worse, to steal his ideas. Although Bell shared the amateur inventor's xenophobia when it came to protecting his invention, Hubbard further fostered his fear, with warnings to not "communicate information, which will set others on the look out." Early on, he even advised Bell not to file a caveat since it might tip his hand.[4] And at one point, in January 1876, Bell felt compelled to move to new, more secure quarters to escape the prying eyes of possible agents for the competition.[5] Considering these concerns, which were bolstered by Hubbard's warnings and admonitions, it's little wonder that Bell might see a spy or secret agent in someone whom he considered unduly curious.

In March 1875, Bell journeyed from Boston to Washington, D.C., to confer with his new patent attorneys. During this visit he detailed his experiences with a possible competitor's agent just before he was to demonstrate his harmonic telegraph scheme to William Orton, president of the Western Union Telegraph Company:

> I had four cells of a battery but no acid. In order to have plenty of battery power that the thing might work well enough, I wished six cells and a mixture of bichromate of potash with some acid (I forgot what).
>
> There was only one electrician in town and I went to him for everything, unfortunately giving him my name. He sent me down two cells of Lockwood's battery and I was surprised that the young man who brought them came right into the parlor and stared about—to see what kind of instruments I had got.
>
> Still further was I surprised to find that the two cells *would not work*. The young man came back with the bichromate solution for the other cells—but I had my suspicions aroused and did not use the solution. On going around to Mr. Maynard's [the electrician], I was met with a face that I did not like. I felt sure there was some underhanded work about the batteries—especially as I could see the man was evidently trying to humbug me. I could have made up two other cells if I had only a large zinc or a small carbon—but would you believe it, Mr. Maynard, who has an electrical establishment, professed not to have a single zinc or carbon—nothing but the battery that would not work.[6]

Rather than any nefarious activity on the part of Maynard, it was most likely Bell's inexperience with a three-terminal, plunge-type bichromate battery that caused it not to work. Unlike the common two-terminal cells used in telegraphy, plunge-type cells had to be connected in a specific way to function. But despite Bell's misadventure with the suspiciously acting electrician, the demonstration went off quite well. So well, in fact, that Orton invited him to repeat the demonstration at Western Union's headquarters in New York.

During the Washington, D.C., demonstration, Orton seemed genuinely interested in Bell's approach. But when Bell accepted Orton's invitation to repeat the demonstration at the New York headquarters, Orton's interest appeared to weaken, or so it seemed to Bell. From Bell's account of his next meeting with Orton, it is apparent that Western Union was curious about his system but may not have been seriously considering it. The meeting did little to bolster Bell's confidence. As he wrote to his parents:

> He [Orton] then informed me that Mr. Gray had called upon him that afternoon and was then in town. He spoke very highly of Mr. Gray and of his invention. Ingenious workman, good apparatus &c. &c.... He then continued speaking very favorably of Gray's apparatus—that mine was crude compared to it.[7]

Orton was a shrewd businessman and a good horse trader. If he were going to do business with Bell, he didn't want Bell to think that Western Union was placing a high value on his invention. It was classic business bargaining, and Bell was never a businessman and certainly no match for Orton—few men were. There is no doubt that Gray's harmonic system was superior to Bell's, which, as it turned out, was never developed. Gray's system ultimately went into commercial service for a short time. But harmonic telegraphy, as we discussed earlier, was a theory ahead of its time. Orton, however, was simply playing on Bell's naiveté, stringing him along and trying to get as much information out of him as possible. Orton, a man of imposing and formidable appearance, knew how to play the negotiating game; and he was hedging his bets. He wanted to keep Bell hanging on in case Bell's system did somehow prove more advantageous than Gray's. Orton was no doubt playing a similar game with Gray.

One factor that weighed heavily against Bell, in Orton's eyes, was his close association with the chief architect of the Hubbard Bill. This bill, should it eventually pass, would sound the death knell for commercial telegraphy in America. As Orton saw it, it was hard to do business with someone who was trying to put you out of business. Orton and Hubbard were outwardly civil to each other, but there was little love lost between them. Hubbard was no doubt also trying to hedge his bets in case the Hubbard Bill didn't pass: if the government's Postal Telegraph Corporation did not materialize, then perhaps Western Union would be interested in Bell's harmonic system. Hubbard was the inveterate promoter and pitchman. Although Orton was fully aware that he had first met Bell at Hubbard's Washington, D.C., home, he feigned surprise when Bell said he was associated with Hubbard. As Bell related:

> Finally just as it was time for me to go, he [Orton] said "Bye the bye, is Mr. Hubbard interested in this matter with you?"
>
> I answered "Yes." He replied "The Western Union will never take up a scheme which will benefit Mr. Hubbard." After a little tirade about Mr. Hubbard we had to leave.[8]

That evening, Bell told Hubbard of Orton's remarks. The next day, following Hubbard's advice, Bell threatened to take his instruments over to the Atlantic and Pacific Telegraph Company, Western Union's chief competitor. Orton retreated somewhat and qualified his stance. He said that Western Union would not *assist* in the development of a scheme in which Hubbard was involved, but, Bell continued, "if the invention is perfected the Western Union would be open to become a purchaser whether Mr. Hubbard was associated with it or not." Orton was not about to close the door if there was a chance to benefit the company. After this New York meeting, Bell would not see Orton again for almost two years.

Bell returned to Boston and on April 3 wrote to his parents, "News has just arrived from Washington—that one of my applications has been allowed and will be issued to bear date next Tuesday."[9] This was the first of five patents Bell would receive prior to Hubbard's incorporation of the Bell Telephone Company. However, only two of them would be remembered, and only one would achieve historic status. Although he had just received his first patent, he realized that it still needed much work before it could be considered a commercially practical system. To achieve this objective, Hubbard would continue to urge the easily distracted Bell to keep plugging away.

Blackmailing Letter

One of Bell's competitors was Elisha Gray, a perception that, if not shared by Gray, was at least fostered by Hubbard and later by Bell's patent attorneys. While it is true that Gray was, in a sense, a competitor, the same could be said of Thomas Edison or any number of other inventors. The idea that Bell was in some kind of technological race with Gray was one of the techniques that Hubbard employed to spur Bell on and to keep him focused on perfecting his harmonic telegraph system.

Months before his meeting with Orton, sometime around October 1874, after he had been experimenting for some time with harmonic telegraphy, Bell went to a local Boston patent attorney, Joseph Adams, and had him draw up a caveat, which was sent to the Patent Office in November 1874.[10] After not hearing from him for a long time, Adams assumed that Bell had either abandoned his idea or had gone to another patent attorney. To see where he stood, Adams asked if Bell still wanted to be represented by him. During a business trip to Washington, D.C., Adams wrote:

> Prof. Bell
> Washington, D.C.
> Feb. 2nd 1875
>
> Dear Sir
>
> I hoped to see you before I left Boston to learn if you had any further use of my services in the matter that formed the subject of your caveat. I presume from my not seeing you in so long a time that you have not, but should like to know from you if I am free to act in the interest of other parties in the matter involving the same subject. Please inform me by return mail and address me in care of B. F. James, Esq. Box 747.
>
> Very truly yours
> Jos. H. Adams[11]

When Bell received this letter, he immediately jumped to the conclusion that Adams was up to no good. Adams could have worded his letter a little better, but it was not the sinister threat that Bell perceived. If Adams were as scurrilous as Bell assumed and had any villainous plans to steal Bell's ideas, he would simply have said nothing. It appears that Adams was being needlessly concerned about any perception of a conflict of interest. However, that's not how Bell saw it. He immediately dashed off a smoldering letter to his parents:

> I received today from Mr. Adams what I consider a dishonorable and blackmailing letter. I at once enclosed the letter to Mr. Hubbard asking him to see Mr. Adams and do what he thought best. At Mr. Sanders' suggestion, I answered Mr. Adams' letter by telegraph saying, "Mr. Hubbard will confer with you."
>
> I also sent a telegram to Mr. Hubbard saying, "Mr. Adams writes me from Washington conveying impression about to be employed by E.G.! Please see him. Address P.O. Box 747." I now await denouement.[12]

If Bell hadn't been so worked up when he wired Hubbard, he would have realized that Hubbard might have had a little problem locating Adams, given only a post office box number. The cryptic E.G., of course, was none other than Elisha Gray. To Bell, Gray was the dragon blocking his way to fame and fortune. In the same letter, he wrote:

> There is no doubt that there is to be a struggle between Mr. Elisha Gray and myself—and to my surprise I find that he has been making overtures to my solicitor [Mr. Adams]. I have been suspicious of Mr. Adams from the moment that he offered to find out for me what Mr. Gray was doing—and I have been careful to avoid letting Mr. Adams know of my latest experiments—as I thought if he could so easily get information for me from Mr. Gray's solicitor, Mr. G. could do the same through him.[13]

Although Gray used a number of patent attorneys, including Alex Hayes also of Boston, there is no indication that he ever employed Adams—or that he ever made "overtures" to him, despite Bell's comment. Except for Hayes, Gray's attorneys were based either in Chicago (Gray's headquarters) or Washington, D.C. Just how much of Adams's alleged offer of espionage is fact and how much is Bell's interpretation is impossible to say. Adams might simply have been offering to conduct a patent search to uncover any prior art in the field of Bell's invention. This is what patent agents routinely do for their clients, and it's perfectly legal. Whether Adams had any other source of illicit information is unknown but doubtful, and he certainly didn't have the Patent Office connection that Bell's next attorney did. Bell would often come to conclusions that were not always supported by the facts, as we shall see from his later court testimony. The irony here is that Bell roundly condemned Adams, whether justified or not, for the very activities he readily accepted from his new patent attorneys.

Pollok and Bailey

After dumping patent attorney Adams, sometime in February 1875, Hubbard arranged for the well-known Washington, D.C., firm of Pollok and Bailey to handle Bell's patent matters. Bell, now convinced that Elisha Gray was the enemy, described his new patent attorneys as though they were being recruited for battle:

> The lawyer engaged on our side is Mr. Pollok and his partner Mr. Bailey. They are the most eminent men connected with the Patent Office. I like the looks of both.[14]

The socially prominent and well-connected patent attorney Anthony Pollok was Hubbard's Washington, D.C., lawyer and also one of his associates in the U.S. Postal Telegraph Bill. As such, he had a vested interest in the bill's success. Hubbard no doubt felt that Bell's harmonic telegraph project was becoming too important to be trusted to just any patent attorney. The Hungarian-born Pollok had built a successful law practice and enjoyed the opulent lifestyle of a prosperous Washington lawyer. His office was a mere half block from the Patent Office. Always with an eye towards ever-greater prosperity, he was willing to do whatever it took to advance the cause of Hubbard's Postal Telegraph Bill.

Pollok embraced the nineteenth-century entrepreneurial philosophy that the ends always justify the means, the ends in this case being the control of a pivotal telegraph patent—specifically, Bell's developing harmonic telegraph patent. Such a patent would go a long way towards injecting the hoped-for new life into the Hubbard Bill. And to supply those means, Pollok turned to his law partner, Marcellus Bailey. In the eyes of Hubbard and Pollok, Bailey had the means to ensure the issuance of that critical patent: a Patent Office official named Zenas Fisk Wilber.

Zenas Fisk Wilber

Zenas Wilber was the principal patent examiner in charge of telegraph-related inventions. Unless overruled by the commissioner of patents,

Wilber decided the fate of all such applications and caveats. His role in telephone history has generally been ignored, yet he was part of a shameless scheme that provided unique advantages to Bell to the detriment of rival inventors. It is tempting to cast him in the guise of a villain, but then that would imply that he was the only culpable one. In reality, he was more pathetic than villainous, a weak-willed man much addicted to what was then the nation's beverage of choice—whiskey. Bell's one-time assistant, Thomas Watson, in his autobiography, described that popular libation and other vices:

> My father and all the stablemen smoked, but tobacco never was a temptation to me. Whiskey and water was the wine of the country and considered necessary to one's well-being. Nearly every man I knew drank several glasses of that beverage every day without any attempt to conceal it. Whiskey was easily accessible to me but I never cared to experiment with it and have been practically a teetotaler all my life.[15]

Wilber came from a prominent Ohio family and was a cousin of Rutherford B. Hayes, U.S. president from 1876 to 1880. During the Civil War he served in the Union army as a lieutenant but without any great distinction. During his military service, he became acquainted with Major Marcellus Bailey, who would later play a vital role in his life.[16] After the war, in 1870, Wilber secured an appointment to the Patent Office as a clerk and steadily advanced through the ranks to patent examiner and, ultimately, in 1877, to examiner of interferences, one of the top positions in that agency.[17] But sometime before he reached that lofty position, he crossed that fine, nebulous line that separates the heavy drinker from the alcoholic.

It is uncertain just when Wilber's drinking problem started, but it caused him to be perpetually short of money and constantly in debt. Strangely enough, in view of his steady advancement in the Patent Office, his alcoholism didn't seem to affect his job performance. However, we must remember that heavy drinking in those days was more readily accepted, or perhaps tolerated. Although the temperance movement had begun in the early part of the century, it had had little effect on the established drinking habits of the country.

At some point during his Patent Office career, Wilber renewed his friendship with the former major, Marcellus Bailey, now a partner in the patent law firm of Pollok and Bailey. Bailey, who still liked to be known as the Major, was now a prosperous patent attorney, and the firm of Pollok and Bailey was well known in Washington, D.C., and elsewhere. Bailey's friendship with Wilber was to be a valuable, though undeclared, asset to the firm.

To ease his money problems, Wilber began borrowing from his former army comrade and was soon heavily in debt to him. To Bailey, though, Wilber's money problems were an investment. Wilber would repay those mounting debts with the favors that only a patent examiner can give. As a patent examiner, Wilber was in the best possible position to help an ambitious, the-ends-justify-the-means patent attorney—and Bailey made full use of him.

Aside from keeping the firm of Pollok and Bailey posted on the most recent patent and caveat applications, an absolute violation of Patent Office confidentiality, nobody could expedite a patent application faster than Wilber and with less scrutiny. Factors that an examiner would normally explore—originality, functionality, prior art, double patenting, and so forth—were obligingly overlooked by Wilber when Bailey so requested. The typical inventor of that period had to wait four to five months from the time of filing until the patent was issued. Edison and Gray frequently waited eight to ten months. But thanks to Wilber, Bell set a Patent Office record for receiving the most patents in the least amount of time. Of the five patents he was issued prior to the start of the Bell Telephone Company, the average wait time was just over three weeks from filing to issue. His last patent was awarded in just 11 days. Considering the usual glacial pace of the Patent Office, this was incredibly fast service. Years later, in a sworn affidavit, Wilber would confess that "such rapid progress from applications to patents is exceptional, and few such instances, if any, can be found outside of Bell's cases."[18] Apparently, Bailey found his investment in Wilber to be a sound one. It seems that Wilber could do just about anything with a patent application except quash an interference. We'll see why shortly.

Wilber left the Patent Office sometime around 1880 and went to work for Thomas Edison as his patent agent. It was not uncommon for former patent examiners to become patent attorneys or agents upon leaving the office. One of Gray's patent attorneys, Alex Hayes, had been a patent examiner at one time. Edison and Wilber had had a long acquaintanceship, and Wilber was a frequent guest at Edison functions. It was Wilber who, in 1878, arranged for Edison to demonstrate his newly invented phonograph at the White House. Wilber simply called up his cousin, President Rutherford Hayes, and told him that Edison would like to demonstrate his latest gadget. Hayes was the first president to use a telephone. It is said that Edison remained at the White House showing off his talking machine until the early hours of the morning.[19]

Edison and Wilber's association as inventor and patent agent was more than just a business relationship; they were also stereopticon fans and frequently shared their extensive collections of stereopticon pictures. But friendship and alcohol don't always mix. Wilber's excessive drinking and related activities took money, money which Wilber "borrowed" from an account intended to pay for patent filing fees. When almost a year and 60 patent applications had gone by without a single patent coming back, Edison's people investigated. After they found a stack of unfiled patent applications and $1,300 missing from the filing fee account, Wilber's career as Edison's patent agent ended.[20] Wilber, who never testified in any of the infringement trials, died in August 1889.[21]

Patent Scam

Immediately after assuming the management of Bell's patent affairs, Pollok persuaded Bell to withdraw the Adams-created caveat and file an actual patent application. In fact, Pollok contrived to turn Bell's single caveat into not one but three separate patent applications. It wasn't that Pollok saw three distinct inventions in Bell's scheme but rather that he saw the basis for a clever patent strategy—actually, an ingenious patent scam. Bell, who was obviously unaware of his attorneys' machinations, naively explained to his parents:

> In regard to the patents. My lawyers—Pollok and Bailey—found on examination at the Patent Office that I had developed the idea so much further than Gray that they have applied for three distinct patents, in only one of which I come into collission [*sic*] with Gray.[22]

This was an extraordinary disclosure. Had Bell realized at the time what was going on, it is almost certain that he would never have revealed what he did. This letter was written on March 5, 1875; the three applications were filed between February 25 and March 10. Incredible as it seems, Pollok knew before he even filed Bell's last application that at least one of them would be in interference with Gray's still-pending, and supposedly confidential, application, the one Gray had filed only a few days before on February 23.

The scam was easy to set up. Since Pollok had illicit knowledge of exactly what Gray and others were claiming, thanks to Examiner Wilber, he drafted one (and perhaps two) of the three Bell applications to purposely conflict with them. The examiner, Wilber, would then have no choice but to declare an interference, and Gray's application, along with one of Bell's "throwaway" applications, would be tied up in interference litigation for months—and possibly years. Bell's second application would soon be in interference with another of his perceived competitors. On April 3, 1875, Bell, still unaware of the sinister business at the Patent Office on behalf of his application, wrote to his parents:

> The other two patents have also been allowed—but are suspended on account of interference with Gray. The Interference is to be declared in a day or two and then my testimony will come in.
>
> I have also been informed (unofficially) that a third interfering party has made his appearance in the shape of a Dane from Copenhagen—a distinguished electrician.[23]

This information, of course, came from Bell's attorneys, who in turn, got it from Wilber. For a patent attorney to be privy to this kind of internal, confidential information before any formal office action had been taken, was blatantly unethical. And in Wilber's case, because he was in the habit of accepting money from Bell's attorneys, it was downright criminal. But that was of little concern: Pollok had effectively blocked Gray's harmonic telegraph application, at least for the time being.

Bell was still confused about Patent Office practice. His other two applications could not have been allowed (as he stated) since they were in interference. And it would be a long time before his testimony would ever be needed. Actually, he wouldn't be called to testify until 1877, almost two years later. The lengthy time involved in adjudicating patent interferences is why they can be so devastating to an inventor. Bell's confusion, though, was caused by his own attorneys, who purposely kept him in the dark on Patent Office procedure. Pollok and Bailey rightly assumed that the high-minded Bell would be appalled if he knew what they were really planning. Remember, too, that Pollok and Bailey were not working for Bell but, in reality, were looking out for the interests of Hubbard and his U.S. Postal Telegraph Bill. It was Hubbard who was running the show and paying the bills. In time, though, the straight-laced Bell would lose some of his naiveté and gradually come to learn how business was done at the Patent Office. But for the moment, the less he knew about these machinations, the better.

Although two of the three applications that were filed shortly after Pollok and Bailey took over were now tied up in intentional interferences, Bell still had one on file. His attorneys never had any doubt that it would be allowed; after all, it was Wilber who would authorize it. On April 6, 1875, Bell's first patent (No. 161,739), was issued, a mere four weeks after it had been filed, thanks to Wilber's incredibly fast service. It was titled "Transmitter and Receiver for Electric Telegraphs" and claimed to be an "autograph telegraph" that would transmit facsimile copies of handwriting and drawings. In other words, it was to be a fax machine. Unfortunately, it required harmonic telegraphy to work.

The Rival

As far as Bell was concerned, Elisha Gray was his bête noire. But was this a long-standing and mutual rivalry: did Gray regard Bell as his major competition? In a letter to his Boston attorney, Gray asks:

> Mr. A. L. Hayes
> March 19, 1875
>
> My dear sir,
>
> Do you know a Professor Bell in Washington? Have you ever had any conversation with him in regard to my invention and what was the character of it. He claimed to Orton [president of Western Union] when he was in Washington that he could antedate me in everything that I ever claimed to do. The coincidence was so remarkable that it looks suspicious.
>
> He told Orton not to tell him how I did what I claimed but let him tell what he did. And then went on and described my method in regard to printing and all. Now I want you to tell all you know for I suspect he never thought of the thing till he got it from my invention.
>
> Yours &c.
> E. Gray [24]

As of the date of this letter, Gray had not yet received a patent on the device he mentions; it was still a confidential (so Gray assumed) patent application. Three weeks later, on April 6, 1875, Bell received his first patent, the one pertaining to a harmonic telegraph device. As discussed earlier, the two other Bell applications that Pollok had filed the month before were tied up in an interference action with Gray's application and that of another inventor, La Cour from Denmark. As soon as Gray received a published copy of Bell's April 6 patent, he fired off another letter to Alex Hayes:

> Apr. 26, 1875
>
> Mr. Hayes
>
> I have read Bell's claims and it seems to me he could not have described my invention better if he had copied it.
>
> How in the name of patent law could Wilber issue that pat. without declaring an interference? It was filed in March long after mine. The best construction you can put on it has a very bad look. I intend to go to the very bottom of the thing now. So everybody connected with the matter who cannot show a clean record had better stand from under. I am mad clear

down to my boots. As I understand the pat. in question it covers broadly the very gist of my invention and I will fight till the pat. expires before I will compromise on such a record.

WRITE IMMEDIATELY YOURS &C.
E. Gray[25]

There is little doubt that Gray did make his feelings about this matter known at the Patent Office, which will become more apparent when we review the events that took place there in February 1876. Examiner Wilber could do various things to help Pollok or Bailey expedite a patent application, but ignoring an interference could prove quite embarrassing to a patent examiner. This perhaps explains why, almost a year later, Wilber was so quick to declare a possible interference in Bell's and Gray's filings on February 14, 1876—not once, but twice.

The application to which Gray refers was the one Pollok had earlier tied up in an interference action. Gray, however, was unaware of the interference at the time. Gray was neither a volatile nor a quick-tempered individual and was slow to anger. The above letter was out of character with his personality, which tended more towards assuming honesty rather than chicanery. In this vein, Gray, too, was perhaps a little naive for a nineteenth century businessman. However, once convinced that he had been wronged, it was another matter. What Gray didn't realize at the time was that he had been the victim of a clever patent scam, one designed to tie up his pending application in a time-wasting tangle.

As far as Pollok's team was concerned, both Gray and the Dane La Cour, were effectively taken out of the game, thanks to Bell's two sacrificial applications. Bell, still unaware of what was going on, now had a little breathing spell in which to perfect his multiple-message harmonic telegraph. But, by mid-1875, he became sidetracked by a fascinating discovery—Bell found a way to transmit vocal sounds.

Notes

1. AGB to parents, March 5, 1875.
2. Bell Telephone Laboratories, *A History of Engineering and Science in the Bell System: The Early Years* (1875–1925), The Bell Laboratories, N.Y., 1975.
3. AGB to parents, March 5, 1875.
4. G. Hubbard to AGB, November 19, 1879.
5. American Bell Telephone Co., *Deposition of Alexander Graham Bell*, 1908, p. 90.
6. AGB to parents, March 5, 1875.
7. Ibid.

8. Ibid.
9. AGB to parents, April 3, 1875.
10. AGB to parents, November 14, 1874.
11. AGB to parents, February 5, 1875.
12. Ibid.
13. Ibid.
14. AGB to parents, February 21, 1875.
15. Thomas A. Watson, *Exploring Life*, D. Appleton, New York, 1926, p. 8.
16. See full text of Wilber's affidavit in chap. 14.
17. *Directory of the Department of the Interior*, 1877.
18. Wilber's affidavit (see chap. 14).
19. Robert Conot, *Thomas A. Edison: A Streak of Luck*, Da Capo, New York, 1979, p. 109.
20. Ibid., p. 214.
21. Elisha Gray Collection, Archive Center, National Museum of American History (NMAH), Washington, D.C.
22. AGB to parents, March 5, 1875.
23. AGB to parents, April 3, 1875.
24. Elisha Gray Collection, Archive Center, National Museum of American History (NMAH), Washington, D.C.
25. Ibid.

Chapter 5

The Day the Patent Was Filed

May 1, 1875–February 14, 1876

For months, Bell had been working hard to achieve the precision tuning needed to make the harmonic telegraph respond properly. If it were to be commercially successful, it would have to handle four or more simultaneous messages. So far, with delicate tuning, he could handle up to three messages. Such tuning took a good musical ear and near-perfect pitch, attributes that Bell possessed to a high degree. The frequency of each receiver had to be matched to that of its transmitter, so that when the latter was set in vibration, the former would vibrate in sympathy. This was the essence of harmonic telegraphy. In Bell's system, tuning was achieved by lengthening or shortening the armature, or reed, as it was called, of each receiver so it would vibrate at the desired frequency.

Although these adjustments were fairly simple for one with a good ear, there could be problems. If one of the transmitter-receiver combinations happened to be set to a harmonic of one of the others, a spurious vibration could be induced in more than one receiver, which, of course, would defeat the purpose of harmonic telegraphy. With finicky adjustments and a careful selection of base frequencies, this could be controlled. However, the likelihood of spurious interferences would increase rapidly as more transmitter-receiver combinations were added. This, it seemed, was one of the inherent problems with harmonic telegraphy.

The tuning procedure, though not difficult, was tedious and required repeated trial-and-error adjustments. Bell had set up three transmitters, each set to a different frequency, and six reed receivers, all connected to the same line. Three of the receivers were in Watson's room, and the other three were near Bell. He had been going over this routine when, for some reason, he failed to get the expected response on one of Watson's receivers. Suspecting a stuck reed on the corresponding receiver, a fairly common problem, he asked Watson to check and, if necessary, to free the reed. Sometimes, if the reed were adjusted too close to the core of the electromagnet, it would magnetically latch onto the core, and residual magnetism would hold it there. To mitigate this possibility, Bell turned off the battery current while Watson investigated.

Suddenly, Bell noticed the reed of another receiver start to vibrate for no apparent reason. He dashed into the room where Watson was checking the faulty receiver and asked him what he had done—and whatever it was, to do it again. Watson replied that he had simply done what he always did: plucked the reed of the stuck receiver to free it up and set it to vibrating again. Watson couldn't help but notice, from Bell's animated state, that something unusual had happened.

For the next hour or so, Bell and Watson plucked the reeds of the various electromagnets and listened to the induced sounds in the other reed receivers. Bell contemplated what he was witnessing. There was, he correctly theorized, enough residual magnetism in the iron cores of the receiver/transmitters that a vibrating reed in one could generate an alternating current sufficiently strong to vibrate the reed in another receiver/transmitter. To Bell, this was a most significant and surprising discovery—it completely dispelled a previous assumption he had made.

Bell was an eager student of the work being done in the field of electromagnetic theory, and he read whatever he could on the subject. He was well aware of the fact that an electrical current could be induced in a wire while it was in a fluctuating magnetic field. However, he greatly underestimated the effect. He had always assumed that a reed vibrating in a magnetic field—especially in the weak field of residual magnetism—would produce currents too feeble to be detected. But he was wrong. The lightly vibrating reed in the unplucked receiver demonstrated otherwise. He had Watson try the other receivers by plucking their reeds. The corresponding receivers near Bell responded in turn. Bell then pressed one of the reed receivers to his ear just enough to dampen the reed's natural frequency. To his amazement, he could hear, ever so faintly, the different pitches of the other receivers as Watson plucked each one in turn. The reed receiver, as he held it against his ear, acted as a crude earphone. When he made the magnetic field even stronger by passing battery current through the receiver's electromagnet, the sounds became noticeably louder.

Bell was extremely excited over this new discovery; he realized that he had greatly overestimated the power it took to make a reed receiver vibrate. Equally important, he learned that, even though a reed receiver had its own natural resonant frequency, it could also respond to any other frequency. As far as Bell was concerned, this was a profound revelation. Ideas began churning in his mind, and a concept evolved that required a more sophisticated experiment.

Gallows Model Telephone

Bell's concept took the form of a crude drawing, which he gave to Watson to be turned into a device that, he hoped, would prove what the reed receiver had merely promised. Watson's embodiment of that drawing was for a device that would later be called the *gallows model telephone* because of its fanciful resemblance to a hangman's scaffold, with the electromagnet suggesting the shrouded body of the condemned. It was a sophisticated refinement of the reed receiver he was then using, inspired by the phenomenon of the plucked reed. It was essentially the armature of a reed relay attached to a drumlike membrane of goldbeater's skin (a thin form of parchment). As we know now, the gallows model had all the elements needed for a basic, functional telephone: an electromagnet, an armature, a sound-activated membrane, and a battery. It would later be classed as a voice-powered, magneto-inductive telephone. However, it had one problem: it didn't work—although theoretically it should have.

Anxious to try it out, Bell connected it to several cells and to one of the reed receivers used in the previous plucked reed experiment. (Based on his later testimony, they were most likely bichromate cells, a popular battery of the period of almost two volts potential.) First, Bell shouted into it while Watson, located in another room, listened on the reed receiver. Watson claimed he could hear something, but he couldn't quite make it out. Then they changed places, and Watson shouted while Bell listened. However, Bell heard nothing, at least nothing like what he had hoped to hear, and he considered the experiment a failure. Then, suddenly the armature, which had been glued to the membrane, broke free and clamped itself onto the core of the electromagnet. When they reglued it with an even stronger bond and tried it again, the membrane tore. This gives us a clue as to why the gallows telephone failed to work.

As we said before, theoretically, the gallows model telephone should have worked. We know from samples still existing and from other reports

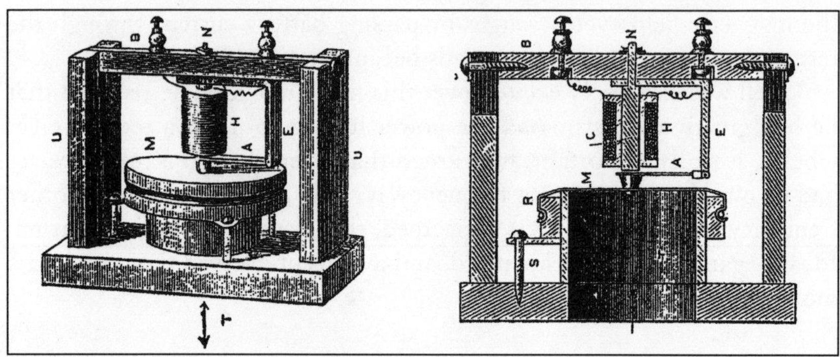

Figure 5–1. Courtroom reproduction of the gallows model telephone of June 1875.

that Bell used electromagnets of rather low resistance, typically from one to ten ohms.[1] As a result, the relatively high source voltage and low circuit resistance created such a strong magnetic pull on the membrane that it could not adequately respond to the voice sounds—it was so highly stressed that it couldn't flex enough to sufficiently activate the armature. In addition, Bell compounded these problems by employing a fairly heavy, pivoted armature, similar to those used in telegraphic service. All in all, his instrument was simply too inefficient to produce recognizable results. (Interestingly, during the 1879 Dowd case, discussed later, a model of the gallows telephone was reconstructed for a courtroom demonstration. Utilizing four years of accrued design knowledge, the engineers and model makers of the Bell Telephone Company were able to produce a gallows telephone that corrected the original faults and actually did work—at least well enough to prove the point.)

Further work on the gallows model was postponed for about a month as Bell and Watson focused once more on harmonic telegraphy. Then, early in July 1875, Watson completed a second gallows model, this one with a lighter but still pivoted armature. The two experimenters repeated their earlier tests, but this time they used the two similar instruments, one as a transmitter and the other as a receiver. The always-optimistic Watson claimed he could hear indistinct but voicelike sounds from the second gallows instrument. These would become the famous "vocal sounds" that Bell would claim in his next patent application. Bell, as before, heard nothing that he considered even close to sending spoken words along a telegraph wire. After this last test, no further work was done on the problem of voice transmission until after Bell received his next patent on March 7, 1876.

However, these failed experiments didn't discourage Bell, and they didn't stop him from including the instrument, in a modified form, in his next patent application. This is the one that would be identified as the famous Telephone Patent, the one historians would label "the most valuable patent ever issued." Although he hadn't been able to transmit articulate speech, as he had hoped, he had managed to transmit something. Watson maintained he had been able to detect, ever so faintly, some kind of transmitted sounds made by the human voice. Bell would be careful in his next patent application not to claim too much for this device, such as actually transmitting speech, lest the patent examiner make him prove it with a working model. Such a model was at the option of the patent examiner, an option that was then still fairly common practice, despite the fact that the Patent Office was running out of space for its ever-growing collection of models. Playing it safe, the most Bell would claim, based on what Watson said he had heard, was that it transmitted "vocal sounds".

Shortly after this experiment in sound transmission, Bell wrote to his friend Sarah Fuller, principal of the Boston School for Deaf Mutes, concerning one of his young pupils, George Sanders. In an unrelated postscript, Bell exclaimed:

> Grand telegraphic discovery today. Transmitted *vocal sounds* for the first time.... With some further modification I hope we may be enabled to distinguish ... the "timbre" of the sound. Should this be so, conversation *viva voce* by telegraph will be a *fait accompli.* [2]

What makes this announcement so significant is that Bell makes a clear distinction between what he calls "vocal sounds" and articulate speech. To Bell, at that particular time, they were two different things. He knew he was on to something, but it seemed just out of his grasp. Bell never did achieve speech transmission with the gallows model nor with the device depicted in his March 7 patent, nor did his patent ever claim to do so.

During one of the many court trials, Bell Telephone Company lawyers, in defending Bell's patent, pointed out to the judge that articulate speech was obviously, and undeniably, a vocal sound. And that, the lawyers argued, specious logic that it was, proved that when Bell used the term *vocal sounds* in his patent, he obviously intended it to mean "articulate speech." Bell of course readily agreed, despite his letter to Sarah Fuller stating otherwise. But more important for the Bell interests, the court also agreed. At the time he prepared his March 7, 1876, patent, although articulate speech was his goal, Bell was astute enough to realize he had not achieved it.

Bell's lack of a more descriptive term for speech, other than that of vocal sounds, was always a weak point in his patent and was frequently cited by opposing counsel. However, by the time Bell gave his deposition in the government's case to annul his patent, he had managed to convince himself that had he used such terms as *articulate speech* or *conversations*, the description would have been inaccurate. As he said:

> I believed at the time I drew my specification, and still believe, that if I described my invention specifically for the purpose of transmitting articulate speech alone, it would have been an inadequate description, not covering fully the scope of the invention.[3]

Just what the fuller scope of his invention entailed, he never said. The fact that other inventors, such as Gray and McDonough (see chap. 12), saw no reason to exclude the specific and concrete terms *speech* and *conversations* from their patent applications shows the weakness in Bell's argument. Oddly, Bell had no hesitation in using the term *articulate speech* in his now-called Second Telephone Patent (January 30, 1877). But, regardless of what he may have believed later on, he knew that in the summer of 1875 he had at least sent a vocal sound over a wire.

Rocky Road to Romance

As much as Hubbard tried to keep Bell focused on perfecting his harmonic system, it seems the young inventor was always being sidetracked by other interesting distractions. His father, more than once, took him to task for jumping from one thing to another, "I feel strongly as Mrs. Hubbard does in reference to your flightiness from theory to theory without working any of them to a practicable issue."[4] But one of the biggest distractions had nothing to do with vocal sounds or harmonic telegraphy—it was Hubbard's own daughter, Mabel. For a long time, Bell had been smitten by the petite and attractive teenager who, when they first met as teacher and pupil in late 1873, wasn't quite 16. By 1875, he could no longer deny it, and he finally admitted to himself—and later to Mabel's parents—that he was in love.

As the summer of 1875 was waning, most of the things in Bell's life were moving favorably for him, except for the blossoming romance with his mentor's daughter. The courtship had been mostly one-sided, mainly at the request of Mabel's mother. Part of the problem was Mabel's age; she was only 17 then, and Bell was almost 11 years her senior. The age difference weighed heavily on Mabel's parents. When they first met him, because of his cultured speech and mature demeanor, they had assumed that he was considerably older than he was. It wasn't that they didn't approve of Bell; on the contrary, they were extremely fond of him. But they worried that Mabel had yet to enter into adulthood. As we might say today, she had yet to find herself, to find out who she was.

At one point in their relationship, sometime during August, when it was not progressing as well as Bell had hoped, he became extremely distraught, almost to the point of being physically ill. For years he had been plagued with splitting headaches, especially when things weren't going as he wished, and he would sometimes take to his bed for several days at a time. He was by nature volatile, high-strung, and given to acting impulsively, especially under stress. A more meditative person would have responded differently.

Apparently, Bell had misread or misinterpreted a letter from his mother concerning Mabel. Jumping to unwarranted conclusions was one of Bell's weaknesses. Feeling pressured from all sides—by his parents, her parents, and perhaps even Mabel herself—he responded by pouring out his frustrations in letters and telegrams to his parents. This prompted his confused father to reply:

> Home, Sunday, August 29th, 75
>
> My dear Aleck,
>
> I "write at once" in reply to your unintelligible telegram.... Your telegram of the day before, addressed to Mamma was also opened by your Uncle, who must be more mystified than even we are. What is wrong with you? When your Mother read your last letter (in your Uncle's study) she almost fainted. They of course asked what was the matter. I could only say that you had imposed absolute secrecy. The letter I did not see for several hours afterwards. Mamma did not wish me to read it at all. She however ultimately gave it to me, and I read it, with what feelings I shall not describe. Since then you have telegraphed "all right now," and the latest telegram to which I am replying, asks us to destroy a letter which has not yet arrived! The extraordinary and unwarranted messages are bewildering.... Never allow yourself to think an evil or unloving thought in reference to your parents! Under all circumstances take for granted their affection and true interest are lifelong. "Honor thy father and thy mother that the days may be long in the land which God giveth thee." Come home and rest.... I took Mamma for a trip to Niagara as an antidote to the effect of your letter. She is better.... With much love I am ever,
>
> Your affectionate father,
> Alex. Melville Bell.[5]

Melville Bell understood well his son's impulsive nature and freely forgave whatever intemperate thoughts he may have expressed. Alexander likewise understood his father's concerns and realized that he had, as he often did, acted in haste and without too much forethought. Soon everything was back to normal as quickly as it had erupted. Melville Bell would dish out fatherly advice ("Put a coat of charity over your porcupine quills in the future!"[6]) whenever he felt Alexander needed it, and Alexander, in turn, was never hesitant about expressing his views on the advice. But in the end, neither would harbor any grudges and the air was always cleared. Alexander and his father maintained a very close relationship until the latter's death in 1905. On August 31, 1875, Alexander wrote to his father explaining the forces that led up to his most recent crisis:

> Dear Papa
>
> ...Please forgive me for my harsh allusions to you—and do not think I do not love you. You do not know how much trouble I have passed through.... It made me feel so bitterly that I could not help writing as I did—but I was sorry for it afterwards.
>
> ...She [Mabel] has been for two months at the sea-side under the care of a guardian who had formed a dislike for me. An *old maid* who has no thoughts of—nor sympathy with—love. She had been so influencing Mabel against me that she had finally formed a deep dislike for me—and distrusted my intentions, and I was powerless to explain. Had she died with these ideas in her mind—I really think I should have committed suicide.[7]

By the time he wrote that letter, Mabel had returned from Nantucket, and she and Alexander had had a long talk on the future of their relationship, which left him feeling much better. The "old maid" was Mary Blatchford, Mabel's older cousin, who later came to idolize Alexander and who, apparently, never did marry. Earlier, Alexander had managed to convince Mabel's parents of his sincerity, and they, in turn, relieved him of his promise not to reveal his feelings towards Mabel. They agreed to let Mabel herself decide the future of their relationship. Mabel's mother also agreed that if he could win her daughter's love, she would not stand in his way. Less than three months later, Alexander wrote to his parents:

> This day—Thursday Nov. 25th—has been appointed by the Governor of Massachusetts—as a Day of Thanksgiving for the Commonwealth—and to me it is truly a day of Thanksgiving—for Mabel has to-day trusted herself to me and has promised to become my wife.
>
> This is her birthday—She was eighteen years old this morning. My heart is too full to allow me to write much to you tonight—so I scribble off only these few lines that you may know of my happiness.
>
> Please write Mabel one of your nicest and kindest letters. It might be well to write to Mr. and Mrs. Hubbard too.[8]

Bell-Brown Arrangement

After his unsuccessful attempts in June and July 1875 to transmit speech and bowing to Hubbard's constant badgering, Bell went back to working on his harmonic telegraph system. Hubbard and his associates had little interest in something as pointless (economically, that is) as sending vocal sounds over a wire. They needed a harmonic telegraph system, and by fall Bell had progressed to the point that he began drafting specifications for yet another harmonic telegraph patent application. He continued to experiment and to refine his specifications until early January 1876, when, as he would testify later, he had them in final form to submit to the Patent Office. This was to be the defining patent for his harmonic telegraph system, the one Hubbard, along with attorneys Pollok and Bailey, had been pushing for—the one they hoped would advance the cause of the Hubbard Bill.

After drawing up the specifications for this latest application, almost as an afterthought, Bell added an illustration roughly depicting his earlier device, the gallows telephone from the previous summer. This would become the famous figure 7 in the patent application he was about to file. He also added a brief paragraph describing the instrument in the illustration. Just what connection figure 7 had to the rest of his patent application, which was for the harmonic telegraph, has forever remained a mystery. His attorneys allowed it, no doubt against their better judgment, simply to appease Bell. They knew they ran the risk of creating a "double patent," two different inventions under the same patent, which was prohibited under patent law.[9]

Even before completing this latest application, starting in about October 1875, Bell had begun considering the feasibility of applying for foreign patents, particularly in England. After all, he was still a British subject. He had made inquiries along these lines with friends still in England but apparently without much success. Later, probably through his father, he learned of a family friend living in Toronto, Canada, who might be willing to help. The Honorable George Brown was editor of the *Toronto Globe* as well as a prominent member of the Canadian Liberal party and the former premier of Canada. Brown, obviously a man of means and accomplishment, would be an ideal choice for such an assignment. He learned of Bell's interest in obtaining British patents and suggested that he and his brother, Gordon, might consider such a venture.

The Browns considered the proposition, not too seriously at first, for several months and finally, on December 29, 1875, agreed to Bell's proposal. Under this agreement, the Browns were to undertake the cost of securing British patents and defending them in court if necessary. George Brown himself would go to England to make the necessary arrangements to obtain the patents. In return, Bell agreed to give them 50 percent of all foreign receipts accruing from the patents. These were for his harmonic telegraphy scheme and had little to do with the telephone—which, of course, didn't exist at the time. In addition, they were to pay Bell $50 a month until the patents were issued, for a maximum of six months. These payments were to allow Bell to move to more "secure" quarters. As he told the Browns, he had been bothered by possible spies at Williams's shop, the place where he was presently conducting his experiments: "I was quite troubled by rumors that had reached me that strangers were visiting Mr. Williams's workshop, and examining my apparatus with curious eyes."[10]

This arrangement was mutually advantageous to both parties since it was generally accepted that successful improvements in telegraphy could be financially rewarding. Assuming that the British patents would be commercially viable, the Brown brothers stood to make a great deal of money, and Bell stood to capture a major foreign market. Both parties were anxious to launch their mutual business venture, and George Brown told Bell he would notify him as soon as he had made arrangements to sail for England.

Bell returned to Boston around the first of January 1876 and began the job of finishing up the specifications for his next patent application, the one destined to become the most valuable patent ever issued. In addition to these details, he was also confronted with the laborious and boring task of preparing numerous copies of his other patent specifications. As he wrote to Mabel:

> I have so much copy work to do that I have employed a copyist but must still do a good deal myself—as I require three copies of each of my four specifications. One for the U.S. Patent Office, one for George Brown, and one for myself.[11]

The "four specifications" he refers to consisted of his first (April 6, 1875) patent, the two applications still tied up in interference actions, and his latest application. Bell completed the final revisions to this latest application around January 12 and forwarded it to Hubbard in Washington. Hubbard, in turn, brought it to Pollok and Bailey, who prepared a neatly written copy,[12] commonly called a "fair copy," and mailed it back to Bell. On January 20, Bell signed it, had it witnessed and notarized, and returned it to Pollok and Bailey with the instructions: do not file; hold until further notice. This simple request, and the mystery surrounding it, goes to the core of the Bell-Gray controversy. As we will see, this instruction played a vitally important role.

Since his Thanksgiving Day engagement to Mabel Hubbard almost two months earlier, Bell had completed the application for his second patent and was now about to obtain his first foreign patents. He also had acquired two new business partners in the persons of George Brown and his brother, Gordon. At long last, or so it must have seemed to Bell, his fortunes were beginning to turn, and at this rate he would soon be financially able to marry Mabel, a goal that was always foremost in his mind.

On January 13, 1876, Bell received the anxiously awaited telegram from Brown: "Sail by *Russia* twenty-sixth. Will be at St. Nichols Hotel N.Y. on twenty-fifth."[13] On January 25, 1876, Bell, Hubbard, Pollok, and George Brown met in New York to go over last-minute details before Brown departed for England.[14] The fact that both Hubbard and Pollok came up from Washington to attend this meeting attests to the importance of Brown's trip. If they could lock in foreign patent rights, especially on this, Bell's second harmonic telegraph patent application, they all stood to make a great deal of money. Hubbard and Pollok apparently felt that with Bell's first patent and this next one they would have patent dominance in the field of harmonic telegraphy. And with that, they could pretty much write their own ticket, assuming, of course, that there were no snags along the way.

We don't know what they talked about—this was never documented—but knowing the nature of the meeting we can be reasonably certain that it focused primarily on the various applications Brown was taking with him. They would have wanted to make certain that Brown fully understood the nature of the patents he was applying for and therefore would have carefully reviewed all the details. In addition, they were probably discussing future business strategies to exploit Bell's patents.

Brown, who had only a cursory knowledge of telegraphy, had previously told them that he intended to discuss Bell's inventions with Sir William Thompson, apparently to get a second opinion. Sir William, later Lord Kelvin, was England's most highly regarded scientist, and securing an appointment with him would have presented no problem to Brown, who had both the social standing and the political clout to arrange such a meeting.[15] Assuming a satisfactory report from Sir William, Brown would then arrange for a patent solicitor to have Bell's specifications worked up into the proper form, along with the necessary drawings, for filing with the British Patent Office. As soon as Brown had attended to all of this business, and the application was safely filed, he would fire off a cablegram to Bell. This would be the all-clear signal for Bell to file his

American application, the one Pollok and Bailey were holding as instructed. There was a sound, legal reason for filing the British patent first.

George Brown was well aware of how the British patent system worked. One point he insisted upon was that he be allowed to file in the British Patent Office before Bell did so in the American office. Under British patent law, to protect the claims in the British patent, it was vital that the invention not be published nor disclosed prior to filing at the British Patent Office. Brown believed that *any* prior filing in the American Patent Office would—or could—compromise the British patent. Consequently, he insisted that Bell promise that the American application would not be filed until *after* Brown had filed in the British office.[16] Brown was not about to waste his time and money on a patent that could be made worthless by such an act as advance filing in America. Of the four applications he was taking to England, only one had been issued a patent. Bell promised that he would honor Brown's wishes and even put it in writing:

> N.B.—It is understood that Mr. Bell will not perfect his application in the American patent office until he hears from Mr. Brown, that he may do so without interfering with European patents.[17]

After Brown sailed for England, two incontrovertible facts emerged: (1) Bell never received the expected all-clear cable from Brown, and (2) Bell's application was hastily filed, under highly unorthodox and irregular circumstances, on February 14—completely contrary to Bell's promise and written agreement with Brown.

Sudden Filing

Brown's failure to send a cablegram was, in all probability, the direct result of the sudden filing of Bell's application (this will be discussed in the next chapter). But in attempting to explain that urgent need to get to the Patent Office on that fateful Valentine's Day, we stumble into a mystery. According to popular history, Hubbard became "impatient" because there had been no word from Brown. And it was this supposed anxiety that compelled him to rush Bell's application to the Patent Office on February 14, 1876. Bell would later testify:

> Mr. Brown neglected to take any action in the matter and sent no cablegram; and Mr. Hubbard, becoming impatient at the delay, privately instructed my solicitors to file the specification in the American Patent Office, and on the fourteenth day of February, 1876, it was so filed without my knowledge or consent.[18]

On the surface, this sounds quite plausible, but on closer examination it just doesn't stand up. It seems rather odd that Hubbard would have acted as he did simply on the basis of "impatience." After all, Bell had given his word, both verbally as well as in a written note on Brown's specification, that he would wait for a cable from Brown. The most compelling reason for waiting was economic: there was the potential for a lucrative British market. But what is even more puzzling about who authorized the sudden filing is that neither Bell nor Hubbard could get their stories straight. During another court case, Hubbard testified:

> He [Bell] did not hear from Mr. Brown as he expected, and finally wrote to me that if he did not hear by a certain day, that I might file it.[19]

Not only do Bell and Hubbard give conflicting testimony on this point, in chapter 9, we will see that Bell offered yet a third explanation on the question of who ordered the filing. About the only thing we know for certain about the filing is that it did occur on February 14, 1876.

Whether Brown was going to England solely for Bell's benefit, we don't know; it's quite possible he had other business to attend to as well. We do know that Brown's ship, the *Russia,* sailed on the evening of January 26.[20] Travel time to England in those days of sail-assisted steamships was highly variable; a traveler could not say for certain when he might arrive. When Thomas Watson, Bell's former assistant, made that same journey in 1881, he spent over two weeks on the water because of weather conditions.[21] Nor was it unheard of to spend three weeks or more battling adverse winds and weather. Bell and Hubbard, both ocean travelers themselves, would have been well aware of these travel vagaries and would—or should—have allowed for them.

If Brown had had a passage like Watson's, he wouldn't have arrived in London until February 11 or 12, just a few days before Hubbard—or someone—rushed to the U.S. Patent Office. It would have been impossible for Brown to have done anything that quickly with Bell's applications. Actually, though, the *Russia* made good time, no doubt aided by favorable westerlies, and Brown arrived in Liverpool on Saturday, February 5, and in London that weekend.[22] Of course, neither Bell nor Hubbard had any way of knowing this. Therefore, Monday, February 7, would have been the earliest Brown could have started the process, assuming he had no other business to attend to. But he still would have needed more time to do all that had to be done: to arrange a meeting with Sir William Thompson, to line up a British patent solicitor, to prepare the specifications, to have patent drawings made, and to process the application. Remember, Bell's specifications had to be prepared in accordance with British Patent Office requirements. It would have been unreasonable and unrealistic for either Bell or Hubbard to have expected Brown to do so much in just a week.

Moreover, if Hubbard had been truly concerned, he could easily have cabled Brown for a progress report and had a reply in a matter of hours or in a day at the most. The argument that Hubbard became impatient with Brown's lack of communication is without merit and simply doesn't stand up in light of what we now know. Lack of communication and impatience had nothing to do with the sudden filing. So what really caused Hubbard to jeopardize the British patents and to forgo a potentially lucrative foreign market? We will never know for certain, since the available records are silent on this point. We can only surmise his motivation based on what we do know. But on this basis, it is obvious that there was a more compelling reason for Hubbard's action than mere impatience.

The only logical hypothesis based on the available evidence is that Hubbard, through the accommodating Pollok and Bailey, became privy to some potentially damaging information. Whatever it was, it was alarming enough to warrant rushing Bell's application to the Patent Office as soon as possible, even if it meant reneging on a potentially valuable business deal. Pollok, of course, had been pushing for an early filing ever since Bell completed the application; it was Bell, with Hubbard's concurrence, who wanted to delay filing until he heard from Brown. So what was the possible nature of this alarming information, and how was it obtained?

This much we know from the record: (1) Bell claimed that his application was filed on February 14 without his knowledge; (2) it was filed in a highly unorthodox manner to bypass normal Patent Office procedure; (3) it was filed without word from Brown; and (4) this act violated Bell's agreement with Brown. The following is the sequence of events that best fits the available evidence.

Elisha Gray's Caveat

Gray had been in Washington since the latter part of January 1876, attending to a variety of patent matters with his attorney, William Baldwin.[23] He was winding down his business at the Patent Office in preparation for a trip to Philadelphia to prepare for the upcoming Centennial Exposition, where he planned a rather extensive exhibition of his telegraphic devices. He also planned to meet with his financial backer, Philadelphia dentist Dr. Samuel S. White. White had amassed a small fortune from his patented method for making porcelain teeth, and he subsidized Gray's inventions and shared in the profits.

However, Gray had one last piece of personal business he wanted to take care of before leaving. He wanted to file a caveat on the "speaking telegraph" he had long been thinking about but never had the time to work on. Just as Hubbard, Bell's financial backer, endeavored to keep Bell focused on telegraphic designs, so did White try to keep Gray focused on his telegraphic devices. Once, during a meeting with White, Gray brought up the subject of transmitting the human voice as a possible invention. As Gray related the conversation some years later:

> I told him I thought it would be very valuable if it worked out. He gave me a look that I shall never forget, but he did not say a word. The look conveyed more meaning than all the words he could have said, and I did not dare broach the subject again.[24]

Knowing White's feelings on the idea of transmitting human voices,[25] Gray said nothing concerning what he was about to do, not even to his assistant, William Goodridge. But then on Friday, February 11, he gave Goodridge a rough drawing he had prepared along with several pages of handwritten text.[26] He instructed Goodridge to have William Skinkle, one of Baldwin's draftsmen, work it up into a drawing suitable for a caveat. Baldwin would handle the rest of the caveat, which, as Gray later recalled, was completed late Saturday afternoon, too late to be notarized.[27] He would attend to that final detail first thing Monday morning, before making arrangements to leave for Philadelphia.

The employees in Baldwin's patent office were soon treated to a rare glimpse into the future. As the caveat's illustration gradually took shape under Skinkle's deft strokes, Gray's invention finally emerged. There it was—a telegraph that could actually transmit the human voice. The caveat's title said it all: "Instruments for Transmitting and Receiving Vocal Sounds." Even to the invention-weary clerks in a patent attorney's office, who were used to seeing all sorts of clever devices, this one was truly special. And it appeared so simple. Once it was explained how it worked, one could only marvel at its ingenuity.

What a choice bit of news: the well-known telegraph engineer, Elisha Gray, had just invented an incredibly simple device that would allow a person to send his voice over a telegraph wire. He had actually done what the scientists and philosophers had long been talking about—what some even said was impossible. And he was preparing to file a caveat to cover it. It was the kind of story that would make the messenger the center of attention.

How then did this intriguing bit of information find its way from Baldwin's office to Anthony Pollok? Based on his correspondence and comments to Bell, Hubbard was somehow always well-informed about Gray's comings and goings as well as his Patent Office business. Although we will never know the precise channel for such covert information, it's sufficient to understand that it could have been passed through a variety of links. The Washington, D.C., patent agent fraternity was a relatively small one, with offices usually located within a block or so of the Patent Office and with many employees living within walking distance of their offices. For example, William Skinkle, the draftsman who worked on Gray's caveat, lived in a boardinghouse just a block from the Patent Office and essentially just around the corner from Pollok and Bailey's office. It's quite possible that an employee or two from that office also lived there or took meals there—and over dinner, they talked shop. But whatever the link, whether it was simply idle, after-work gossip or intentional espionage, knowledge of Gray's caveat got back to Pollok and Bailey sometime between that Saturday evening and early Monday morning.

We don't know how much detail was revealed in that covert report, but to Bell's attorneys, this knowledge of Gray's caveat was quite unsettling, especially the part about "transmitting vocal sounds." Those were the very words Bell had used in the application Pollok and Bailey were holding for him. But now they had a serious problem. From what they had learned of Gray's as-yet-unfiled caveat, there was a good chance that the Patent Office would have to declare a possible interference with Bell's as-yet-unfiled application. Both Bell and Gray were claiming the transmission of "vocal sounds," which alone would be sufficient grounds for such a declaration. The great irony was that Bell now faced the same Patent Office action that Pollok had masterminded so effectively against Gray and La Cour when he tied up their harmonic telegraph applications.

To understand the problem now facing Bell's application, we must look first at the Patent Act of 1836, the one in force at the time, as it pertains to caveats. The portion that concerns us is explained in the *Guide to the Practice of the Patent Office*:

> The primary object [of a caveat], however is to prevent the issuing of a rival patent for the same thing to a subsequent inventor. Before the issuing of a patent, the caveats which have been filed within the year preceding the application are carefully searched. If one is found which may conflict with the proposed patent, the issue is suspended. Notice is thereupon given to the person who filed the caveat so found, and he is required to complete his application within three months. Unless he complies, the Office will proceed with the other case, regardless of the caveat. If, on the other hand, he files his application as required, and it is found to cover the same ground with the one already in the Office, an "interference," as it is termed, will be declared between the two.[28]

In other words, only after a conflicting caveat has been turned into a patent application can the examiner determine whether an actual interference exists; until then, it's only a *possible* interference. But during the three months given to the caveat holder to complete his patent application, the other application is suspended. However, the exact phrasing of the statute pertaining to interferences with caveats, as found in Section 4902 of the Patent Act of 1836, left room for a most remarkable interpretation. It was upon this interpretation that Pollok and Bailey devised a rather ingenious, two-part scheme to circumvent any possible interference action with Bell's latest application. It's important to realize that their scheme would work *only* if they knew Gray was filing a caveat. If Gray were filing a regular patent application, there would have been no need to rush Bell's application to the Patent Office that Monday morning—they could have waited for as long as it took for Brown's cablegram.

This brings us to the crux of the problem that so alarmed Pollok and Bailey. Because of the way the patent law was written regarding conflicts between caveats and patent applications (Section 4902), an interference could result *only if Gray filed his caveat before Bell filed his application*. If it were the other way around, if the application were filed before the caveat, then an interference could not be declared. Therefore, to prevent the possibility of Bell's application being tied up in a long, drawn-out interference action, it was essential that Bell file before Gray—or at least have it *look* like he filed first. But neither Pollok nor Bailey knew when Gray would file his caveat. Fortunately, Hubbard was still in Washington, and Pollok wasted no time in spelling out the problem and listing the options.

Hubbard's Dilemma

For almost a year, Hubbard had been doing all he could to keep Bell focused on perfecting his multiple-message harmonic telegraph invention. Only the previous fall, Hubbard had rebuked Bell for his tendency to "undertake every new thing that interests you & accomplish nothing of value to anyone."[29] Hubbard and his associates considered Bell's harmonic telegraph vital to the U.S. Postal Telegraph Bill. But based on the information they now had of Gray's caveat, Pollok and Hubbard came to a startling realization.

It now appeared that Bell's seemingly fruitless dalliance with the gadget that he hoped would transmit voice messages, a sketch of which he had included in his application, might not have been so frivolous after all. Here was the highly esteemed Elisha Gray—in Bell's mind, his most formidable competitor—with an invention that claimed to do just that:

to transmit the human voice over a telegraph wire. Suddenly, Bell's experiments in transmitting vocal sounds had taken on new meaning. One thing was certain though: they would have to get more information on the caveat.

Hubbard now faced a dilemma. He had to decide whether to file immediately to avoid a threatening and time-consuming interference action and, as a result, most likely lose the hoped-for British patent or wait until Brown's cablegram arrived before filing and still gain the potential British market. The second alternative, because of the filing delay, would almost certainly lead to a possible interference, but unlike the first alternative, would not affect the British patent. It was a tough call. Both alternatives presented serious problems, but Hubbard no doubt reasoned that if he had to make a choice, he would choose an American over a British patent. He selected option one.

In light of their knowledge of Gray's caveat, Pollok and Bailey were now aware of certain discrepancies in Bell's application that would have to be addressed. But now that Hubbard had made his decision, the immediate task was to avoid what they knew would almost certainly be an interference. Timing was the critical element in this case. Because of the intervening weekend, it was quite possible that Pollok and Bailey didn't learn of Gray's caveat until sometime Sunday or early Monday morning. If such were the case, fast action was called for, since they would have no knowledge of when Gray would actually file his caveat. If they assumed a worst-case scenario, Gray would file on Monday, February 14.

Pollok's "Proof"

To put the first part of their scheme into operation, as Pollok and Bailey had scripted it, Bell's application had to get to the Patent Office before Gray's caveat. And even if it didn't actually get there first, it had to *appear* to have arrived first. This bit of legerdemain would be accomplished by a daily journal, or log book, called the "cash blotter."

The cash blotter was kept in the chief clerk's office and simply listed the applicant's name and amount of the filing fee.[30] It was basically an accounting record used to tally up the day's receipts and to provide a checklist of the documents received that day. It was not intended to show any chronological sequence. In fact, it would have been impossible to show any particular order since it included both hand-delivered and mailed-in applications.

We don't know who actually delivered Bell's application; Bell himself was still in Boston. But, as we saw earlier, whoever it was insisted that the application bypass the normal channel and be hand carried directly to Room 118, the office of Principal Patent Examiner Zenas F. Wilber.

The clerk's procedure for managing the cash blotter never varied: all of the documents received by mail, both morning and afternoon, were recorded first; this was followed at the end of the day by the hand-delivered ones taken from the in baskets.[31] As we know, Bell's application was brought in shortly before noon, just after the clerk in charge of the cash blotter started to enter the applications and caveats from the morning mail.[32]

Ordinarily, Bell's hand-delivered application would simply have been tossed into the in basket, as Gray's had been, where it would remain until later in the day. At that time, the contents of the basket would be removed and sent to the chief clerk's office, where they would be recorded as the final entries in the cash blotter. After this, they would be combined with the mailed-in applications and readied for distribution the next day to the appropriate patent examiners.

But that didn't happen. The person who brought in Bell's application demanded that it be taken immediately to Room 118. Because of this unusual request,[33] it was not thrown into the in basket. Therefore, before heading for Room 118, the clerk had no choice but to stop at the chief clerk's office, and request that Bell's application be entered immediately into the daily blotter, thus interrupting the process of entering that morning's mailed-in applications. The chief clerk's assistant had just finished entering the first four documents from the morning's mailbag when Bell's application arrived. Bell's application, therefore, became the fifth entry on that day's cash blotter.

Because Gray's caveat was still in the in basket, it wouldn't be recorded until later that day, when all the other hand-delivered documents were taken to the chief clerk's office. It would become the 39th entry on the blotter. But as Pollok and Bailey would soon discover (as if they didn't already know), this would be the perfect "proof" they needed—the proof, they hoped, that would forestall any possible interference action with Bell's application and forever perpetuate the myth that Bell had arrived two hours ahead of Gray. There was nothing for Pollok and Bailey to do now but wait to implement step two of their scheme.

Notes

1. Bernard S. Finn, "Alexander Graham Bell's Experiments with the Variable-Resistance Transmitter," *Smithsonian Journal of History* 1, no. 4 (Winter 1966), p. 14.

2. Robert V. Bruce, *Alexander Graham Bell and the Conquest of Solitude,* Cornell University Press, Ithaca and London, 1990, p. 149.
3. *Deposition of Alexander Graham Bell*, New York, p. 178.
4. AMB to AGB, May 3, 1876.
5. AMB to AGB, August 29, 1875.
6. AMB to AGB, October 24, 1875.
7. AGB to AMB, August 31, 1875.
8. AGB to parents, November 25, 1875.
9. *Guide to the Practice of the Patent Office*, Washington, D.C. 1853, p. 449, "But where the contrivances are independent of each other, and effect objects entirely distinct, they must be protected by separate patents."
10. American Bell Telephone Co., *Deposition of Alexander Graham Bell*, 1908, p. 90.
11. AGB to Mabel Hubbard, January 19, 1876.
12. The typewriter had yet to be introduced into general use.
13. AGB to G. Hubbard, January 13, 1876.
14. 126US231, October 1887, *The Telephone Cases* United States Supreme Court Reports, vol. 126, 1888.
15. Bruce, p. 165.
16. *Deposition of Alexander Graham Bell*, p. 81.
17. Bruce, p. 165.
18. *Deposition of Alexander Graham Bell*, p. 82.
19. Dowd case, p. 435. *Bell Telephone Co. et al. v. Peter A. Dowd.* Circuit Court of the U.S., Dist. of Mass. Filed Sept. 12, 1878.
20. South Street Seaport Museum, New York, shipping records for *Russia*, Cunard Line.
21. Thomas A. Watson, *Exploring Life*, D. Appleton, New York, 1926.
22. South Street Seaport Museum, New York, shipping records for *Russia*, Cunard Line.
23. *Petition of Elisha Gray to Re-open Interference Hearings*, 1888, p. 50.
24. Elisha Gray, *Nature's Miracles*, Baker and Taylor, New York, 1900, p. 142.
25. White would later change his mind and become a major stockholder in the American Speaking Telephone Company.
26. *Petition of Elisha Gray to Re-open Interference Hearings*, p. 50.
27. The six-day work week was standard in the nineteenth century.
28. "Report of the Commissioner of Patents," *Guide to the Practice of the Patent Office*, Washington, D.C., 1853, p. 450.
29. G. Hubbard to AGB, October 29, 1875.
30. *Petition of Elisha Gray to Re-open Interference Hearings*, p. 68.
31. Ibid.
32. Pollok and Bailey to Commissioner of Patents, n.d. (c. February 19, 1876).
33. There is no evidence that this unusual procedure had ever been carried out before. It would serve no legitimate purpose.

Chapter 6

Inside the Patent Office

February 15–March 7, 1876

George Brown, after arriving in London, never did send Bell that anxiously awaited cablegram, the one that could have said: patent application safely filed in compliance with British law. That message would have been Bell's signal to file his American application, knowing that it would not compromise his British patent. At least that was the way it was supposed to work, the way Bell and Brown had agreed. But somehow something went wrong, and it seems that it was Bell himself who was most responsible.

Unsent Cablegram

Actually, George Brown did send a cablegram from London that February—but not to Bell. It went instead to his brother, Gordon, in Canada and informed him to contact Bell and tell him that the telegraph deal they had so eagerly embraced just a month ago was off. The Brown brothers were washing their hands of the whole matter.[1]

Before leaving for England, Brown had said that he intended to speak with Sir William Thompson concerning Bell's patent application for the harmonic telegraph system. Contrary to popular accounts, it had nothing to do with a telephone, which Bell had yet to make work. With George

Brown's political connections, he would have had little trouble arranging such a meeting. Whether he actually spoke to Sir William we don't know, but if not he would most certainly have spoken to a qualified engineer. Bell's harmonic telegraph, as described in this latest application, was not a complete or fully functional system; the depicted design merely illustrated an approach to harmonic telegraphy, a concept. If the harmonic device shown in the application had been built, it would have been useless for transmitting messages. Regardless of whom Brown went to for technical advice, this fact would have been pointed out, along with several other design anomalies in the application. Such a report would not have bolstered Brown's opinion of the deal and would probably have dampened his initial enthusiasm.

However, aside from any negative evaluation of Bell's application, the real reason for abandoning the patent deal can be traced directly to Hubbard's surprise filing on February 14. Ironically, it was Bell himself who alerted George Brown to this breech of promise. As soon as Bell, who was still in Boston, learned what Hubbard had done, he immediately attempted to mitigate any possible damage by advising the Browns to file for British patents as soon as possible, naively hoping that if the matter could be handled quickly enough, no harm would occur. Shortly after learning of the sudden filing, Bell wrote to his parents:

> Telegraphed Gordon Brown—Toronto—and he replied that he cabled his brother to secure patents abroad instanter. Gordon Brown wanted specifications to apply for Canadian Patents.[2]

From George Brown's perspective in London, his brother's cablegram revealed a most egregious act. Bell had committed an unpardonable business sin: he had reneged on a deal. Bell had sworn—given his word in writing—to wait until after Brown cabled him before filing the American application. Now Bell had broken that promise. And by doing so, had compromised any potential British patents, at least in the eyes of George Brown. Without a valid patent to back them up, the Browns would have no way of protecting their investment against any competitors. Bell's seemingly cavalier disregard for their agreement, which Brown considered extremely important to their future business relationship, was quite likely interpreted by Brown as both unethical and unprofessional. And in light of this, he probably wanted no more to do with the unpredictable Bell, his questionable telegraph scheme, or his shoddy way of doing business.

Whatever it was that happened in London that February, it caused George Brown to drop the whole scheme, including the promised $50 a month to Bell for rent expense.[3] This must have been a major decision for Brown, because he and his brother would have received 50 percent of the foreign profits resulting from the commercial exploitation of the patents.

Brown would later claim—according to Bell—that Bell's telegraph scheme could never be made profitable in England because of government control. In a letter to his parents, Bell wrote, "George Brown has thrown up telegraphy as it cannot be made a commercial success in England—telegraphy being there a government concern."[4]

However, the fact that other British inventors had made money from their telegraphic inventions discredits that explanation. If Bell's system had lived up to its promise, there would have been a ready market, government control or not. No doubt this was Brown's polite excuse for not going ahead with the original plan. After all, the Brown family and the Bell family, especially Alexander's mother and father, were still on friendly terms. George Brown, out of respect to the Bell family, would see no need to detail the real reason behind his abandonment of Alexander's business deal.

This wasn't the last of the Browns, however; their names would pop up again before the decade ended.

Inside the Patent Office

The fascinating story of what took place after Bell and Gray filed their respective documents that Valentine's Day is recorded in the internal office memos as well as the letters that flowed between Bell's attorneys and the Patent Office. Sometime during the week of February 14, the patent examiner in Room 118, Zenas Wilber, had time to read and compare Gray's caveat of February 14 with Bell's patent application of the same date. In his opinion, claims 1, 4, and 5 of Bell's application might possibly interfere with the subject of Gray's caveat. Because of past problems, Wilber was not going to overlook a possible interference—especially one involving Gray.[5] Therefore, on February 19, following standard Patent Office procedure, Wilber notified Pollok and Bailey, as well as Gray's attorney, William Baldwin, of this and stated that Bell's patent would be suspended for 90 days. This was the prescribed practice, as defined by law, whenever there was a potential interference between a patent application and a caveat. The caveator (caveat holder) was given 90 days to complete his invention and file a regular patent application.[6] Only after this was done could the examiner determine if an interference, in fact, did exist.

Examiner's Room No. 118
U.S. PATENT OFFICE
Washington, D.C., Feby 19, 1876

A. G. Bell
Care Pollok and Bailey
Present

TELEGRAPHY Feby 14, 1876

In this case it is found that the 1st, 4th & 5th clauses of claim relate to matters described in a pending caveat.

The caveator has been notified to complete and this app'n is suspended for 90 days as required by law.

Z. F. Wilber, Exr[7]

Considering what they had learned of the similarities between Bell's and Gray's documents just before Monday's filing, Pollok and Bailey were not surprised to get this letter. Although potential interferences between patent applications and caveats were not everyday events, they were fairly routine matters, and the Patent Office procedures for handling them were well established. Notice that Wilber did not refer to Gray by name, which would have been a breech of confidentiality. However, he should not have specified which claims were involved, since it could not be determined whether an interference would exist until after Gray actually filed his patent application. This disclosure was a breech of regulations, although not a major one. After receiving the directive from Wilber, Gray was given just three months to complete or perfect his invention and apply for a patent.

The interference action that Pollok and Bailey were expecting had happened, and they now started step two of their scheme to kill it. The first step had already been carried out: getting Bell's name near the top of the cash blotter—and ahead of Gray's. The fact that Bell's application got into the hands of Patent Examiner Wilber a whole day before Gray's did was just an extra bonus.

Although they were not too surprised at Wilber's declaration, the last thing they wanted to contend with was the possibility of a long, drawn-out interference, such as the one Pollok had engineered a year earlier against Gray and La Cour. Ironically, the situation was reversed—now it was Hubbard and his Hubbard Bill associates who were facing this unwanted nuisance, one that could tie up their much-hoped-for harmonic telegraph patent for who knew how long.

At this point one might ask: if Wilber were essentially in the pay of Bailey, why didn't Wilber simply ignore this possible interference and issue Bell's patent in his usual expeditious manner? The answer is that he couldn't take the risk. If he did, both inventors would become aware of the conflict when one or the other of their patents was issued. That was exactly what happened after Bell's patent of April 6, 1875, was issued. Gray was outraged and, no doubt, complained loudly that an interference should have been declared. Apparently, Gray had made enough noise at the Patent Office over the affair that Wilber didn't want to precipitate another incident like that, especially one involving Bell again. Ignoring a legitimate interference would, in effect, create two patents, each claiming a portion or the whole of the same invention—an embarrassing situation not only for the examiner but for the Patent Office as well.

The problem now facing Pollok was to avoid this interference action and get Bell's patent issued as quickly as possible. Like the shrewd lawyers that they were, Pollok and Bailey were carrying out a contingency plan that, if properly executed, would circumvent the pending interference. But before they proceeded with the next step, they needed to verify an important point.

One or the other went to the Patent Office and, under some pretext, was allowed to examine the cash blotter. As we learned earlier, this was the daily log that was kept in the chief clerk's office and simply listed the applicant's name and the amount of the filing fee. However, the examination of the blotter by Bell's attorney was a direct violation of Patent Office rules. It was a serious breach of an applicant's confidentiality, since no one, except authorized Patent Office personnel, had a right to know who had filed an application or caveat. The fact that they were allowed to look at it at all shows the considerable influence they had at the Patent Office and underscores the lack of security. The nineteenth-century Patent Office was not a tightly run ship.

As they had suspected, the blotter revealed that Bell's name was near the top, the fifth entry, and Gray's was near the bottom, the 39th entry. Of course, Pollok and Bailey had a pretty good idea that this would be the case, since they knew exactly how the cash blotter was handled. This was no fortuitous accident.

Clearly, they would proclaim later, this was conclusive evidence that Bell had arrived first—the essential element in their scheme. Later, this "proof" would play well in the press and, later still, in all of the popular Bell biographies and histories. Like so many stories that have no basis in fact, it took on a life of its own. Thanks to its frequent recitation by Bell's attorneys, it soon became an accepted "fact," or common knowledge, that Bell (actually Hubbard or one of his attorneys, since Bell was still in Boston) had arrived at the Patent Office exactly two hours ahead of Gray. Even the courts, during the numerous trials to follow, would make reference to this so-called fact. The reason this myth was so easy to sell was that the public, as well as the press, had little understanding of how patents were awarded when two inventors claim the same invention. The public readily accepted the erroneous belief that the patent always goes to the inventor who gets to the Patent Office first.[8]

But in reality, the blotter's order of entry was meaningless and couldn't possibly have indicated any chronological sequence since the bulk of the entries were from mailed-in documents. Recording the time of day for these, since they all arrive at the same time, would have been pointless. There are only three available documents that shed any light on the question of who arrived first: Gray's last letter (see app. B), Wilber's office memo of February 25 (this chap.), and the 1885 report of the Secretary of the Interior.[9] The preponderance of the evidence is in favor of Gray arriving first. However, even if this question could be unequivocally answered, it is totally irrelevant. Had the proper Patent Office procedures been followed, as they always had been in the past, it would have made no difference who arrived first.

Having completed their preliminary investigation of the blotter, Pollok and Bailey next sent a letter to the commissioner of patents.[10] Their letter was actually received and acted on by Ellis Spear, the acting commissioner of patents. The letter was not dated, but according to a notation added at the Patent Office it was received on February 24. Bell's attorneys were careful not to admit to too much knowledge about the caveat, requesting that the Patent Office make the necessary inquiries—but carefully detailing where those inquiries should be made. However, they already knew what such an inquiry would yield. A good lawyer seldom asks a question to which he doesn't already know the answer. The letter reads:

> In the matter of the application of
> A. Graham Bell for Impts in
> Telegraphy—filed Feby 14/76
> Hon. Commr. of Patents
>
> Sir: In this matter we beg to acknowledge receipt of official letter notifying us of the suspension of our application for completion of an interfering caveat.
>
> We respectfully request, before it is concluded to suspend our application for 3 months, that you determine whether or not our application was not filed prior to the caveat in question.
>
> We have inquired the date of filing of this caveat (inasmuch as we are entitled to this knowledge) and find it to be February 14, 1876—the same day on which our application was filed. If our application was filed earlier

in the day than was the caveat, then there is no warrant for the action taken by the Office.

We suggest that an examination of the books in the Examiner's, Mr. Moore's [a clerk] and the Chief Clerk's rooms, be made with a view of determining this question.

We can say that our application was filed early in the day on Feby 14, and at our request was on the same day sent to the Examiner. We also call attention to the fact that our client's oath of invention is dated Jany 20/76

Respectfully
Pollok & Bailey
Attys.

Notice that they say, "We have inquired as to the date of filing of *this* caveat." Since filings were supposed to be confidential, how did they know to *which* caveat the letter referred? Wilber's letter never disclosed that fact. There's a subtle mystery here. How did Pollok and Bailey know that the interference was with Elisha Gray, the 39th entry on the blotter? Merely looking at the cash blotter (which itself was a violation of the rules), even if they did see Gray's name on it, wouldn't disclose that information. And how did they know that the conflicting caveat was even filed on February 14? Actually, the caveat in question could have been filed by anyone months before—in fact, up to a whole year before. The answers to these questions simply confirm what was covered in the previous chapter. The details of Gray's caveat that they didn't get from their clandestine report of February 12–13, they got from Examiner Wilber, the only other person who would know.

Notice also in the last paragraph, "our application ... was on the same day sent to the Examiner." This explains the mysterious request made by the person filing Bell's application. This action, too, was not only unorthodox but a breech of Patent Office procedure. But the real question is: why were Pollok and Bailey in such a hurry to have Bell's application reach the examiner?

To find the reason for their haste, we must pay particular attention to their statement "If our application was filed *earlier in the day* than was the caveat, then there is no warrant for the action taken by the Office." That statement goes to the crux of the issue and defines their strategy to defeat the impending interference action. It would be unrealistic to assume that this letter was the only communication Pollok or Bailey had with Acting Commissioner Spear. There was too much at stake not to follow it up with a personal visit, especially since the Patent Office was only a few minutes' walk from their office. The argument that Pollok hoped to make would have required a personal visit and a little discussion.

It was the phrase "within one year from the *time* of filing," which is found in Section 4902 of the Patent Act, on which Pollok based his argument. He argued that the year did not begin until the *instant* that the caveat was filed. If this were true, according to Pollok's argument, and had Bell's application been filed, ever so shortly, before Gray's caveat, then clearly Bell's application would have been filed *before* Gray's year began. And if that were true, there would be no cause to declare an interference. This was why it was so important—solely for the purpose of Pollok's argument—to have Bell's filing take place before Gray's, or at least have the appearance of being filed first.

This was the legal argument Pollok offered to Spear. It's hard to fault Pollok for making the argument; as an attorney, he was simply doing what he could for his client—and, of course, for himself and Hubbard's Postal Telegraph Bill scheme. What is so surprising, though, is that Acting Commissioner Spear accepted it. Ellis Spear, himself a lawyer, no doubt appreciated, as only another attorney could, this imaginative interpretation of the law that Pollok had advanced. But while Pollok may have been congratulating himself on what he probably felt was an extremely clever and original argument, Spear had heard it all before. As we will discover later, it was nothing new to him.

After receiving Pollok and Bailey's letter, Spear contacted Wilber to ask why he had suspended Bell's application. In response, Wilber, on February 24, sent a written reply to Spear requesting his guidance in the matter. In all the years Wilber had been with the Patent Office, on the occasions when this question had come up before, he had always followed standard office procedure. Spear, who also had come up through the ranks of patent examiners, was well aware of this procedure. Wilber wrote:

> Examiner's Room 118
> Feby 24—1876
>
> Respectfully referred to the Hon. Com'r for instructions. The regular practice in the Office has been to determine dates of filing by *days alone*, and in accordance with such practice I suspended the application herein referred to on a/c [account] of a caveat, the application and caveat being filed upon the same day, viz. Feby 14'—1876.
>
> In view of the practice above noted, I have paid no attention to the alleged differences between the times of the filings on the same day.
>
> Resp. Submitted
> Z. F. Wilber
> Exr.

As you can see, Wilber, correctly, didn't put any stock in the "alleged" times of filing, insisting that only the *date* of filing was the determining factor and that that was standard Patent Office practice. However, Acting Commissioner Spear soon set Wilber straight on that point. The following day, February 25, Spear replied:

> The application in order to become liable to suspension to await the completion of his application by a caveator must have been filed "within the year" of the life of the caveat. Ordinarily, the day of filing is not computed, this is considered *punctum temporis* [the shortest space of time]. Yet where justice requires it the exact time in the day, when an act was done, may be shown by proof—Kents Com. 95. The examiner will be guided by this rule in the present case, and if the record shows that the application was filed earlier in the day, then the caveat should be disregarded and otherwise not.
>
> Ellis Spear
> Actg. Com'r
> 25, 2, 76

The tone of Spear's memo to Wilber left little doubt as to what he was expected to find and what action he was supposed to take. Spear injected yet another argument to support Pollok and Bailey's position. The point of law he attempts to make (Kents Com. 95) assumes extraordinary situations in which the precise time of day may be used to resolve the problem. However, this point applies only to exceptional cases, not to such a common and routine situation as a possible patent interference. We will consider this a little later. Examiner Wilber got the message—he knew exactly what was expected—and the same day promptly fired back a reply to Spear:

> Exr's Room 118
> Feby 25—1876
>
> The cash blotter in the Chief Clerk's room shows conclusively that the application was filed some time earlier on the 14th—than was the Caveat.
>
> The app'n was received also in 118 by noon of the 14th—the caveat not until the 15th.
>
> Z. F. Wilber
> Exr.

Notice the second paragraph in the above memo; this simply backed up Pollok's original argument. Later that day, Wilber sent a terse letter to Pollok and Bailey informing them that the suspension had been lifted. Thanks to the benevolence of Acting Commissioner Ellis Spear, their strategy had worked just the way they had planned. They were home free—almost.

Examiner's Room No. 118
U.S. PATENT OFFICE
Washington, D.C., Feby 25, 1876

A. G. Bell
Care Pollok and Bailey
Present

TELEGRAPHY Feby 14, 1876

The suspension of this app'n having been declared in misapprehension of Appt's rights, is withdrawn.

Z. F. Wilber
Exr

But just when they thought the battle had been won, Wilber came up with a surprise. Gray had filed yet another document, this one on January 27, that also appeared to conflict with Bell's February 14 application. Since it had been filed more than two weeks before Bell's filing, it couldn't be summarily dismissed as Spear had done with Gray's February 14 caveat. As Bell explained in a letter to his father:

> The Examiner was about to issue my patent when he discovered that Mr. Gray had applied for a caveat for something similar before my patent appeared. He had applied on the 27th of January and my papers were sworn to before a Notary Public in Boston on the 20th of January. Still this altered the aspect of affairs and judgment was delayed and my attorneys sent for me to come to Washington.[11]

Bell may have been a little confused on the nature of Gray's January 27, 1876, document. He refers to it as a caveat, when in reality it was most likely a patent application.[12] However, it made no difference, since either one could have precipitated the interference. Notice that Wilber had been ready to issue (i.e., allow to be published) Bell's patent on February 25—just 11 days after filing—meaning that it would have been officially published the following week, on February 29, 1876.

However, the possible interference with this other Gray document caused Wilber to proceed with caution. A possible interference, as discussed earlier—and especially with Gray—was something Wilber had to deal with carefully. Wilber was not about to open up another can of worms. When Pollok and Bailey were notified of yet another potential interference, they immediately telegraphed Bell, who was still in Boston. He arrived in Washington on Saturday morning, February 26. After checking in with his attorneys, he went directly to the Patent Office to confer with Wilber. In the same letter to his father, Bell continues:

> It was then my right to see the portions of Mr. Gray's specification which came into conflict with mine. I could not however see the caveat, but the examiner told me the point of issue. Mr. Gray made a sudden change in the intensity of the current without actually making or breaking the circuit—and the Examiner thought that this constituted an "undulatory current." I explained that it did not—and that even if it did, I had mentioned the *same thing* in my application filed *Feb. 1875* just over one year ago. The Examiner handed me my paper of that date and I was able to point out the exact passage describing what Mr. Gray had only now taken out a caveat for. The Examiner said that was so and that he had not noticed that passage before as bearing on the subject. He allowed me to make an amendment upon my specification so as to refer to that application and the patent was handed in this morning (February 29th).
>
> The Examiner however feeling that this is a very important case could not decide to render judgment at once, and I am only waiting in Washington for the denouement.[13]

Bell had been misinformed about his rights regarding Gray's caveat (or application). Either Pollok or Bailey deliberately misinformed Bell, or he confused himself. Pollok and Bailey were in the habit of flattering Bell and telling him whatever was convenient or expedient, whether factual or not. In either case, he had no business even knowing that the possible interference was with Gray. That would be a matter for the examiner of interferences to handle. If Wilber had suspected a conflict, he should have suspended Bell's application for 90 days, just as he had attempted to do with Gray's caveat of February 14. Or, if the conflicting document was a patent application, an interference should have been declared, and the matter turned over to the examiner of interferences. Either way, Bell's patent should never have been issued without first resolving the interference. That was the law.

However, Wilber was understandably reluctant to tread that path again, especially since Pollok's previous argument regarding Gray's February 14 caveat would not apply. Wilber was in a most awkward position. As discussed before, an unresolved possible interference could prove extremely embarrassing. The easiest course for Wilber, and one that would show Pollok and Bailey that he was doing all he could to help them, was to allow Bell to make an amendment to his current application. This was stretching the Patent Office's code of ethics to the breaking point, but the legalities could be argued. Amendments are permissible for the purpose of clarification as long as they don't change the meaning and scope of the original application. However, in this case, the "clarification" was for the sole purpose of avoiding an interference. It was based on illicit knowledge of Gray's January 27 patent document and, as such, constituted an illegal act.

Accordingly, on February 29, Wilber received a letter from Pollok and Bailey requesting that certain changes, a total of three amendments, be made to Bell's original specifications and claims. The four paragraphs beginning with the phrase, "In a pending application for letters patent filed in the U.S. Patent Office February 25, 1875" were added at this time.[14] This first amendment was to preclude a possible interference with Gray. The other two amendments were essentially word changes in the claims. For example, the word *gradually* was used in place of the original word *alternately*, in the fourth claim. None of these changes had anything to do directly with variable resistance. Three days later, on March 3, 1876, Patent No. 174,465 was approved for issue to A. G. Bell; it was published in the *Official Gazette* on March 7, 1876.

Apparently, Bell's attorneys were delighted when he showed up in Washington that Saturday morning. There was a lot riding on his patent application, not so much for Bell as for Hubbard and Pollok. It just might be the patent that could resurrect Hubbard's Postal Telegraph Bill. Because of this, Bell's relationship with his attorneys was far more than the usual attorney-client alliance. They treated him more like a valued business associate—or visiting royalty. As Bell later described, Pollok rolled out the red carpet upon his arrival:

> Mr. Hubbard handed me over to Mr. Pollok my solicitor and I am now his guest. Mr. Pollok has the most palatial residence of any that I have ever seen. It is certainly the finest and best appointed of any in Washington. Mr. Pollok & his wife occupy it alone with a large suite of colored servants. None of the rooms are less than fifteen feet high. The portico is also about fifteen feet high—supported by massive polished Aberdeen-granite pillars.
>
> Mr. Pollok has been introducing me to some of the elite of Washington. Yesterday we called upon Mrs. Bancroft (wife of the historian)—we did not see Mr. Bancroft as he was not very well. Today we called on Prof. Henry of the Smithsonian—and on Saturday Mr. Pollok gives a party in my honor—and I expect to meet Sir Edward Thornton and the members of the other foreign Embassies. So you see I am having a gay and happy time.[15]

Lest one assume that Pollok was just a typical, workaday patent attorney, his opulent lifestyle indicated much more. If Bell ever questioned why he was being treated in such royal fashion, he kept it to himself. Remember, Pollok was as anxious as Bell to have this latest patent issued, and it was most likely Pollok's vividly glowing promises that inspired Bell to exclaim to his parents, "*the whole thing is mine* and I am sure of fame, fortune and success," to which he added as an anticlimactic afterthought, "if I can only persevere in perfecting my apparatus."[16]

This last observation was a valid concern, because even after he received his patent, he still did not succeed in transmitting more than three simultaneous messages on his harmonic telegraph—far short of the hoped-for 30 or 40 messages. And the device shown in figure 7 of the patent, which was supposed to transmit "vocal or other sounds," had yet to utter so much as a syllable. Popular history tells us that this was Bell's famous telephone patent, but this became true only in retrospect and only in a legal sense.

When this patent was issued, it was considered by Bell and his associates to be a multiple-message telegraph device that would compete with, or surpass, the four-message quadruplex system. If anyone held any thoughts of cashing in on transmitting voice messages, it could only have been Elisha Gray, who had specifically claimed as much in his caveat. Even Bell stopped short of claiming the transmission of speech, alluding only to "vocal sounds." While Bell may have dreamed of someday sending the human voice over a wire, this was the furthest thing from anyone's mind—except Gray's.

The extraordinary decision that Acting Commissioner Spear made in this case would forever skew the patent claims in favor of Bell and against Elisha Gray, and it has turned out to be one of the most far-reaching decisions ever made by the Patent Office. As we will see next, Spear's action in this matter would later be condemned by the Department of the Interior, the agency then in charge of the Patent Office.

Notes

1. AGB to AMB, March 8, 1876.
2. AGB to parents, February 20, 1876.
3. American Bell Telephone Co., *Deposition of Alexander Graham Bell,* 1908 p. 90. Bell had complained to the Browns about spies trying to learn of his experiments and said he needed more secure quarters.
4. AGB to parents, March 10, 1876.
5. See Gray's letter to Alex Hayes, April 26, 1875, chap. 4.
6. See *Guide to the Practice of the Patent Office*, chap. 5.
7. Patent Office memo to Pollok and Bailey; February 19, 1876.
8. When patents interfere, the patent goes to the inventor who can prove priority of conception.
9. *Report of the Department of the Interior* (per Jenks), 1885: "as if the book [cash blotter] gave any reliable information it would seem to prove that Gray's caveat was first filed." Quoted in *Petition of Elisha Gray to Re-open Telephone Interference Hearings*, n.p., 1888, p. 68.
10. All correspondence with the Patent Office is addressed to the commissioner of patents.

11. AGB to AMB, February 29, 1876.
12. Gray did file an application for "Electro Harmonic Telegraph" on this date. It was issued almost a year later as Patent No. 186,340 on Jan. 16, 1877.
13. AGB to AMB, February 29, 1876.
14. See Bell's Patent No. 174,465 in Appendix D.
15. AGB to AMB, February 29, 1876.
16. Ibid.

Chapter 7

Decision That Changed History

The Unexplained Order of Acting Commissioner Spear

On February 25, 1876, Acting Commissioner of Patents Ellis Spear made Patent Office history. Seldom, if ever, had a top-level Patent Office official used his power to bestow favors on one inventor over the rights of another. His actions would later be condemned by his superiors at the Department of the Interior (then overseer of the Patent Office), yet his reasons for doing what he did would forever remain an enigma.

On that date, Spear instructed Patent Examiner Zenas Wilber to use the nonexistent *time of filing* to decide the Bell-Gray interference issue. Wilber, operating under Spear's order to disregard standard Patent Office policy, then claimed that the cash blotter showed "conclusively" that Bell had filed sometime ahead of Gray. And then, still following Spear's directive, Wilber canceled the pending interference action, and eight days later issued Bell's patent. All in all, despite the challenge of not just one but two interference actions it had taken only 17 days to issue Bell's second harmonic telegraph patent, the one historians would immortalize as the "most valuable patent ever issued."

Of course, at the time, neither Spear nor anyone else knew that history had been made. While the final decision was ostensibly left up to Wilber, it was actually Spear who told him what that decision must be, based on the entries in the cash blotter. And although it was Pollok and Bailey who crafted the whole scenario and who recruited Acting Commissioner Spear to their scheme, the responsibility for this egregious bit of skullduggery lies solely with Spear. This was the decision that forever skewed the course of telephone history away from Elisha Gray and towards Alexander Graham Bell.

What might have been the outcome had Wilber's original decision to proceed with the interference action remained unchanged? Gray, through his attorney, William Baldwin, had been notified of the possible interference. It is reasonable to assume that Gray would have then proceeded to complete his patent application in the required three months. There would have been little reason for him not to; after all, a caveat was simply the first step to an eventual patent. And the fact that a possible interference had been declared would have told him that he was on to something and that others were thinking along the same lines. This alone would have sparked some interest in a "speaking telegraph," most likely from Western Union, with which Gray was already negotiating his harmonic telegraph system. Despite Baldwin's apparent initial reluctance to pursue the matter, after more consideration he probably would have concluded that there would be nothing to lose by proceeding.

Just how effective Baldwin was as Gray's patent attorney is questionable. He and Gray would later have a falling out with Gray charging that Baldwin had not truly represented his best interests in the Dowd case and in other actions. This suspicion ultimately proved correct. It turned out that Baldwin was on the payroll of the Bell Telephone Company at the same time he was supposedly representing Gray in a Patent Office action involving that very company. Although Baldwin presented Gray with a bill for his services, Gray ignored it—and Baldwin never asked for payment.[1] As we considered previously, it is quite possible that one of Baldwin's employees inadvertently (or otherwise) revealed some confidential information regarding Gray's telephone caveat to one of Pollok and Bailey's employees.

The Bell-Gray interference, of course, never happened, much to the relief of Hubbard and his associates. Pollok told Spear what the law was in this case (Pollok's interpretation). Spear agreed and then essentially told Wilber to disallow the interference. Spear claimed that special circumstances prevailed and that long-established Patent Office procedures did not apply in this particular case. Wilber, of course, was correct in claiming that the standard Patent Office policy, in cases of simultaneous filings such as this, was to ignore any "alleged" time of day. The fact that Wilber, initially, did not accept Pollok's argument shows that he was simply following prevailing policy. Ellis Spear, who had been with the Patent Office for over ten years and who had come up through the ranks of patent examiners, was as aware of that policy as was Wilber. One could argue, as Pollok no doubt did, that the portion of the Patent Act covering caveats was, perhaps, vague on this issue and never spelled out precisely how it was to be applied in the case of simultaneous submissions. But one could also make the persuasive counterargument that, if the time of day were important in interference situations, the Patent Office would have required that the time of filing be recorded. Even after the Bell-Gray incident, this never became a filing requirement. Any argument made on behalf of time-of-day filing falls apart when one tries to equate mailed-in applications with carried-in applications. Time of day simply cannot be a factor.

Popular history, and even the courts, have made an issue out of Bell's supposed and often-quoted two-hour advantage over Gray. How they knew it was two hours has never been explained. But it really makes no difference. To interpret the Patent Act as Pollok did, and to support that interpretation as Spear did, was a clear violation of Gray's rights. Surprisingly, the legality of Spear's decision never came up in the various court cases, although it did during the investigation by the Department of the Interior. But if it had, it would have been a crucial bit of evidence in all of those cases. By the same token, however, there were other equally compelling issues, for example, double patenting, which could also have been brought up in subsequent trials but for unexplained reasons were never addressed.

We will never know why Spear made the decision he did. Was he consciously trying to help or conspire with Pollok for some reason? Or did he just accept Pollok's argument at face value? From what we know of Spear's background, we have to reject any hint of collusion; there simply doesn't seem to be any point to it. There certainly could have been no monetary incentive, as there might have been in Wilber's case, as he had an expensive habit to support. At $3,500 a year, Spear was near the top in government service. His Civil War military record was exemplary, and he had received several commendations for meritorious service on the field of battle. He had risen through the ranks to become a 31-year-old brevet brigadier general by the war's end. He had started at the Patent Office in 1865 at one of the lower levels and had advanced steadily to second in command as the assistant commissioner of patents. During the Bell-Gray affair, he was serving as the acting commissioner of patents in the absence of the appointed commissioner, Robert H. Duell. He resigned his post on March 20, 1876, just two weeks after Bell's patent was issued.

After a brief one-year stint as a patent attorney in the law firm of Hill, Ellsworth and Spear, he received a presidential appointment as commissioner of patents and served from January 1877 through October 1878.[2] Yet, despite this impressive resume of achievement and character testament, there is one troubling fact we must consider, a fact that casts great suspicion on Spear's decision to favor Bell at Gray's expense.

The Bell-Gray Decision vs. the Essex Decision

Just three weeks before Spear made his decision in the Bell-Gray matter, the *Official Gazette* published a decision he had made in a case virtually identical to the Bell-Gray situation. But in this instance, his decision was directly opposite the one he made in the Bell-Gray case. In the earlier case, Jeremiah Essex filed a patent application for "Improvements in Cop-Tubes" (devices for a spinning machine). On the same day, another inventor filed a caveat for essentially the same invention. The patent examiner in this case (not Wilber) made the standard office decision to suspend the Essex application for three months to allow the caveator to "mature" his invention and file an actual patent application. In making his decision, the examiner, citing standard Patent Office practice, stated:

> Where a caveat and an application for a patent were filed upon the same day, and for the same invention, by different parties, the Office will presume that they were filed simultaneously and the caveator notified under the provisions of the law.[3]

Inventor Essex, fearing a possible protracted interference action, appealed to the commissioner of patents, as was his right, to set aside the decision of the examiner. Here is what Acting Commissioner Spear said in reply, as reported on February 3, 1876, in the *Official Gazette*, in what is called the Essex decision:

> In order to free the application from suspension and possibly from interference with the application filed by the caveator it must appear that the application was filed prior to the caveat. That does not appear. The bounds of the lifetime of both application and caveat are in this respect the same. I cannot take into consideration any representation of special hardship in this case, because it would be manifestly improper to consider any *ex parte* statement whatever. There would seem to be nothing in the attitude of either a caveator or an applicant to entitle one more than the other to invoke any special equity in the case. I do not see why the law should not be strictly applied and the caveator notified and direct that it be done.[4]

In the Essex case, Spear ruled that, since both the application and the caveat were filed on the same day, the time of filing had no bearing, and he *agreed* with the decision of the patent examiner. He also declared that it would be "manifestly improper" to listen to only one side (*ex parte*) of the case. Yet in the case of Bell and Gray, less than three weeks after his Essex decision, Spear reversed himself on both counts: (1) he listened to and accepted Pollok's argument concerning the time of filing without ever consulting with Gray or his attorney, and (2) he decided that the *alleged* time of filing, to use Wilber's description, was the determining factor.

Of particular interest in the Essex decision is that no mention was ever made of the cash blotter, although this played a key role and was the deciding factor in the Bell-Gray decision. Spear specifically states: "There is nothing in the records of the Office to show which, if either, was, in point of fact, filed first."[5]

Why Spear did what he did in the Bell-Gray case we will never know. It's just another of the holes in the telephone's history. The most plausible explanation is that he did this merely as a little favor to the firm of Pollok and Bailey. There is nothing to indicate that it was anything other than a favor. We know nothing of the personal relationships of Spear, Pollok, and Bailey. As former army officers, they may have met during the war. Spear knew that in a few weeks he would be leaving the Patent Office and joining the brotherhood of patent attorneys—and one never knows when one might need a return favor. At the time, he must have known that he was bending the rules a little. A bit unethical perhaps, but who would ever know—or even care? As far as Spear could tell, this was just another run-of-the-mill patent application, no different from any of the other 15,000 or so that would pass through the Patent Office that year. Although there was no justification for Spear's action, this much we do know: he had absolutely no idea what impact his decision would have. Yet, if historians had to pick the one pivotal point in telephone history, it would have to be the instructions that Acting Commissioner Spear gave to Examiner Wilber on February 25, 1876.

Report of the Department of the Interior

Almost ten years later, Spear's Bell-Gray decision was to come under scrutiny by the Secretary of the Interior, who was then holding hearings on a suit brought by the federal government to annul the Bell patents. At that time, the Patent Office was under the jurisdiction of the Department of the Interior. Secretary Lamar was attempting to determine if there was sufficient evidence to justify such a suit, and, if so, if it should be handled by the Patent Office or by the court. In a report dated December 22, 1885, prepared by Assistant Secretary of the Interior George A. Jenks, the 1876 decision of Ellis Spear came under sharp attack. In his report, Jenks discussed the Patent Office events of February 25, 1876, and stated:

> In this part of the proceedings the action of the Commissioner was exceptional. It was contrary to the former practice of the Office. It was in distinct contradiction of his own ruling on the same subject made on the 3rd of February 1876, in the Essex case.[6]

Assistant Secretary Jenks then goes into a discussion of the role of the cash blotter in the chief clerk's office. As we saw in Wilber's office memo of February 25 to Acting Commissioner Spear, Wilber stated that the cash blotter "shows conclusively" that Bell's application was filed earlier than Gray's caveat. But by 1885, Wilber had changed his story. As Jenks reported:

> On the 10th of October, 1885, his [Wilber's] affidavit is made that the book [cash blotter] he referred to fix the time in his entry would give *no* reliable information on the subject. Upon examination of the book his oath seems to be entitled to greater credence than his written entry [on the back of Gray's caveat] as if the book gave any reliable information it would seem to prove that Gray's caveat was filed first.[7]

All of the available information seems to confirm that Gray actually did file his caveat before Bell. How the Patent Office managed the cash blotter has been fully covered in chapter 5. Gray himself attests to the fact that he filed his caveat on the morning of February 14 (see app. B). There was never any testimony as to the filing time from the person who submitted Bell's application. Wilber stated in his office memo that Bell's application arrived at his desk just before noon on the 14th. Bell's attorneys relied solely on the entries in the cash blotter to "prove" that Bell had filed earlier. But as we have seen, this was a groundless argument.

The *time of day* of filing was also of no consequence and had no legal status. No provision had ever been made, neither in the Patent Act itself nor in Patent Office practice, to record the time of day when an application was submitted. Since it was filed on the same day, Bell's application did fall within the one-year scope of Gray's caveat, and Wilber's original declaration of a possible interference should have stood. That was what Spear had ruled just three weeks before in the Essex case and what he should have ruled in the Bell-Gray case. But because of his decision in the Bell-Gray matter, that never happened, and out of this grew the myth—widely publicized by Bell's attorneys—that Bell had filed his application two hours ahead of Gray. So pervasive and persuasive was this myth that even Gray himself believed it to be true—at least for a while.[8]

This same myth has led to the widespread but unfounded belief that, in the case of duplicate inventions, the one who gets to the Patent Office first gets the patent. While this may be true in many other countries, it is not true in the American patent system. In America, in the case of duplicate inventions, the patent goes to the inventor who can show priority of conception, regardless of who files first, as long as the filings take place within a one-year period.

This fact is further proof that Pollok and Bailey not only knew that Gray was soon to file a document in the Patent Office, but that they knew precisely that it would be a caveat and not a patent application. Had it been a patent application, Pollok and Bailey would have known that there would be no need to rush to the Patent Office that Valentine's Day. They could then have waited for Brown's cablegram and filed the application afterwards, just as Bell had promised. Whether an interference would have been declared is problematical. But of this much we are certain: Gray filing a caveat instead of an application was Bell's luckiest break.

Jenks concluded his report with observations on several other anomalies involved in the Bell patent application. He noted that of the seven applications filed in the same department on February 14, only Bell's reached the examiner's room on the 14th. The other six, including Gray's, didn't arrive there until the 15th, which was the normal time interval.[9] He noted also the great rapidity, a mere 17 days, with which Bell received his patent once the interference was lifted, and he made the comment, "It will be noted that all irregular and exceptional action in the case was favorable to Mr. Bell, and tended to great haste in the result."[10] He closes his report to the Secretary of the Interior with this observation:

> If in passing through a forest the woodsman should come upon the course of a tornado, and finds the tops of the trees all pointing in one direction he would be as firmly convinced of the direction the wind had blown as though he had been an eye witness to the storm. In this one-sided contest between the Bell application and the Gray caveat the tree tops all point one way.[11]

Ellis Spear left the Patent Office on March 20, 1876, just three weeks after his decision in the Bell-Gray matter. He became a partner in the patent law firm of Hill and Ellsworth, which was then renamed Hill, Ellsworth and Spear. It was not unusual for patent examiners, in which capacity Spear served for a number of years, to go into the lucrative practice of patent law. In an interesting twist, Spear's new law partner was Lysander Hill, the attorney who would later (1888) bring to the Supreme Court charges that Bell's patent was obtained by fraud.

The final issue to be addressed in this matter is the role Wilber played. Wilber is hardly innocent, since he was the one who supplied Pollok and Bailey with the illicit information on Gray's caveat. But Wilber had several problems. He had to do what his boss, Ellis Spear, had so clearly told him to do. And, for financial reasons, he had to keep Pollok and Bailey happy. But most important, he had to look out for himself. A little bribe money was one thing, but if he bent the rules too far he could jeopardize his $2,500-a-year position, a salary that would be hard to duplicate.

If we look just at the events of February 19 through February 25, we have to conclude that Wilber was merely doing his job. The fact that he declared an interference between Bell and Gray certainly indicated that he was not going out of his way to help Bell, as has been suggested by some historians. He may well have had a self-serving interest in declaring an interference and probably felt he had little choice.

Less than a year earlier, when Bell received his first patent, Gray had complained bitterly that Bell had copied the "gist" of his invention.[12] He questioned why Wilber had not declared an interference in that instance. Wilber, of course, had no way of knowing how Gray would look upon Bell's latest application. Wilber, therefore, prudently decided that it would be better to declare a possible interference than to ignore it, and he did have what seemed to be sufficient grounds. As it turned out, because of the vagueness of Bell's patent, Gray did not immediately recognize the similarities between his caveat and Bell's patent, and he raised no objections. It would be years before Gray would find out that Bell first obtained transmission of articulate speech with an instrument uncannily similar to the one in Gray's caveat.

Notes

1. "Speaking Telephone," *Chicago Tribune*, November 17, 1885, p. 3.
2. *Journal of the Patent Office Society* 18, no. 7 (1936), p. 183–185.
3. "Commissioner's Decision of February 3, 1876," *Official Gazette*, March 14, 1876, p. 1.
4. Ibid.
5. Ibid.
6. *Petition of Elisha Gray to Re-open Interference Hearings*, 1888, p. 67.
7. Ibid., p. 68.

8. Gray to AGB, February 21, 1877. See Chapter 9.
9. *Petition of Elisha Gray to Re-open Interference Hearings*, p. 68.
10. Ibid., p. 69.
11. Ibid., p. 69.
12. Gray to Alex Hayes, April 26, 1875, Gray Collection, Archive Center, National Museum of American History.

Chapter 8

"Mr. Watson, Come Here"

The Closely Guarded Secret of March 10, 1876

March 3, 1876, was a doubly important day for Alexander Bell: it was not only his 29th birthday but also the day his most famous patent was granted. It has long been standard Patent Office practice to date all patents on the Tuesday following the week in which they are granted, this being the date they carry when published in the *Official Gazette*. Therefore, although Patent No. 174,465 was granted on March 3, its official publication date is March 7, 1876.

Bell had been in Washington, D.C., since Saturday, February 26 as the result of an urgent telegram from Hubbard. Just the day before, Bell's attorneys had received word from Patent Examiner Wilber that the interference on his most recent application had been withdrawn by order of Ellis Spear, acting commissioner of patents. However, there was still the matter of the interferences between the applications he had filed almost a year earlier and those of Gray and La Cour. These were officially declared to be in interference on February 16, 1876. This came as no surprise to Bell, since he had known for almost a year that it would happen and had expected it much sooner than this. It would be almost another year before he would be required to testify in the matter, so this was not the reason he had been suddenly called to Washington.

Wilber, it seems, had discovered a second possible interference with yet another Gray document, not a caveat this time, but a patent application filed sometime earlier. (Bell mistakenly referred to it as a caveat.) Wilber, quite understandably, wisely chose to proceed with caution when dealing with possible interferences between Bell and Gray; he had no desire to precipitate another incident. Wilber thought Gray was using an undulatory current in this application, and therefore it might conflict with Bell's present application. "I explained that it did not," Bell later wrote to his father, "and that even if it did, I had mentioned the *same thing* in my application filed *Feb. 1875*."[1] To get around this potential problem, Wilber suggested that Bell make several amendments to his application. Amendments to a pending patent application are allowed only for purposes of clarification; they cannot be used to change the scope of the application. Wilber was satisfied that Bell's "clarifications" would eliminate the possible interference, and the patent was duly granted on March 3.

Having wrapped up his patent business, Bell left for Boston and home on or about March 6. His attorneys said they would mail him his patent certificate, his second since becoming an inventor. Knowing that it had been granted was enough to satisfy Bell; it wasn't worth hanging around Washington just waiting for a piece of paper. By now, he had been away from home and Mabel for almost ten days, and besides, he was anxious to continue a series of experiments on his multimessage system that he had begun on February 18. Even though he had just received his second harmonic telegraph patent, he knew there was still considerable work to be done before it could become a practical, commercial system.

While in Washington, during one of his discussions with Patent Examiner Wilber, Bell picked up a bit of information concerning Gray's confidential caveat. This is an area of great mystery, and over the years historians have drawn various conclusions. Was it merely an innocent slip on the part of Wilber, as Bell maintains, or was there more to it? We'll see what Wilber had to say on this point in a later chapter, but for now we'll look at what Bell testified to during the telephone company's first infringement lawsuit, the famous Dowd case of 1879. During cross-examination, Bell was asked how he learned about the operating mode of Gray's liquid, variable resistance transmitter as described in his February 14, 1876, caveat:

> *Cross-Int. 251.* ...How did you come to know as much as that about the nature of a paper [Gray's caveat] in the confidential archives of the Patent Office?
>
> *Ans.* ...I found that there had been two interferences declared with my application. The first was with a caveat filed the same day as my application, and

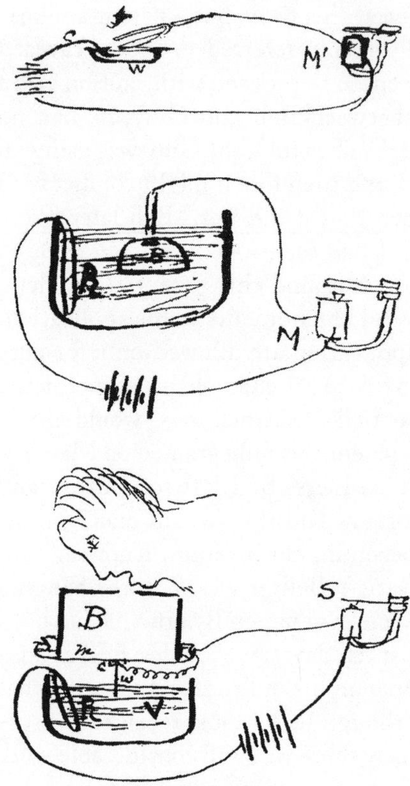

Top: ***Figure 8-1. Vibrating a tuning fork in a dish of acidulated water with a reed receiver as listening device. (From Bell's laboratory notebook for March, 1876.)*** **Center:** ***Figure 8-2. Substituting a bell for the tuning fork. No response. (From Bell's laboratory notebook.)*** **Bottom:** ***Figure 8-3. Bell's first liquid transmitter. (From Bell's laboratory notebook.)***

had already been dissolved. The examiner declined to show me the caveat, as it was a confidential document, but he indicated to me the particular clause in my application with which it had conflicted. I therefore knew it had something to do with the vibration of a wire in a liquid. I do not now remember what it was that led me to suppose that that liquid was water.[2]

As Gray would later exclaim, "A wire vibrating in water was the whole thing!"[3] We can possibly excuse Bell for asking Wilber about the caveat, since what little knowledge he did have of Patent Office practice was oddly twisted, thanks to his attorneys. However, he did know that caveats were supposed to be confidential, since he had mentioned this fact in letters to his parents: "it [his original caveat] will be filed in the secret archives at Washington."[4] But there is no excuse for Wilber, who should never have even hinted to Bell the nature of the interference, much less reveal who the caveator was. Some have dismissed Wilber's breech of confidentiality as of little consequence; after all, the interference in question had been dissolved. Others are not so sure; the caveat was still valid and confidential.

Bell would later testify that the clause referring to the variable resistance method was added to his patent application at the last minute: "producing electrical undulation by varying the resistance occurred to me while I was making the final revisions of the specifications for the U.S. Patent Office, and almost at the last moment before sending it off to Washington to be engrossed."[5] He mailed the finished application to Hubbard in

Washington, D.C., about January 12. However, what is rather curious about Bell's previous testimony regarding this clause, which he said suggested a wire vibrating in water, is that the application specifically describes mercury:

> For instance, let mercury or some other liquid form part of a voltaic circuit, then the more deeply the conducting-wire is immersed in the mercury or other liquid, the less resistance does the liquid offer to the passage of the current. Hence, the vibration of the conducting-wire in mercury or other liquid included in the circuit occasions undulations in the current.[6]

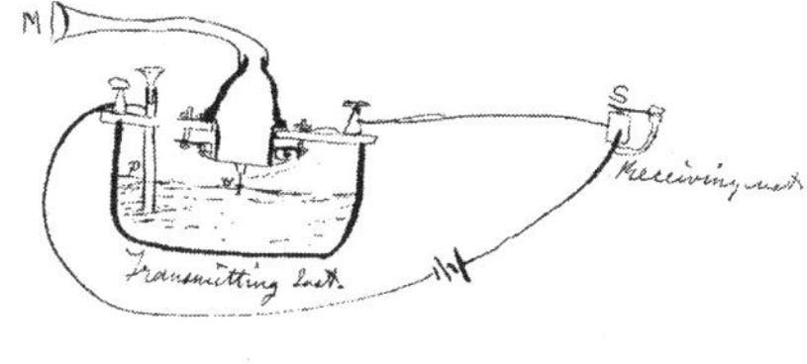

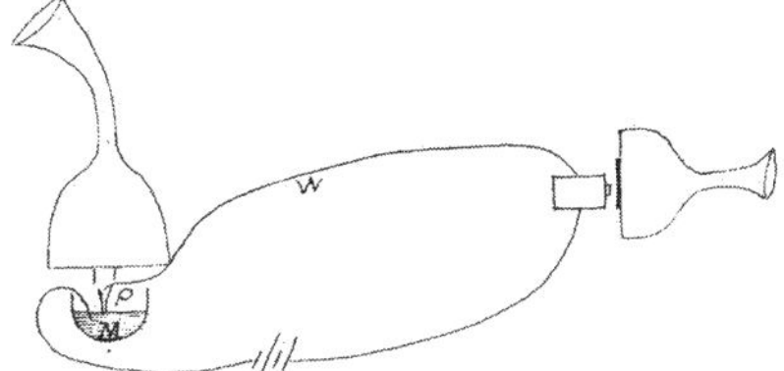

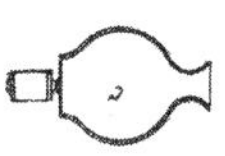

Top: ***Figure 8-4. An improved liquid transmitter. (From Bell's laboratory notebook.)*** **Bottom:** ***An experiment to test the effectiveness of mercury. A proposed electromagnetic receiver replaced the previous reed receiver. Note the similarity to Gray's caveat receiver (From Bell's laboratory notebook.) Note the similarity to Gray's caveat receiver shown in lower right.***

Sometime around March 7 or 8, Bell started to investigate the concept of "a wire vibrating in water." The idea was simple enough: vibrate a current-carrying electrode in a conductive liquid, and the variations in current will be equivalent to the frequency and amplitude of the vibrations. In modern terminology we would call the current variations an AC (alternating current) signal. Since that term didn't exist in Bell's day, he chose to call it an *undulating current.*

To verify the concept, Bell hastily connected a tuning fork, a battery, and one of the reed receivers he had been using in his experiments with the harmonic telegraph. These elements were connected in serial fashion to a bowl of slightly acidic water. Bell held the reed receiver, which functioned as a crude earphone, against his ear and then struck the tuning fork. Holding the tines of the vibrating tuning fork almost parallel to the water, he slowly immersed just the very tip into the water while listening to the reed relay. To his surprise and delight, he could hear clearly but faintly the sound of the tuning fork coming from the reed receiver. He had converted the audible sound of the tuning fork into an electrical current—an undulating current—and then converted it back into an audible sound at the reed relay.[7]

There was no doubt that the pitch of the tuning fork was being reproduced at the reed receiver. He added a little acid to the water, and the sound became "much louder." Obviously, Bell reasoned, the undulating current was caused by the variation in the resistance between the tuning fork and the acidic water as the excursions of the vibrating fork advanced or retreated within the liquid. It was just as his patent had theorized, but it had never been tried.

He experimented further and discovered that the excursions of the fork had to be perpendicular, or nearly so, to the liquid to produce an undulating current. In other words, the tines of the tuning fork had to be nearly parallel to the acidulated water. If the fork were allowed to vibrate laterally in the liquid (i.e., the tines perpendicular to the surface), no sound was heard. He also discovered that the greatest variation in resistance, and hence the loudest sound, occurred with minimal contact with the liquid. The sound would become loudest just before surface tension broke the connection between the vibrating tuning fork and the liquid.

Armed with this knowledge, Bell, with the aid of a crude sketch, instructed Watson to construct a diaphragm-type device with which voice sounds could be used to vibrate a wire in a conductive liquid. Although he now knew that acidulated water worked very well, he planned to try a variety of liquids to see which worked the best. The first instrument Watson created was a rather crude device, not at all like the more refined version he would construct later on—the one popular history always shows as being the "original telephone" first used by Bell to transmit articulate speech.

The instrument was completed on March 10, just three days after the official date of his telephone patent. Bell wasted no time in setting it up and by that same afternoon had completed the initial tests. That evening he wrote the results of those tests to his father:

> I write to announce a great failure and a great success. George Brown has thrown up telegraphy as it cannot be made a commercial success in England—Telegraphy being there a Government concern. The success is this. Articulate speech was transmitted intelligibly this afternoon. I have constructed a new apparatus operated by the human voice. It is not of course complete yet—but some sentences were understood this afternoon.
>
> I was in one room at the Transmitting Instrument and Mr. Watson at the Receiving Instrument in another room—out of ear-shot.
>
> I called out into the Transmitting instrument, "Mr. Watson—come here—I want to see you." And he came!

> He said he had heard each word perfectly distinctly come from the electro-magnet at the other end. We then exchanged places. Mr. Watson sang an air. Every note was audible. He then read from a book and the voice came from the electro-magnet in a curious half muffled sort of way.
>
> The sense was not intelligible but I caught a word here and there such as "to"—"out"—"further."
>
> The last sentence I heard very plainly and distinctly. It was "Mr. Bell, do you understand what I say?" We tried other sentences, "How do you do" and etc., with satisfactory results.
>
> This was a great day with me. I feel that I have at last struck the solution of a great problem—and the day is coming when telegraph wires will be laid on to houses just like water and gas—and friends converse with each other without leaving home.

It truly was a great day for Bell. For the first time he had actually heard articulate speech transmitted electrically over a wire. His use of the expression *articulate speech* is significant since it clearly demonstrates that he makes a distinction between that and the *vocal sounds* mentioned in his patent.

His famous request, "Mr. Watson—come here—I want to see you," has been linked to the name of Alexander Graham Bell for all eternity. It seems that this is the one Bell anecdote that people remember from their school days. But, unfortunately, they always get the details mixed up. The oft-told story that he had spilled acid on his pants and was calling to Watson for help is just that, a story with little factual basis. Robert Bruce, in his biography of Alexander Graham Bell, debunks the myth by pointing out that Bell never mentioned this alleged mishap in either his lab notes or his letters.[8] And knowing Bell's penchant for minutiae, we can be fairly sure he would have made some comment had it actually happened. The story first aired in 1926 in Watson's autobiography, *Exploring Life*. As Bruce points out, Bell probably did spill acid on his pants at one time or another but not on that eventful afternoon of March 10, 1876. We can certainly forgive Watson, who, in looking back through the mists of a half century, mistakenly combined two unrelated events into a charming, apocryphal anecdote.

One would think that such a scientific breakthrough—the actual electrical transmission of speech—would have been a rather auspicious occasion. Bell must certainly have assumed that he was the first person ever to have transmitted a human voice over a wire. Knowing Bell's fondness for publicity and recognition, one would also think that there would have been some public announcement, a press conference perhaps or an article in some scientific journal. But this never happened. We know from later events that Bell was not reticent when it came to media attention;

he sought it out and reveled in it. Above all, he wanted the public to know and recognize the name of Alexander Graham Bell. We shall see later, in the Bell-Gray letters, just how upset he can become when he believes he is cheated of his rightful recognition.

With the exception of this letter to his father and a few notations in his laboratory notebook, however, it would be many years before Bell would make any further mention of his March 10 telephonic breakthrough. It was to remain a secret for over six years, only to be revealed by Watson during a court trial in 1882.[9] Although Bell did make occasional references to a liquid variable resistance transmitter in later lectures and demonstrations, he apparently never used it after March 1876. Bell claimed in later testimony that he had had a liquid transmitter at the Centennial Exposition in Philadelphia, but he never used it. However, Bell had good reason to keep this device secret. Gray attended the exposition and saw—and even participated in—Bell's demonstration of his telephones. But these were voice-powered, magneto-inductive instruments similar to the one depicted in his patent. Gray claimed he never saw Bell's liquid transmitter there and, of course, had no idea that Bell first transmitted speech with such a device. He assumed that Bell had achieved his success with an instrument similar to that shown in his patent of March 7 and that Bell knew nothing of Gray's liquid transmitter.

After the initial discovery that speech could be transmitted electrically, Bell continued his experiments to learn more about the nature of the liquid variable resistance transmitter. He experimented with different liquids, even cod liver oil, which, of course, produced no sound. He also tried mercury and got no sound. Strangely enough, in his patent specifications, mercury was precisely what he (or someone) declared should be used to produce undulatory currents.

The only effective mode for the liquid variable resistance transmitter was a wire vibrating in acidulated water. Even this mode was not without its problems. Too much current flowing through the system would cause gassing at the electrodes. This, in turn, would create a background noise that would, if too loud, interfere with speech transmission. A source voltage of four to six volts would provide a good compromise between sufficient loudness and minimal background noise. What Bell's experiments with the liquid transmitter illustrate is that he never tried them before writing his patent specifications. What he says in the patent about the use of mercury may sound plausible on paper, but it just doesn't work that way in practice. In other words, Bell's invention had never been reduced to practice, in the true sense of that phrase, prior to filing the application.

Even after his success at transmitting speech, first with the liquid transmitter and then with the electromagnetic device similar to that of his patent, Bell still did not foresee a dazzling future for his telephone nor for harmonic telegraphy. So far, all he had done was prove that it was possible to send words through a wire. While it might have been a great scientific achievement, it was a long way from paying the rent. With the prospect of marriage coming up, and none too soon as far as Bell was concerned, he had to find a way to earn a living. Oddly enough, he had never really had what could be called a "regular job." He had conducted classes from time to time or taken on private students but nothing on a regular schedule. This was a great concern to his future father-in-law, who wrote to him in April shortly after he received his latest patent:

> I had a letter from Mrs. Hubbard yesterday in which she says you have received an offer of a professorship at the Washington College. I think it would be a mistake for you to accept it because I fear if you were tied up to rules and hours it would be very irksome and hard—that if you were also married you would feel compelled to remain and there would thus be a constant struggle and life would go hard.
>
> You are not like other men and you must make allowance for your peculiarities. I do not mean to praise your peculiarities for they are a very great injury to you. If you could work as other men do you would accomplish much more than with your present habits. But you must overcome those habits by your own will, and not by rules imposed by a college faculty and President.
>
> I believe there is money in your patents and that if you would take Mr. Williams' man as I propose and work with him or let him work steady on *one thing* until you had perfected it you would soon make it a success. While you are flying from one thing to another you may accidentally accomplish something but you probably will never perfect anything.
>
> ...I like you so much that I want to see your life a success and it will be unless you neglect all your opportunities and talents. With my best love.[10]

Whether Hubbard's admonitions had any impact is doubtful; however, they may have spurred Bell to more actively promote his telephone. Bell reveled in lecturing and demonstrating his new instrument. For the next year, he would be his own public relations agent, lining up lectures and talks wherever he could. He addressed learned bodies willingly without charge, but for the public ones he charged a fee. He did earn a modest income from this source, but not as much as he had originally hoped. Shortly after starting his lecture circuit, he wrote to his parents:

> Dear Papa & Mama,
>
> There is nothing like putting up a bold front after all. I feel myself borne

up by a rising tide. The meeting at the Academy was a grand success.

I had a telegraph wire from my rooms in Beacon Street to the Athenaemic building, and my telephonic organ was placed in my green reception room under the care of Willie Hubbard.

When the proper time came I rose to address the dignified assembly of grey heads before me and telegraphed to Willie Hubbard for some music. While I was speaking out burst the notes of the "Old Hundred" from an instrument upon the table to the delight of all.

When I spoke of the simultaneous transmission of musical notes I sent a telegraphic signal to Willie and in response came some rich chords—and then an air with its proper accompaniment.

Everything was most successful, and when I sat down I was somewhat surprised to be greeted by a hearty round of applause—which, I am informed is such an unusual thing at the Academy....

Your affectionate son
A. Graham Bell[11]

This was the beginning of what would be many demonstrations before the Bell Telephone Company would begin business a little over a year later. But what is of special interest in the above letter is that no mention is made of transmitting articulate speech. He had to signal Willie Hubbard by telegraph to start the music, and his instruments were being used to transmit musical tones only, essentially what Gray had been doing for several years when demonstrating his harmonic telegraph system. Bell still had a long way to go before he would have a marketable telephone.

Notes

1. AGB to AMB, February 29, 1876.
2. Dowd case, p. 531, *Bell Telephone Co. et al, v. Peter A. Dowd.*
3. See Appendix B.
4. AGB to parents, October 20, 1874.
5. American Bell Telephone Co., *Deposition of Alexander Graham Bell*, 1908, p. 87.
6. Patent No. 174,465, Appendix D.
7. Bernard S. Finn, "Alexander Graham Bell's Experiments with the Variable-Resistance Transmitter," *Smithsonian Journal of History* 1, no. 4 (Winter 1966).
8. Robert V. Bruce, *Alexander Graham Bell and the Conquest of Solitude*, Cornell University Press, Ithaca and London, 1990, p. 182.
9. Ibid.
10. G. Hubbard to AGB, April 26, 1876.
11. AGB to parents, May 12, 1876.

Chapter 9

Bell-Gray Letters

Revealing Correspondence Between Two Adversaries

Bell and Gray met for the first time at the Centennial Exposition in Philadelphia in June 1876. However, both had been aware of the other long before this. Bell, who was always a little apprehensive on the subject of spies, was convinced that Gray, somehow, was trying to spy on him. Gray, on the other hand, and with some justification, was quite suspicious of Bell. As we saw earlier, Gray vented some of his frustrations in a letter to Alex Hayes, one of his patent agents at the time: "Do you know a Professor Bell in Washington?... He claimed to Orton [president of Western Union] when he was in Washington that he could antedate me in everything that I ever claimed to do. The coincidence was so remarkable that it looks suspicious."[1]

Shortly afterwards, on April 26, 1875, Gray followed up with yet another letter to Hayes in which he said: "I have read Bell's claims and it seems to me he could not have described my invention better if he had copied it.... I am mad clear down to my boots. As I understand the pat. in question it covers broadly every gist of my invention and I will fight till the pat. expires." We know now that the source for most of these Patent Office leaks was Patent Examiner Wilber, who fed confidential patent information to Pollok and Bailey. They, in turn, passed it on to Hubbard who, in turn, relayed the essential elements to Bell in the form of a mentor's advice. Hubbard was careful not to let the high-minded Bell believe there was anything illicit about such "advice."

Hubbard, an attorney himself and well-versed in patent matters, knew that this kind of information was privileged, but he was apparently willing to overlook it. In fact, Hubbard even warned Bell at one time against filing a caveat because it could "tip his hand." Hubbard was well aware of the confidentiality breech at the Patent Office. If Wilber were willing to give information to Pollok and Bailey, he would, Hubbard reasoned, quite likely pass it on to others. It was probably not a coincidence that Thomas Edison, a friend of Wilber's, started conducting experiments with a liquid transmitter little more than a month after Gray filed his caveat.[2] Bell, a naive novice in the world of invention and patent office practice, probably didn't realize the nature of the intelligence he was receiving and, therefore, didn't suspect any underhanded activity. If he did, he didn't reveal it in his letters. On several occasions, he wrote to his parents boasting of the progress he was making on his inventions and how he was so much further ahead than his rival, Elisha Gray. This information came from his patent attorneys, Pollok and Bailey.

Gray and Bell both had exhibits at the Centennial Exposition in Philadelphia that summer. Gray's, of course, was focused on his harmonic telegraph system; Bell's, a last-minute entry arranged through Hubbard, was less extensive but centered around his harmonic system and his "speaking telephone." They knew who each other was, but that was about all. Gray, who was among a group that watched Bell's telephone demonstration, recalled seeing several versions of his telephones at the centennial. But, as they would later testify, neither Gray nor his assistant, William Goodridge, had seen Bell's liquid transmitter at that time. Although Bell never demonstrated the liquid transmitter at the exposition, he did claim, some years later, to have had it with him. If so, he wisely kept it out of Gray's sight.[3]

One evening, after the exposition had closed for the day, Bell and Gray met at Bell's hotel and, as Bell wrote in a letter, had a pleasant discussion about harmonic telegraphy. The telephone was not mentioned. After having met Gray, Bell concluded that "he was an honorable man & an independent inventor" [4] and entertained no more thoughts that Gray was spying on him.

Gray would, on occasion, give lectures and demonstrations on the instruments he either had or was in the process of developing. On February 27, 1877, at McCormick Hall in Chicago, he planned to give a lecture on his own telephonic developments and wished to include the work Bell had done along the same lines. Gray was a popular lecturer and could always be counted on to put on a good show; describing Bell's approach, Gray thought, would simply round out the program. We must remember that at this time Gray had no idea—and would not have for a number of years—that Bell had used a liquid variable resistance transmitter to make his first transmission of the human voice. Gray simply assumed that Bell was using an instrument based on the description in his patent of March 7, 1876 (No. 174,465), specifically the one depicted in figure 7.

It was in this light that Gray, ever the proper gentleman, requested permission from Bell to include his instruments in Gray's upcoming lecture. Thus, he wrote to Bell:

> Chicago, Feb. 21, 1877
> Prof. A. G. Bell:
> *My dear Sir*:
>
> I give a lecture in McCormick Hall, this city, Tuesday evening, the 27th inst., on the *telephone*, as I have developed it. I also connect with Milwaukee, and have tunes and telegraphing done from there. I should like to explain and exhibit *your* method of transmitting vocal sounds as well, but do not feel at liberty to do *more* without permission from you. I should explain it as *your* method, and not mine, although the *Office* records show a description of the talking telegraph filed by me the *same* day yours was filed. The description is substantially the same as yours. I was unfortunate in being an hour or two behind you. There is no evidence that either knew that the other was working in this direction.
>
> With our facilities I can get up an apparatus on a day's notice that will answer. I have a copy of your last patent. Please telegraph at my expense, on receipt of this, yes or no, and I will act accordingly.
>
> Yours truly,
> Elisha Gray
> 220 Kinzie St. Chicago
>
> I send this care of Mr. Hayes, as I do not know your address. I received a line from you through Mr. Baldwin, for which please accept thanks.

Bell's knowledge of current events, especially those pertaining to electrical developments, was not restricted to the Boston newspapers but included those of Chicago as well. He may even have employed a clipping service for this purpose. Apparently, the *Chicago Tribune* had recently printed a brief article in the "Personal" column to which Bell had taken great exception. He promptly fired off a telegram to Gray:

> Boston, February 24, 1877
> Elisha Gray,
> *Western Electric Manufacturing. Co.*
>
> If you refute in your lecture, and in the *Chicago Tribune*, the libel upon me published in that paper February sixteenth, I shall have no objection. Please answer.
>
> A. Graham Bell.

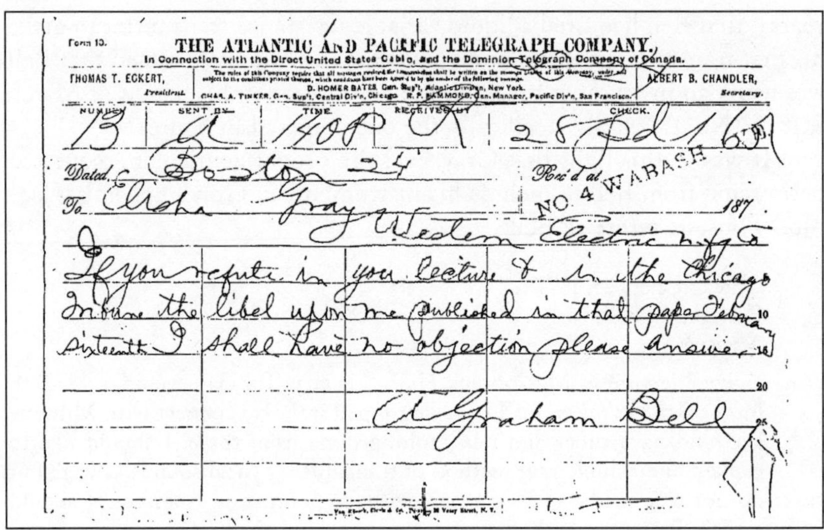

Form 10.

THE ATLANTIC AND PACIFIC TELEGRAPH COMPANY.

In Connection with the Direct United States Cable, and the Dominion Telegraph Company of Canada.

THOMAS T. ECKERT, President. D. HOMER BATES, Gen. Sup't, Atlantic Division, New York. CHAS. A. TINKER, Gen. Sup't, Central Div'n, Chicago. R. P. HAMMOND, Gen. Manager, Pacific Div'n, San Francisco. ALBERT B. CHANDLER, Secretary.

NUMBER	SENT BY	TIME	RECEIVED BY	CHECK.
13	G	140P	R	28 Pd 16

Dated Boston 24 Rec'd at NO. 4 WABASH 187.

To Elisha Gray Western Electric Mfg Co

If you refute in your lecture & in the Chicago Tribune the libel upon me published in that paper February sixteenth I shall have no objection please answer.

A. Graham Bell

Figure 9–1. Bell's telegram to Gray telling him to "refute ... the libel upon me."

This was not quite the answer Gray had expected; he was taken aback by the curtness of Bell's reply. Gray, it seems, was not the ardent newspaper reader that Bell was and professed ignorance of the problem. That same day, he replied to Bell:

> Chicago, Feb. 24, 1877
> Prof. A. G. Bell
> *Sir*:
>
> Your telegram received. In answer, I would say, first, that I do not know what article you refer to, but will see the paper of that date. I have seen one or two articles lately that ventured to assume that you were not the only man in the world who had contributed to the development of the telephone. If such assertions are "*libels*," then you have been *libelled*. So far as I know, the "libels" are mostly on the other side, if assertions of *originality*, etc., may be so considered. The papers here have been full of articles of late, copied from Boston papers, claiming the whole development of the telephone for you. It would not be strange if someone, knowing the facts, should speak, and in doing so may have done you an injustice.
>
> You seem to assume that I am responsible for all the newspaper articles that are not in your favor. I assert here that I have never said a word about you in the public prints, and I have always—even to the degree of offending some of my friends—defended you when I have heard disparaging remarks made about you. Since I made your acquaintance I have taken the ground that we were both independent inventors. Now, if we are going into the refutation business I suggest that it be mutual. So far as I know there

is quite as much needed from your side as from mine. I am always willing to correct any wrong done to you, even if I am not responsible. If we undertake to follow up the newspapers we will have our hands full. I shall not show your apparatus, as I do not want any conditions imposed until I know what I am to refute. I do not know but that it is to deny all claim to the invention. Allow me to suggest that your telegram was just a little indiscreet, as it contained an assumption very unjust to me.

I do not know your address, so I send through Mr. Hayes.

Yours truly,
Elisha Gray

P.S. You should have sent your dispatch collect, as I requested it be sent.

The "Mr. Hayes" referred to in the above letters is Alex Hayes of Boston, one of Gray's patent attorneys. After mailing his reply to Bell, Gray sought out the *Chicago Tribune* article in question. We have to keep in mind that the newspapers of that era were a little more provincial than they are today. Although Gray lived in the Chicago suburb of Highland Park, a Chicago reporter would have considered him a native Chicagoan when compared to a Bostonian such as Bell. The somewhat biased reporting of the *Tribune*, while perhaps not in the best journalistic spirit, is at least understandable.

> Many of the Eastern newspapers are favoring their readers with sketches of Professor A. M. Bell, "the inventor of the telephone." Meanwhile, the real inventor of the telephone—Mr. Elisha Gray, of Chicago,—minds his own business, and apparently concerns himself not at all about the spurious claims of Professor Bell. Persons acquainted with the subject need not be informed that Mr. Gray's claims are incontrovertible. Science long since recognized them. They were established in the columns of the *Tribune* years ago, before Professor Bell was so much as heard of. They are officially approved in the Patent Office at Washington, and they have already brought in large returns in money as well as in reputation to the inventor. Talking by telegraph and other sport of that description Mr. Gray has not paid much attention to as yet, because there is no present indication in it of anything more than sport; but the principles involved in it were discussed by him and have all been used by him in a practical manner. (*Chicago Tribune*, Feb. 16, 1877)

It's easy to see what so upset the always impetuous and frequently hot-headed Bell. Perhaps the most biting part was the reference to "Professor A. M. Bell." Obviously, the reporter had confused young Alexander with his very successful father, Alexander Melville Bell. This would have been especially distressful to the prideful son, who was still struggling for recognition in his own name. This unintentional journalistic snub was no doubt what sparked his brusque telegram to Gray. That the reporter didn't get all his facts straight—not an uncommon situation—and was a little confused about the subject matter is readily apparent. However, it is just as apparent that the reporter had also interviewed Gray, since the article reflects Gray's then-opinion as to the commercial limitations of the telephone.

Despite the negative tone of the *Tribune* commentary, after receiving Gray's letter, Bell simmered down considerably, and he finally got around to writing a more temperate and conciliatory reply:

> Boston University, March 2, 1877
> Elisha Gray, Esq., *Chicago.*
> *My dear sir:*
>
> I was somewhat hasty, I must confess, in sending my telegram, for, of course, you are not responsible for all the ill-natured remarks that may appear in the newspapers concerning me.
>
> I am sorry that my telegram should have prevented you from making the experiments you desired, for it is my sincere desire to oblige you in any way that I can. I am glad that you are willing to do me justice, and I must thank you for saying a good word for me occasionally. I may say that it has uniformly been my custom to make honorable mention of your name in multiple telegraphy, and to give you the credit of being an independent inventor.
>
> I have not generally alluded to your name in connection with the invention of the electric "telephone," for we seem to attach different significations to the word. I apply the term only to an apparatus for transmitting the voice (which meaning is strictly in accordance with the derivation of the word), whereas you seem to use the term as expressive of any apparatus for the transmission of *musical* tones by the electric current.
>
> I have no knowledge of any apparatus constructed by you for the purpose of transmitting vocal sounds, and I trust that I have not been doing you an injustice. It is my sincere desire to give you all the credit that I feel justly belongs to you.
>
> I do not know the nature of the application for a caveat, to which you have referred as having been filed two hours after my application for a patent, excepting that it had something to do with the vibration of a wire in water, and therefore conflicted with my patent. My specification had been prepared *months* before it was filed, and a copy had been taken to England by a friend. I delayed the filing of the American patent until I could hear from him. At last the protests of all those interested in my invention, deprecating further delay, had their effects, and I filed my application without waiting for a conclusion of negotiations in England. It was certainly a most striking coincidence that our applications should have been filed on the same day.

I have been kept so busy the past few days correcting the examination papers of my normal school, that I have been unable to write.

In haste.
Yours truly,
Alexander Graham Bell

This was a rather curious letter. Not because of Bell's almost-apology, but because of his emerging position with regard to the telephone and the harmonic telegraph. On January 30, 1877, Bell had received what is now called the Second Telephone Patent (No. 186,787). Although this patent, like the first telephone one, was still closely tied to the concept of multiple or harmonic telegraphy, it clearly marked a turning point in Bell's objective. By this time, he had virtually abandoned the idea of the harmonic telegraph, with which he had never been successful, and was concentrating solely on the telephone. This was why he was so willing to give full credit to Gray for work on harmonic telegraphy, while reserving the credit for telephonic development for himself.

The letter is also curious for what it says concerning Gray's caveat. Remember, a caveat was a confidential document, and Gray's caveat was still valid, having just been renewed for another year. Although Gray had said in his letter that he had filed it on the same day as Bell's application, Gray made no disclosures as to its contents. Yet Bell knew it "had something to do with the vibration of a wire in water," which was the essence of Gray's invention. We know now, from later testimony, that Bell got this information from Patent Examiner Wilber. But at the time, Gray had no idea that Bell knew the full nature of his caveat, which is why it is so strange that Bell would even mention the incriminating "vibrating wire in water." The only conclusion we can come to is that Bell was still very naive about confidentiality at the Patent Office.

However, what he said about the preparation and filing of his application is especially puzzling. In January 1876 letters to Mabel and his parents, he claimed that he was still working on the application just a week before he sent it to his attorneys. Yet in his letter to Gray he states that his application (the specification) had been prepared "months in advance." This could be construed as just a little harmless hyperbole, until we consider what he also said immediately afterwards. Here he states that *he* ordered his attorneys to file the application. As we saw earlier, this is in direct contradiction to his court testimony a few years later:

> Mr. Brown neglected to take any action in the matter and sent no cablegram; and Mr. Hubbard, becoming impatient at the delay, privately

> instructed my solicitors to file the specification in the American Patent Office, and on the fourteenth day of February, 1876, it was so filed without my knowledge or consent [Deposition of A.G. Bell, p. 82].

What is even more puzzling is that Gray never picked up on Bell's surprising disclosure concerning his knowledge of Gray's caveat. It wouldn't be until many years later, after it was too late to make a difference, that Gray would realize that Bell's statement "it had something to do with the vibration of a wire in water" was the whole crux of his "confidential" caveat (see app. B). However, Bell's letter of March 2 seemed to mollify Gray and prompted him to make this fatal reply:

> Chicago, Mar. 5, 1877
> Prof Bell
> *My dear Sir:*
>
> I have just received yours of the 2nd instant, and I freely forgive you for any feeling your telegram had aroused. I found the article I suppose you referred to in the personal column of the *Tribune*, and am free to say it does you an injustice.
>
> I gave you full credit for the talking feature of the telephone, as you may have seen in the associated press dispatch that was sent to all the papers in the country—in my lecture in McCormick Hall, Feb. 27th. There were four different papers represented at the lecture, but only one—the *Tribune*—alluded to my mention of you, except the "press" dispatch. I described your apparatus at length by diagram.
>
> Of course you have had no means of knowing what I had done in the matter of transmitting vocal sounds. When, however, you see the specification, you will see that the fundamental principles are contained therein. I do not, however, claim even the credit of inventing it, as I do not believe a mere description of an idea that has never been *reduced to practice*—in the *strict sense* of that phrase—should be dignified with the name invention.
>
> Yours very truly,
> Elisha Gray

Gray made reference in this letter to the fact that he was planning to turn his caveat into an actual patent application, which when issued would be available for public inspection—hence his phrase "when ... you see the specification." In light of this statement, it seems incredible that he would turn around, and in the same letter, disclaim credit for having invented it. In evaluating his statements, we have to remember that Gray was totally in the dark regarding Bell's activities. Gray honestly, but erroneously, believed that Bell had achieved his telephonic results with the electromagnet device depicted in figure 7 of his March 7, 1876, patent.

And he would continue in this belief for a number of years. Despite Bell's slip of the pen in his previous letter, in which he revealed illicit knowledge of the caveat, Gray gave no outward sign that he suspected anything out of the ordinary. Years later, though, he would vividly remember Bell's comment. But at the time he wrote his so-called fatal letter, he hadn't yet realized that he had shown Bell the way to telephonic success.

Several years later, Gray's alleged "disclaimer" would come back to haunt him. However, to be fair, it should not be taken out of context but judged on the basis of his full statement. What he actually said was "I do not, however, claim even the credit of inventing it, as I do not believe a mere description of an idea that has never been *reduced to practice*—in the *strict sense* of that phrase—should be dignified with the name invention." At the time of his caveat, he had not yet made a model of his invention (nor was he required to) and, obviously, could not have reduced it to practice, as is required for a full-fledged invention. Therefore—in Gray's mind—it was not yet a true *invention.*

It is inconsistent to assume that Gray actually meant to disclaim any credit for inventing *it* (*it* being the telephone device in his caveat). It is more logical to assume that he was simply trying to make a point. In his previous letter, he left little doubt that he considered it his invention. Few inventors, if any, ever disclaim their inventions. If he were trying to make a point, which is the only logical explanation, it was this: a mere idea is not an invention until the inventor can prove by actual demonstration that it truly works. That is the definition of *reduction to practice* as embraced by most engineers and is the one Gray followed. Remember, a caveat did not require, nor did it preclude, that an invention-in-process be reduced to practice at the time of filing. The fact that Bell had never achieved voice transmission before his patent was awarded would raise the reduction-to-practice issue in the telephone trials that would follow. Gray's problem was that he was just a little too straight for his own good.

Whatever interpretation we choose to make of Gray's final reply to Bell is immaterial; it had no legal significance. What *is* important, is that Bell's lawyers used that letter to devastating advantage in subsequent court battles. In preparation for the Dowd case, discussed later, Gray had to give his deposition. One can almost hear the Bell company counsel, as he shoved the fatal epistle in front of Gray and asked, "Is this the letter you wrote on March 5, 1877, to Alexander Graham Bell in which you said, 'I do not, however, claim even the credit of inventing it'?" Bell took special delight in relating this incident to his parents:

> Poor Elisha Gray looked very much disconcerted when our Solicitors handed this letter to him and asked him whether he acknowledged it as

his. He turned to his solicitor and said: "I will have to swear to it and you can swear at it."[5]

Although Gray's so-called disclaimer to the invention of the telephone had little legal significance, it did have immense value as a public relations tool. There had been stories going around—vicious, unfounded

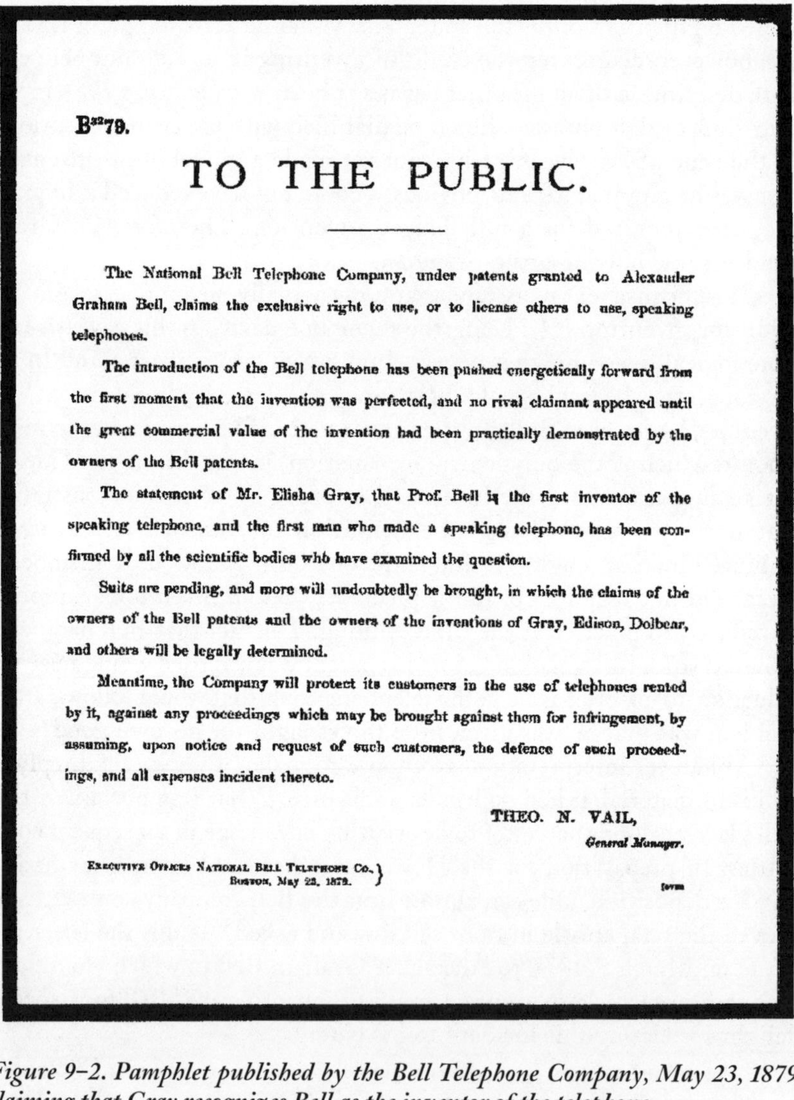

B[32]79.

TO THE PUBLIC.

The National Bell Telephone Company, under patents granted to Alexander Graham Bell, claims the exclusive right to use, or to license others to use, speaking telephones.

The introduction of the Bell telephone has been pushed energetically forward from the first moment that the invention was perfected, and no rival claimant appeared until the great commercial value of the invention had been practically demonstrated by the owners of the Bell patents.

The statement of Mr. Elisha Gray, that Prof. Bell is the first inventor of the speaking telephone, and the first man who made a speaking telephone, has been confirmed by all the scientific bodies who have examined the question.

Suits are pending, and more will undoubtedly be brought, in which the claims of the owners of the Bell patents and the owners of the inventions of Gray, Edison, Dolbear, and others will be legally determined.

Meantime, the Company will protect its customers in the use of telephones rented by it, against any proceedings which may be brought against them for infringement, by assuming, upon notice and request of such customers, the defence of such proceedings, and all expenses incident thereto.

THEO. N. VAIL,
General Manager.

EXECUTIVE OFFICES NATIONAL BELL TELEPHONE Co.
BOSTON, May 23, 1879.

[illegible]

Figure 9–2. Pamphlet published by the Bell Telephone Company, May 23, 1879, claiming that Gray recognizes Bell as the inventor of the telephone.

rumors, according to the Bell interests—that Gray was the real inventor of the speaking telephone. This, the company said, was undermining public confidence in the newly formed National Bell Telephone Company as well as its counterpart in Canada.

Properly utilized, Gray's damning letter could go a long way towards refuting those stories and improving the image of the Bell interests. Bell, himself, for purely personal reasons, was chomping at the bit to use the letter as proof of his claim to be the inventor of the telephone. For a long time, he had been pestering his attorneys for permission to publish it. As he wrote to his parents:

> These horrid law suits are dragging to a close and there can be no doubt in regard to the termination. If there is justice anywhere the case *can not* go against us. I shall know tomorrow whether we can publish Gray's *disclaimer* of Invention or not. This will be a great step towards public confidence.[6]

To Bell, this was one of the most important issues in the entire Dowd case. Although he naturally wanted victory for the National Bell Telephone Company, as far as he was concerned, the Dowd case was also a vehicle to announce to the world that he was the true inventor of the speaking telephone. It was a matter of honor.

Notes

1. Gray to Alex Hayes, March 19, 1875, National Museum of American History.
2. Robert Conot, *Thomas A. Edison: A Streak of Luck*, Da Capo, New York, 1979, p. 83.
3. *Petition of Elisha Gray to Re-open Interference Hearings*, 1888, p. 121.
4. Robert V. Bruce, *Alexander Graham Bell and the Conquest of Solitude*, Cornell University Press, Ithaca and London, 1990, p. 198.
5. AGB to parents, April 11, 1879.
6. AGB to parents, April 20, 1879.

Chapter 10

Birth of the Bell Telephone Company

Telegraphy Gives Way to Telephony

Sir William Thompson (later Lord Kelvin), England's most respected and distinguished scientist, was called to testify at a patent infringement trial in Edinburgh in 1882. The complainant's attorney questioned Sir William, who had witnessed Bell's demonstration at the Philadelphia Centennial Exposition in June 1876, as to what he had seen—or rather, heard.

> Q. You were one of the judges at the Philadelphia exhibition, and when there was your attention called to some device of Bell for reproducing sounds?
>
> A. Yes.
>
> Q. After Bell had shown these [Bell's harmonic telegraph devices] did he show you anything else?
>
> A. Yes; he showed us something which he said he would hardly call an invention, but which might ultimately become an invention.

Q. What did he show you? (The witness was here shown the telephone given him by Bell.) The telephone shown, was it to be used in connection with a battery and a line wire?

A. Yes.

Q. What did Bell say about them?

A. He said he could show us something which would speak, and on that occasion, in the presence of the Emperor of Brazil, and after some troublesome adjustment, it was made to speak. I heard the vowel "o" and "to be or not to be," and "there's the rub."

Q. He stuck to monosyllables?

A. Yes.

Q. And was this after troublesome adjustment and many orders to his assistant, and he had tried to see whether it would do?

A. Yes. I felt so very much interest that I went too far and said the thing is done. I urged Mr. Bell to go on, and before the close of the meeting he had improved his adjustment. My friend Watson [Prof. James C. Watson] heard it very faintly. It required very minute attention but I am absolutely convinced that I did hear it. [1]

The voice-powered telephones that Bell demonstrated at the Centennial Exposition in Philadelphia were extremely weak, but they did prove that it was technically possible to transmit the human voice over a telegraph wire. Just a year later, on July 9, 1877, with telephones not much different from those used in the centennial demonstration, the Bell Telephone Company went into business.

Even after Bell had demonstrated to his father and Hubbard that he actually had transmitted articulate speech, sometime in March 1876, they were still pushing him to perfect his harmonic telegraph system. Apparently they weren't too impressed as to the telephone's commercial value. As late as May, his father wrote:

> The only hope so far as I can see, for the immediate pecuniary benefit from your scientific work, is in the autograph! [Bell's as-yet-unperfected patent of April 6, 1875, for a "fax" machine] Make it produce an income and you can ride the electric hobby. At present you have no stable for such a horse and you should deny yourself till you get one.[2]

But Bell was beginning to lose interest in telegraphy matters; the telephone was his all-consuming enterprise now. In May he gave several lectures to scientific groups in Boston, which were well received, but apparently the news didn't reach the general public.[3] And then he had an opportunity, through the well-connected Hubbard, to display his system of harmonic telegraphy as well as his telephone instruments at the prestigious Centennial Exposition in Philadelphia. On June 25 he gave his now-famous demonstration before such notables as the Emperor of Brazil, Dom Pedro, and England's Sir William Thompson, who was one of the Centennial judges. Even Elisha Gray, Bell's long-time nemesis, witnessed his telephonic performance.[4]

Following his success in Philadelphia, Bell began to demonstrate his telephone whenever he could. In August he put on a show for his father and friends in Brantford, Ontario, and by October he was carrying on two-way conversations. By December, using the telegraph lines of the Eastern Railroad, he carried on a "long-distance" call between Boston and North Conway. Perhaps one of the most convincing demonstrations occurred when Bell showed that the telephone could even transmit conversations in Japanese. Of course, the whole idea of putting on these shows was to obtain press coverage, which was generally favorable. But demonstrations are always risky, especially when using borrowed telegraph lines. The one Bell put on in Lawrence, Massachusetts, on May 28 was close to a failure. Thomas Watson, whose voice was supposed to emanate from the receiver on display, was not to be heard. The next day the Lawrence *Daily American* reported on the event in a multistanza verse entitled "Waiting for Watson":

> To the great hall we strayed,
> Fairly our fee we paid,
> Seven hundred there delayed,
> But where was Watson?
> Was he out on his beer?
> Walked he off on his ear?
> Something was wrong, 'tis clear.
> What was it, Watson?[5]

In late 1876, it is said, Hubbard, Sanders, Watson, and Bell offered to sell their patent rights, actually the patents assigned to the Bell Patent Association, to Western Union for $100,000. This would have yielded the partners a handsome profit for a mere two-year investment. But William Orton, president of Western Union, turned them down with the comment, according to one source, "What use could this company make of an electrical toy?"[6] Another commentator claimed that Orton just laughed at them. Whether he felt that Bell's patents weren't worth that much or whether he didn't see any advantage for Western Union, we really don't know. But we do know that Western Union had close ties to Thomas Edison as well as Elisha Gray and probably felt that it could get a similar system from one of these sources.

Although this story of Hubbard's offer to sell Bell's patents is widely quoted and apparently accepted by all of Bell's biographers and historians, there is little documentation to support it. As voluminous a letter writer as Bell was, there is nothing in his correspondence to indicate such an offer, and nobody seems to know where the story originated. Knowing the long-standing animosity between Hubbard and Orton, Hubbard could not have had a high expectation of success with Western Union, if the story of the offer is true. Hubbard, being the good promoter that he was—and he was one of the best—probably reasoned that the worst that Orton could do was to say, "No."

As for the telephone concept itself, this was only a minor part of Bell's patent (No. 174,465) and was still considered only a scientific curiosity. Bell had put on a few public telephone demonstrations, something that he did well, and had gotten some favorable, although not glowing, press coverage, but that was about all. Although these demonstrations had been written up in the newspapers and some of the science-oriented magazines, they were not treated as major technological breakthroughs. As far as Hubbard, Sanders, and, especially, Orton were concerned, there simply was no commercial market for Bell's gadget, the one he claimed would transmit "vocal sounds." If that were the only device that Hubbard was pitching to Western Union, it is little wonder that Orton turned him down.

However, even before Hubbard approached him, Orton had asked Edison to look into the matter of voice transmission and had furnished Edison with all of the available data on Philipp Reis's telephonic devices. Orton was a good businessman and wasn't about to close the door on something that might have commercial potential in the future. He was astute enough at least to look into the matter.

Most likely, Hubbard offered Orton all of Bell's patents, which of course included his March 7, 1876, patent with its brief and fuzzy description of his telephone device. George Prescott, Western Union's chief engineer, had previously studied and evaluated Bell's harmonic telegraphic idea and concluded that it still needed a lot more development, despite Bell's naive enthusiasm over Orton's initial interest.

It is important to realize that the general public was neither looking for nor eagerly awaiting a speaking telegraph. Just the decade before, something as bizarre as a device called a "telephone" was enough to get at least one person into a lot of trouble. A Boston newspaper of 1865 reported:

> A man about 46 years of age giving the name of Joshua Coppersmith, has been arrested in New York for attempting to extort funds from ignorant and superstitious people by exhibiting a device which he says will convey the human voice any distance over metallic wires so that it will be heard by the listener at the other end.
>
> He calls the instrument a "telephone" which is obviously intended to imitate the word "telegraph" and win the confidence of those who know of the success of the latter instrument without understanding the principles on which it is based. Well-informed people know that it is impossible to transmit the human voice over wires as may be done with dots and dashes and signals of the Morse code, and that, were it possible to do so, the thing would be of no practical value.
>
> The authorities who apprehended this criminal are to be congratulated and it is to be hoped that his punishment will be prompt and fitting, that it may serve as an example to other *conscienceless schemers* who enrich themselves at the expense of their fellow creatures.[7]

One can only wonder whatever happened to the scheming Coppersmith and his improbable "telephone." Was it just a scam, or did he really have a device that would send the voice over an electrical wire? He could have. There certainly were no technical barriers, and everything he needed already existed. This was about the same time that men like Reis, McDonough, and Drawbaugh (to be discussed later) were experimenting, with varying degrees of success, with their versions of speaking telephones. But the public, it seems, just wasn't ready for something called a "telephone."

Moreover, this was also an era when a clever speaker could turn any reference to "talking by telegraph" into a surefire laugh-getter. A reporter gives us this account of a speech by Sir Edward Thornton, British ambassador to the United States, at an 1868 banquet honoring telegraph inventor Professor Samuel Morse:

> Should I have the good fortune to live to the age of the venerable professor, I still hope to see some such improvements as will enable us to carry on the *viva voce* conversation by means of the Atlantic cable (laughter).... We shall hear, perchance, some love-stricken youth of London or Paris whispering soft nothings along the cable to one of those bewitching sirens of New York at so much an hour (laughter), she tempting him all the while to throw himself into the gulf which separates them (laughter). We shall have statesmen, aye, and in those days of progress, even stateswomen (laughter and applause) discussing international questions across the water at so much a conference (laughter).[8]

Telegraph Experts

It is almost impossible for us now to understand how intelligent, sophisticated businesspeople failed to grasp immediately the commercial potential of something as unique as the telephone. One would think that they would be doing everything possible to exploit this uncommon device and to reap the rewards of a virgin market. The simple fact was that they just couldn't see it, especially those in the best position to exploit its potential—the telegraph experts. This anomaly is well explored by David Hounshell in his article "Elisha Gray and the Telephone: On the Disadvantages of Being an Expert."[9]

As Hounshell points out, not only did the telegraph people fail to see the potential, Gray himself greatly underestimated it. Telegraph men, of which Gray was one, looked upon the telephone as merely a substitute for the telegraph key. From their perspective, only trained telegraph operators had the technical skills needed to use a telephone to transmit messages. They envisioned "telephonic telegraphy" as simply a keyless or codeless way to send a telegram. As they viewed it, a customer would go to the telegraph office, write out his message, the rate being predicated on the number of words, and hand it to the telegraph operator. The operator would then read the message over the telephone to the telegrapher at the destination point, who would write it down in shorthand, later transcribe it to longhand, and then deliver it to the recipient. It never occurred to them that ordinary people, untrained and unskilled in telegraphy or any other science, could do the same thing. Nor did it occur to them that the telephone, as a communication device, could ever be utilized outside of a telegraph office. This was the mindset of the telegraph experts.

Even Gray pointed out that the present telegraph, with the multiple transmission capabilities of the quadruplex system, could already send more messages in a given time than would be possible with the single-line telephone. In a November 1, 1876, letter to Alex Hayes, one of his patent attorneys, Gray commented:

> As to Bell's talking telegraph, it only creates interest in scientific circles, and, as a scientific toy it is beautiful; but we can already do more with a wire in a given time than by talking, so that its commercial value will be limited so far at least as it relates to the telegraphic service.[10]

Despite the fact that Gray himself had invented a workable telephone, he still considered it somewhat of a novelty and certainly nothing that could compete with the venerable telegraph. Telegraphers knew that for error-free transmission, you had to speak very slowly and distinctly through a telephone, and this could be a disadvantage. Then there was the question of numbers. To the pragmatic telegraph experts, four messages at a time with the telegraph but only one message at a time with the telephone was an economic fact. And once the harmonic telegraph scheme was commercially perfected (which, of course, except for Gray's brief success, never actually happened), it would be impossible for the telephone to compete. It was a simple matter of bottom-line economics as the telegraph experts saw it.

By early 1877, Bell had made a number of public demonstrations of his telephone and had received some generally favorable local press coverage. But even in these accounts, the press never treated the news that the human voice had been transmitted over a wire as a blockbuster scientific breakthrough. The highly regarded *Scientific American* in September 1876, after the centennial demonstration, devoted only one brief column to it. After first describing the so-called lover's telephone, or string telephone, the article continued, "Professor Graham Bell, by a device somewhat analogous, has succeeded in transmitting the tones of the human voice by telegraph." The article further elaborated, "Several familiar questions were, it is said, understood after a few repetitions.... Now and then, however, a sentence comes out with startling distinctness." Not exactly a glowing tribute to what would soon become one of the world's greatest inventions.

The main problem with the telephone in its earliest stages was simply one of application: no one knew what to make of it or what to do with it. It was a mysterious, marvelous, almost magical instrument—but for what purpose? It was not something for which society had been longing. Many couldn't see any real point to it. Why would anyone want to talk to somebody they couldn't see? Many people felt downright silly talking to a box, especially if you had to shout at it; they felt as if they were talking to themselves. Some had to be instructed in how to speak on a telephone and even then would go through a period of tongue-tied self-consciousness. Some media commentators, searching for any redeeming social benefits from the telephone, suggested that one could listen to concerts and symphonies—perhaps even opera—from the comfort of one's own living room. The idea that one could carry on a conversation with a friend was overlooked. So despite the telephone's amazing capabilities, there was a lot of social and cultural inertia to overcome.

Bell delighted in demonstrating his mysterious talking telegraph whenever he could, lecturing being the most common but not the only method. Once he approached a group of Baltimore women, who were holding a charity bazaar to raise money for the city's orphans, to feature his telephone as a rather novel and unusual fundraiser. After much discussion, they finally agreed to let Bell set up his "coffee grinder," as some described it, in a booth at the bazaar. For ten cents, all of which would go to the orphans, a visitor could actually talk by electricity to someone at Barnum's Hotel several blocks away. But for some reason, this attempt at public relations was not a smashing success. The attendees didn't exactly stand in line to try this new marvel of communication. As the chairwoman confided later, "Mr. Bell called often during the two weeks of the bazaar. He was very much worried because the people did not seem to grasp the significance of his idea." Bell's charity booth netted the orphans of Baltimore all of $10.10. Perhaps people felt a little foolish talking to something that resembled a coffee grinder. Or perhaps they were afraid of what a coffee grinder might say in reply.[11]

Hubbard had followed up on Bell's demonstrations and media coverage by inducing several companies with multiple facilities to install a few interoffice telephones. These were, for the most part, direct line or point-to-point telephones; the concept of the central switchboard was yet to come. Although the users of these first telephones could not selectively call other users, the fact that the boss in the front office could talk directly to the warehouse or the shipping dock was little short of a miracle. Some of these business owners also had telephones installed between their offices and their homes, more for show than anything else—a rich man's toy.

With these modest successes, the telegraph industry was beginning to take notice and perhaps worry a little over the telephone's growing acceptance. In response, a telegraph trade journal, the *Operator*, in an apparent effort to assuage the concerns of its readers, posed some questions in a brief article:

> A correspondent asks: "Do you think that the telephone will take the place of the telegraph now in use?" As this question is one which a great many are now asking, we would say that we do not. It may perhaps supersede the Morse system to some extent for private lines and the like, and, possibly, may be utilized somewhat in forwarding press reports; but for regular commercial telegraphing, it does not appear to us to possess, as it now stands, any advantages. In the first place, messages would require to be taken down in short hand by the receiving operator, and afterward copied in long hand; and we all know the liability to error, not to speak of the great delay of such a system. Then, again, while "Auld Lang Syne," "Home, Sweet Home," or anything with which we are perfectly familiar, could be very easily recognized, it is questionable if regular messages could be "telegraphed" without serious errors occurring. It is very much like talking through the little toy "lover's telegraph," or an ordinary speaking tube. If great care is taken

> to speak slowly and distinctly, and you have an idea of what is coming, you can generally make out enough to understand what a person is talking about. But it seems to us that nobody would care to trust important messages, sometimes involving life and death, or thousands of dollars, to be sent in this manner. We chronicled, issue before last, a ludicrous mistake made just this way. A reporter telegraphed over the police wires to the editor of a Brooklyn paper that he was at the lunatic asylum, where he had gone on business, and could not get back in time for the afternoon edition. The sergeant told a policeman to step around the corner to the newspaper office and inform the editor that Koselowski (the reporter) was at the lunatic asylum. The policeman misunderstood the message, and reported to the editor that Cardinal McCloskey was insane and had been removed to the lunatic asylum. For the above reasons we do not think that telegraphers need have any fears about the telephone usurping, to any great extent, the place of the system handed down to them by Professor Morse.[12]

While the editor of that telegraphers' journal may have been somewhat biased as he tried to reassure his readers, there was also much reality in what he said. As to the quality of transmission, the comparison to the "lover's," or tin can–and–string telephone was pretty much on target. The allusion to popular songs was a poke at the early telephone promoters, such as Reis and Bell, who used the trick of singing to demonstrate their gadget. Once you recognized a tune's melody, you subconsciously recognized the words, even if you didn't hear them too clearly. Although the article implied that messages sent by telegraph were inherently error-free, this was not always the case. Contemporary newspapers and magazines delighted in recounting the frequently comedic consequences of telegraphic blunders.

Although American telegraph experts were doubtful as to the telephone's efficacy in message transmission, German officials decided to give it a try but under strict procedures. This was their method for sending a "telephonic telegram":

> The transmission will take place as follows: The sending office will request the receiving office to prepare the instrument; as soon as the tubes are adjusted, the sending office will give the signal for dispatching the verbal message.
>
> The sender must speak slowly and clearly, without raising his voice; each syllable must be distinctly pronounced; the final syllables especially must be well articulated, and there must be a pause after each word, to give the receiver time to write it down.
>
> When the telegram has been received, the employee at the receiving office must verify the number of words; then he must repeat through the telephone the whole message without pausing, so as to make sure there is no mistake.

In order to insure secrecy, the telephones are placed apart, where persons unconnected with the service cannot hear the verbal message, and the employees are forbidden to reveal to anyone the names of the correspondents.

The charge for telephonic messages, as for the ordinary telegraphic services, is at a rate of so much a word.[13]

Commercial Telephony Begins

The telephones that started the Bell Telephone Company on July 9, 1877, were based on the instruments covered in Bell's Second Telephone Patent of January 30, 1877, not the device shown in figure 7 of his first telephone patent. These later instruments were entirely voice-powered (batteries not required), employing permanent magnets and metallic diaphragms, and were notably weaker when compared to what Western Union would introduce just a half year later. They had improved somewhat over the ones Sir William Thompson testified about but not by much. The illustrations of users holding two Bell receivers to their ears were not exaggerations. This technique was absolutely necessary if you were to hear the message with any degree of clarity. Fortunately for the users, either instrument could function as a transmitter or a receiver. But despite their low volume level, they had one sterling quality: there was so little to them—just a coil of wire, a magnet, and an iron disk—that they were virtually trouble-free. Even today, if the magnets are charged, those early telephones are still capable of functioning as well as they did originally.

Western Union's negative attitude reversed itself after the formation

Figure 10–1. The Bell company's voice-powered telephones (no batteries required) were usually rented in pairs to improve listening.

of the Bell Telephone Company in mid-1877 and word of the orders for the speaking telegraph began coming in, slowly at first, and then with rapidly increasing volume. By the time the Bell Telephone Company opened its doors on July 9, 1877, there were almost 300 sets installed. From that point on, the number of installed sets would increase almost geometrically every few months.

Obviously, Western Union had misjudged the commercial potential of the telephone—if they had considered it at all. The electrical equipment shops, such as Charles Williams's shop in Boston and the Western Electric Manufacturing Company in Chicago, which primarily made telegraph equipment, were now producing telephones on a production basis. It wasn't exactly mass production, but it did attract the attention of Western Union. And what the company saw sparked its interest.

The Western Union Telegraph Company decided then to test the fresh waters of telephony. Less than six months after the Bell Telephone Company was formed, Western Union created a new subsidiary called the American Speaking Telephone Company. It would operate under the auspices of yet another subsidiary, the Gold and Stock Company. Its agent, Peter A. Dowd, was in charge of telephone distribution and apparently was quite good at his job. By the time the case that bears his name was settled in 1879, he had overseen the installation of more than 30,000 telephones,[14] a figure that ultimately climbed to over 50,000.

To understand better the nature of the Dowd case, the Bell company's first significant patent infringement case, we must first examine the two combatants. The Bell Telephone Company began commercial life on July 9, 1877, with Gardiner Hubbard as president and Thomas Sanders as treasurer. Sanders was not only the treasurer but the whole treasury as well. Despite Hubbard's high social and political position and his wife's wealthy family, he did not seem to have a lot of ready cash, although he was considered quite well-to-do.

The entire burden of financing the newly created Bell Telephone Company fell to Sanders: he personally supplied funds and also finagled cash out of his friends and relatives. Sanders eventually invested some $110,000 of his personal wealth, essentially all he could scrape together, before the company started to make money.[15] This was a substantial sum of money in those days, considering that even high-level corporate executives made less than $5,000 a year. A few years later, Sanders, along with the other Patent Association members (Bell, Hubbard, and Watson), would retire from the telephone business, once more a wealthy man. Unfortunately, he suffered reverses in his later business ventures and lost most of his fortune.

Despite Hubbard's skill as an organizer and promoter, the Bell Telephone Company would have failed almost as soon as it began had it not been for Sanders. Even though he was a successful executive, he extended himself far beyond what a prudent businessman should have done. It could only have been because of the personal bond he had with Bell. Hubbard, always the visionary, perceived only the "big picture." He did not concern himself with such petty, day-to-day details as where the money was coming from to pay the vendors. That was Sanders's worry; and this conflict of perspective was a constant source of irritation for the pragmatic Sanders.

Unfortunately, popular history has shown little inclination to credit either of these men—Gardiner Greene Hubbard or Thomas Sanders—as the ones most responsible for the early success of what would eventually become the Bell System. Had it not been for both of them, operating in concert if not always in harmony, each with his own unique contribution, Alexander Graham Bell would be remembered, if at all, only as the son of the famous speech therapist, Alexander Melville Bell. It is doubtful whether either Sanders or Hubbard alone could have succeeded without the other. Although it was Sanders who supplied the capital, it was Hubbard who supplied the vision and, most important, the plan. It was Hubbard's marketing plan, the one that initially kept the lilliputian Bell Telephone Company on the brink of financial disaster, that in the end made it one of America's most profitable corporations. All the people involved in the birth of the company, including Hubbard's wife, wanted simply to get an immediate return on their investment by manufacturing and selling telephones—everyone, that is, except Hubbard. He had a better plan.

At one time Hubbard either had been, or was associated with, the counsel for the Gordon McKay Shoe Machinery Company, a manufacturer of shoemaking equipment. Unlike most manufacturers, this company did not sell its patented equipment. Instead, the company leased it.[16] It proved to be a most effective marketing device. The company's customers could have the use of an expensive piece of equipment without incurring a large initial capital investment. This was a good marketing strategy. In return, the McKay company had a steady income from each product throughout its productive life. And when it wore out, the company replaced it and, of course, issued a new lease. This was the marketing plan Hubbard insisted upon for the fledgling Bell Telephone Company, and it was to be the best business decision the company ever made. In the beginning, residential users could lease a pair of telephones for $20 a year; commercial users paid $40 a year. And the telephone company took care of everything else. The annual charge would later be reduced.

On July 11, 1877, two days after the official beginning of the Bell Telephone Company, Alexander Bell married Mabel Hubbard and left on a year-and-a-half honeymoon. On August 4, after a short visit to his parents in Canada, he and Mabel sailed for England, where they remained until the end of October 1878. During his extended stay, he put on several telephone demonstrations, similar to those he had done previously, including a personal demonstration for the Queen of England. By all reports, the queen was quite impressed with the telephone. When Bell, Mabel, and their six-month-old daughter, Elsie, returned to America, the company that now bore his name was embroiled in its first major patent infringement case—the now-famous Dowd case, then in its third month.

Notes

1. *Electrical World*, December 3, 1887, p. 296.
2. AMB to AGB, May 3, 1876, Bell Collection, Library of Congress.
3. John Brooks, *Telephone: The First Hundred Years*, Harper & Row, New York, 1975, p. 51.
4. *Petition of Elisha Gray to Re-open Interference Hearings*, 1888, p. 121.
5. Alvin F. Harlow, *Old Wires and New Waves*, D. Appleton-Century, New York, 1936, p. 369.
6. Herbert N. Casson, *The History of the Telephone*, A.C. McClurg, Chicago, 1910, p. 58.
7. Francis Jehl, *Menlo Park Reminiscences*, Edison Institute, Dearborn, Mich., 1938, vol. 1, p. 101.
8. Ibid., pp. 102–104.
9. David A. Hounshell, "Elisha Gray and the Telephone," *Technology and Culture*, April 16, 1975.
10. Gray to Alex Hayes, November 1, 1876, National Museum of American History, Washington, D.C.
11. "Recollections of Mrs. W. J. Cole of Long Island," *New York Times*, August 6, 1922.
12. "Professor Bell's Talking Telephone," *Scientific American*, June 9, 1877, reprinted from the *Operator*.
13. Count Du Moncel, *The Telephone the Microphone and the Phonograph*, Harper & Brothers, New York, 1879, p. 226.
14. George D. Smith, *The Anatomy of a Business Strategy*, Johns Hopkins University Press, Baltimore, 1985, p. 161.
15. Robert V. Bruce, *Alexander Graham Bell and the Conquest of Solitude*, Cornell University Press, Ithaca and London, 1990, p. 259.
16. Ibid., p. 227.

Chapter 11

THE FIRST CHALLENGE

The Dowd Case

From the time Hubbard formally launched the Bell Telephone Company on July 9, 1877, until the end of that year, the little startup company had the telephone market to itself. Bell's earlier public relations efforts (demonstrations followed by press notices), although popular and well attended, had been less than spectacular in promoting telephone usage among the general population. However, the business community was beginning to take notice. A businessman could use a telephone to advantage and afford the tariff, a message not lost on that sleeping giant, the Western Union Telegraph Company.

On December 1, 1877, the American Speaking Telephone Company, a newly created subsidiary of the Gold and Stock Company (which itself was a subsidiary of Western Union), went into the telephone business.[1] Its agent in charge of telephone distribution was Peter A. Dowd, by all accounts a man well suited to the job. Hubbard realized the implications of this new situation, with its threat of formidable competition, and soon after the first of the year opened negotiations with Western Union. In a letter to his new son-in-law, honeymooning in England, Hubbard laid out the proposed plan:

> I had a conference with the officers of the West. Union Tel. Co. yesterday & I am satisfied from their conversation that they will make an offer, which

> I shall hardly have the strength of mind to resist. They will give us the equivalent of $500,000 in stock guaranteed by them at the rate of 7 per cent a year. This would give us an annual income of $35,000, one third of which, $12,000, a year, would belong to Mabel. Perhaps we may get better terms than those by taking the same rent in stock not guaranteed, and an annual rental of $1.00 a year on every phone rented by them. I do not like the arrangement, but on the one side is a long law suit of one or more years long, possibly three or four, tho not likely, and necessity of raising money to defray the expense of this litigation, and the care and management of the company and this litigation. Mr. Sanders is no help to me.[2]

Hubbard may have estimated a little high on the distribution of revenue, based on the terms specified in the Bell Patent Association agreement (the previous year, Thomas Watson had been made a 10 percent partner, creating a 30–30–30–10 split). Still Mabel would receive an annual income that would put her well into the nation's top 5 percent earnings bracket. Even high-ranking government officials, such as the commissioner of patents, made only $4,500 a year. Although it was usually the male spouse who handled the family's financial affairs, Bell earlier had agreed, apparently as a wedding gift, to sign over to Mabel the bulk of his share (30 percent) in the original Patent Association. It's quite possible that Mabel's father, putting her best interests first, may have been influential in this decision. Bell did, however, keep ten shares in his own name. If the Western Union deal fell through, Hubbard was prepared for the final, desperate strategy—an infringement law suit. The negotiations with Western Union would drag on for several months, with Hubbard keeping Bell, still in England, up to date on all the corporate conflicts, both internal and external (GGh to AGB, Bell collection):

> February 7, 1878: Mr. Chauncey Smith [Bell company lawyer] called last evening—He is indisposed to have us make any arrangement with the Western Union, except an outright sale to them. I do not agree with him as I think the proposed arrangement if carried would be greatly for our interest.

> February 22, 1878: Our negotiations with the West. Union Tel. Co. are at an end. They made a proposition, particulars of which I wrote, which we declined. We then made one which they declined, and Mr. Cheever [Bell official], by my request, then wrote declining to enter into further negotiations that we might be at liberty to negotiate with other parties.

> March 5, 1878: We have made no arrangement with the West. Union Tel. Co. as I was not satisfied with any of their propositions,—I did not fancy giving everything up to them.—Our agents are generally doing well, my

> great trouble is with Mr. Sanders, who has not carried on his end of the business. He has no pluck, is easily frightened, and wants to sell out at almost any price he can get.

By the time Western Union decided to go into the telephone business, it controlled all the telephone patents and pending patents, of such engineering notables as Elisha Gray, Amos Dolbear, and Thomas Edison. Edison had recently made a breakthrough in transmitter design—a carbon transmitter—that was a vast improvement over Bell's magnetoinductive instrument. A carbon transmitter, unlike Bell's voice-powered instruments, derived its power from batteries, which, in effect, amplified the voice. Edison's transmitter not only was louder but could transmit farther and, with further refinement, would eventually permit long-distance transmission. Back in 1878, long distance was anything over 30 or 40 miles, but, with voice-powered instruments, even those distances were unattainable for all practical purposes. To survive in what was becoming more and more a one-sided battle, the struggling Bell company urgently needed a better transmitter—or less competition. It would eventually get both. As Thomas Watson, recalling that shaky year of 1878, revealed later:

> Now we began to hear rumors of a powerful battery transmitter that Edison had invented and sold to the Western Union Company, with which, its agents boasted, they were going to drive the Bell people out of business. I soon had an opportunity to try one of the Edison Carbon Button transmitters. I found it startlingly loud and clear in its articulation. Then, my other troubles became trifles under the shadow of this new cloud on our horizon. We had no transmitter equal to the Edison, but that didn't worry me much for I felt sure I could devise one as good.[3]

The rumors that Watson and the Bell people had been hearing were more than just rumors. Their customers were complaining that the Bell instruments were not nearly as powerful as those of the American Speaking Telephone Company, the Western Union subsidiary. Theodore Vail, the new general manager of the Bell Telephone Company, in a letter to Watson, stated the problem quite bluntly:

> My Dear Mr. Watson:
>
> They are getting up considerable excitement over the [Western Union] Carbon Telephone; in fact, they say too much for their own good. People can be deceived but they will not stay in that happy condition a great period. Still we want a carbon microphone bad; it has now become a necessity.[4]

Ever since Western Union entered the telephone business, featuring from the start its superior transmitter, the tiny Bell company had been searching desperately for an equivalent transmitter. Thomas Watson devoted most of his time to this quest. Chauncey Smith, the Bell company's counsel, instructed Watson to find a transmitter that worked as well as Edison's but that did not use carbon. Smith believed that a transmitter employing carbon would infringe on Edison's pending patent. As it turned out, carbon proved to be the perfect material and would dominate transmitter design for the next hundred years. Other materials would work but not nearly as well as carbon. At the time, though, Watson didn't know this, and he experimented with a wide variety of noncarbon, metallic electrodes. In light of future court arguments, his comments on the results of his search for a noncarbon transmitter are most enlightening:

> During the rest of the summer of 1878 I devoted all the time I could spare from the routine work of the telephone business to experiment on battery transmitters, using contacts of polished steel, oxidized steel, platinum, brass, zinc, antimony, bismuth and many alloys, avoiding the use of carbon under advice of our counsel. I made transmitters in which I used all these materials, except carbon, with single contacts, with multiple contacts, with polished surfaces and with surfaces coated with various materials. Steel contacts were the best but the adjustment of them was all too delicate for practical use. I also experimented with Berliner's pivoted contact transmitter using metal contacts in it. *They all talked, some of them very well.* [emphasis added][5]

In other words, Watson was successfully experimenting with the Reis telephone, an instrument utilizing metallic contacts, which—supposedly—operated by making and breaking the circuit. This was the instrument that would play such a vital role in the early infringement trials and the instrument the Bell lawyers would later claim could not possibly work. (The Reis enigma is discussed more fully in chap. 13.) The remarkable contradiction here is that while Watson was verifying in the laboratory that a Reis-type transmitter truly did work and was capable of transmitting articulate speech, the Bell lawyers were preparing their case that a Reis transmitter could *not* work. It was based on a "false theory," they would claim. (The Reis telephone theory is much like the Bumble Bee Paradox: according to aerodynamic principles, the bumble bee can't fly. But knowing nothing of aerodynamics, it flies anyway.) Establishing that the Reis transmitter could not and did not work was vital to the Bell company's case, because if it were ever established that it did indeed work, Bell could not claim to have discovered *the art* of electrical voice transmission. It was that broad claim, later endorsed by the courts, that Bell was the original discoverer of the art, or method, of voice transmission, not just the inventor of a particular apparatus, that allowed such an all-encompassing interpretation of his patent. Without that wide-ranging claim, his patent would have been seriously crippled, and no Bell Telephone monopoly could have existed.

After Hubbard's initial negotiations with Western Union came to naught, and after he saw the inroads it was making, particularly in New York, the company's headquarters, and in Chicago, he launched his final strategy. On September 12, 1878, he and Sanders filed suit for patent infringement, ostensibly against Peter A. Dowd, but in reality against the Western Union Telegraph Company, which would pay all of Dowd's legal expenses. From the Bell company's perspective, it had been backed into a corner—it was now all or nothing. In reality, the company had nothing to lose and everything to gain—if it were successful. At the time, it was a desperate act of survival, and the Bell faction doubtlessly felt that they had only a slight chance of winning. Although some may dispute this, a sad fact about patent infringement litigation is that too often the probability of success is directly proportional to the net worth of the litigants: it's usually Goliath who slays David. In the case of the cash-poor, debt-ridden, near-bankrupt Bell Telephone Company against the $40 million Western Union Telegraph Company, the outcome should have been obvious. But as the case progressed, as the testimony and depositions accumulated, the case took on a new perspective. It became not a question of winning or losing but of negotiation.

Dowd Case

Although Hubbard (for the Bell Telephone Company) and Sanders (for the New England Telephone Company, a licensee of the Bell company) filed suit against Western Union (actually, against Peter Dowd) on September 12, 1878, depositions did not begin until the following January. Bell, who had just returned with his family from England two months earlier, traveled from his new home in Washington, D.C., to Boston for the taking of depositions. When he arrived, he found the company that bore his name in a sad state:

> Tremont House, Boston
> January 21st, 1879
> My darling little wife:
>
> The change from Washington to Boston is in every sense a violent one—and I wish I was back again with you. It is too wintery here! Ice and snow everywhere, even in the Telephone office! Indeed telephonically a storm is

brewing! Thermometer ever so far below zero—and Bradley, Sanders, Vail and etc., shivering over the ashes of the Bell Telephone Company.

I must say I do not understand the stormy look of things. One man speaks of "bankruptcy" and another of "selling Chicago." Bradley has one plan—Sanders another—Vail a third—and I—well I'm sure I don't know anything about the matter—but I suspect that the real core of the trouble is—*the number of managers!* "Too many cooks" you know "spoil the broth." I fancy that any one of their plans consistently carried out would bring us out of our difficulties. Our great enemy I think is actual suspicion and distrust. We have far more to fear from internal dissensions than from the opposition of Western Union. I must say I don't like Mr. Sanders' proposition. He bribes the Bell Telephone Company with the offer of thirty thousand dollars—the conditions appearing to be that the Company is to be bound hand and foot and delivered over to him—to be disposed of as he thinks fit. I am very much afraid that his solution of the difficulty would be—to roll the Company right into the rapacious jaws of the Western Union Telegraph Company.

I have spent the greater portion of the afternoon at Mr. Williams' workshop—and with Mr. Chauncey Smith. Mr. Renwick "the expert" (whatever that means) is to be here tomorrow, and I wanted to help him try certain experiments to see whether the form of telephone shown in my first patent will work—and to be present at the opening scene of the contest with Western Union Telegraph Company. I hope I may return on Thursday. And now darling goodnight.

Your loving husband,
Alec.[6]

Bell's suspicions concerning Sanders could well have been true. After all, Sanders had been carrying, essentially alone, the financial ball for the Bell Telephone Company since its beginning. He had invested a large portion of his personal fortune in the company and obviously wanted to protect it, but selling out to Western Union would have been an option of last resort. The last paragraph in the above letter is particularly revealing. When Bell's application was filed that Valentine's Day in 1876, because of its unusual and unique claim of transmitting vocal sounds, he should have been required to furnish a working model to show that the invention had been reduced to practice; in other words, to prove that it truly did work. But this never happened. Examiner Wilber, no doubt at Pollok or Bailey's request, waived the requirement. So far, based on his gallows telephone of June 1875, Bell had been unsuccessful. Now, three years later, a model was finally built, based on the accumulated knowledge those three years had brought, and the Bell lawyers waited hopefully to see if it really did work. It did. Ironically, this was the issue Gray raised in his fatal letter to Bell on March 5, 1877—an invention is not an invention until it has been *reduced to practice*.

The early months of 1879 were dark times for the Bell Telephone Company, and drastic changes in management were shaping up. As the company's electrician, Bell was still, technically at least, an employee, although his current role was more like that of spectator. Bell minced no words as he laid out the company's dire situation, as well as offering his character analysis of some of those involved:

> Milton Hill
> Friday, January 24, 1879.
> My darling May:
>
> Here I am still and I don't know when I am to get away. Our case has not been opened yet and I am sick of the telephone and of everything else.
>
> The Bell Telephone Company seems on the verge of bankruptcy and the gentlemen who have put in money into the Company believe that everything has been mismanaged and are now taking the control into their own hands to save their own credit and the credit of the company. I cannot explain everything to you by letter and shall therefore have to wait till I see you. The condition of affairs has reached a crisis and the company finds itself without any money in its Treasury and about $42,000 in debt. The gentlemen who have recently taken stock in the company are raising heaven and earth to avoid a calamity.... The Executive Committee has been abolished and other radical changes have been made....
>
> A meeting of the Stockholders is to be held to consider the advisability of dissolving the present Company and of forming a new Company with enlarged capital. I will explain everything to you when I return—for you—as the largest stockholder—must make up your mind upon the subject—and vote one way or the other. I wish your father could be here to consult with these gentlemen—for evidently a crisis has arrived....
>
> I wish we had some other man to testify for us than this "expert." I don't like the look [*sic*] of him. He seems to be a *professional witness* who will swear for any person who will pay him.
>
> He does not impress one as a gentleman—and I find that his brother is the "expert" who is engaged *on the other side*! This looks bad—and I don't want to see any such men as this appearing as a witness on our behalf.[7]

The two "experts" to whom Bell refers were Henry B. Renwick, a 61-year-old civil and mechanical engineer and former patent examiner from New York, and his brother Edward S. Renwick, a 56-year-old civil and mechanical engineer from New Jersey.[8] Henry Renwick testified for the Bell company and Edward for Western Union. Despite his characterization of Henry Renwick, Bell was pleased with his performance: "I admire exceedingly the way Mr. Renwick gave his testimony.... All the same it is my private opinion that the man is no gentleman and I would not trust him further than a hundred dollar bill could reach him."[9] In the

January 24, 1879, letter to Mabel, Bell extolled the virtues of William Forbes, a well-to-do Bostonian, who would replace Hubbard as the head of the reorganized Bell Telephone Company, soon (March 1879) to be merged with the New England Telephone Company and rechristened the National Bell Telephone Company:

> He seemed to have stamped on his features the words "Integrity—Fairness—Good Sense and Experience"—well I have never met a man who reminded me so strongly of Mr. Morgan's [a Hubbard family friend] cast of head and inspired in me so much confidence as this Mr. Forbes.... To be true I know absolutely nothing of him—but I judge a great deal from appearances. I like and dislike—trust and distrust people—without the remotest reason very often....
>
> I wish I could get over instinctive feelings. Now there is Mr. Pollok who has been as good and kind to me as any man could possibly be—and who has done all he could to show his interest in my work—well—I like him—and like him very much—and yet there is an instinctive something in my heart—a sort of guilty feeling of distrust without cause.[10]

This is as close as Bell ever came to questioning the activities of his patent attorney, Anthony Pollok. Had Bell finally come to accept that all those Patent Office miracles were not of divine origin? And how much did he really know, or how much did he really want to know? After all, Hubbard, Mabel's father, had been closely associated with Pollok. Bell could not help but have suspicions but most likely chose not to ask and then dismissed it from his mind.

Businesses make the best decisions they can based on what they see at the time and what they perceive to see for the future. This was certainly true of the legal sparring that took place between the Western Union Telegraph Company and the Bell Telephone Company between September 1878 and November 1879. This year-long event became famous as the Dowd case, the first significant patent infringement action brought by the Bell interests. It would set the pattern for all of their future infringement cases. There had been a few minor infringements prior to this case, but these had been quickly and easily settled. In one sense, this case was a dress rehearsal for the real contests that were to follow.

The Dowd case was never adjudicated. The parties reached an amicable—and mutually profitable—out-of-court agreement after a year of testimony and negotiation. Aside from the pecuniary advantages that accrued to both parties, in the long run the agreement was to prove most valuable to the Bell Telephone interests. In addition, the testimony it engendered, a two-volume report known as the *Dowd Case Record*, would be introduced by stipulation into the infringement cases that followed.

In the settlement, both companies gained something and conceded something. As for Western Union, it agreed that Alexander Bell, as he demanded, was the inventor of the telephone and that his patents were valid. This cost Western Union nothing but helped assuage the ego of Alexander Bell. The most important concession was that Western Union agreed to get out of the telephone business. Reciprocating, the Bell Telephone Company agreed not to go into the telegraph business (interestingly, Hubbard had earlier proposed, when technology allowed, to go into the long-distance "telephonic telegraph" business).[11] Western Union also agreed to assign all of its 84 telephone patents to the Bell Telephone Company. There was no reason not to, since it had decided to quit the telephone business. Again, this cost the company nothing.

As for the Bell Telephone Company, it agreed to buy Western Union's existing telephone system, initially some 30,000 telephones, using the stock of the newly created National Bell Telephone for payment. The Bell company also agreed to pay Western Union a 20 percent commission on the annual rental charge on every telephone the Bell company installed over the next 17 years from the date of the agreement, November 1879. Western Union had originally sought a much higher commission, but it was negotiated down to a more realistic and workable 20 percent.[12]

There was another stipulation in the Dowd agreement that was especially advantageous to Western Union. Article 15 of the agreement directed all Bell licensees to route all telegram requests to Western Union offices:

> The second party [Bell Telephone] will turn over and deliver to the Western Union Telegraph Company of the first part, or its agents, exclusively, all messages for transmission to other points by telegraph.[13]

One of the benefits of having a telephone was the ease with which you could send a telegram. Instead of having to go personally to a telegraph office, or signal for a messenger, telephone customers could simply call the central exchange, which would then connect them to a telegraph office—in this case, a Western Union office.

With this stipulation, Western Union acquired a lucrative and captive audience for its telegraph business. It exemplified the dovetailing of the Bell Telephone Company and the Western Union Telegraph Company, which was the essence of the Dowd agreement. The Bell Telephone Company would manage all local communications, which, for the most part, the telegraph couldn't effectively handle, and the Western Union Telegraph Company would take care of all long-distance communications, which at the time the telephone couldn't handle. For businesspeople, this was the ideal arrangement, a perfect blending of the local telephone network with the long-distance telegraph network. A New York businessman, for example, could pick up his telephone, send a telegram to a San Francisco associate, and receive a reply within an hour or less. Compared to the ten-day delivery of the short-lived Pony Express less than 20 years earlier, this was little short of a miracle.

The agreement also stipulated that the Bell telephone was not to be used for transmitting stock quotes nor for transmitting news dispatches, such as those handled by the Associated Press. The AP and Western Union had had a long and profitable relationship, and the telegraph company didn't want to give it up. Nor did the Gold and Stock Company want to give up the business of stock quotes. Just how this restriction was to be enforced is unclear, since it would be essentially impossible to monitor phone calls. However, most of the AP dispatches were of a long-distance nature, which at first could be sent only by telegraph. Actually, telegraphic news dispatches would be around for many years, long after long-distance telephoning was established.

As we know now, from today's vantage point, Western Union got the short end of the deal, and the Bell company, in the end, was clearly the victor. Many historians attribute this ultimate victory to the invincible position of the Bell patents. According to popular legend, George Gifford, the chief counsel for Western Union, became convinced that Bell's patents could not be overturned and, therefore, recommended that Western Union settle for the best terms it could get, lest it get trounced by a mighty midget. While this certainly seems like a plausible explanation, suggesting that David did indeed slay Goliath, it may not be completely accurate.

In George David Smith's *The Anatomy of a Business Strategy*, an alternative explanation is offered, one that probably comes closer to the truth. Although we know now that the Dowd settlement was not in the best long-term interest of Western Union, at the time it seemed to the company like an ideal situation. Consider the situation as it existed: Western Union, then a leader in the telegraph industry, had a sound, stable business. It was a mature, profitable industry with few, if any, surprises in the foreseeable future. The telephone business, on the other hand, was an enigma, a question mark, so to speak. It was a pioneering industry, following an uncharted course, with a lot of potential pitfalls. Was this a gamble Western Union really wanted to take, or should it stick to what it knew best?

As Western Union saw it, the Bell Telephone Company was taking all the risks. Technology was changing almost daily, and the Bell equipment, based on Bell's two patents, was not the best. The magnetoinduction phones the Bell company were using during the 1877–1878 period were limited to relatively short distances. Long distance, as we know it today, was out of the question. Being batteryless and voice-powered, Bell's early telephones simply didn't have the power for distant calling. In fact, they had barely enough power for local calling. However, by 1879, after the company filed suit, it did adopt a carbon transmitter, designed by Francis Blake, which was similar to Edison's transmitter.

As depicted in figure 10-1, it was essential that the listener hold a telephone receiver to each ear in order to make out what the caller was saying (remember, these "receivers" functioned as both receiver and transmitter). It took a robust voice to speak over these phones; soft-spoken callers had difficulty conversing. Thomas Watson, who certainly knew the facts, commented wryly on those early Bell instruments: "It was simple and reliable, but it required loud talking on the part of the user ... they used to say that all the farmers waiting at a country store would rush out and hold their horses' heads when they saw anyone preparing to use our telephones."[14] After the initial miracle of voice transmission became more accepted, customers also became more critical of telephone performance. Telephone users now had a way to compare performance.

So here was the Western Union Telegraph Company, with a sizable block of Bell company stock (payment for Western Union's installed telephones), profiting to the tune of 20 percent of Bell's business and getting all of Bell's telegram request business—all that, and with none of the headaches. Now, the recently restructured American Bell Telephone Company had to string the lines, install the phones, service the customer, and attend to all the other problems that plague any new venture. As Western Union regarded the Dowd settlement, it was a pretty good deal and one it wanted to preserve.

And to preserve it, Western Union had to help the Bell company fend off any and all challengers. If the Bell company had competition, Western Union, in effect, had competition; it would lose revenue from the Bell company's loss of new customers. By the terms of the Dowd agreement, Western Union would pay 20 percent of the legal costs for infringement cases. It was a curious reversal of roles; the former antagonists were now allies. In retrospect, some commentators have speculated on just how "antagonistic" the two parties really were.

The next real challenge after the Dowd settlement was the one now known as *Spencer v. American Bell Telephone Company* June 1881. When this case came to trial under Judge Lowell, the same judge who signed the Dowd decree, Western Union's chief counsel, George Gifford, was only too happy to testify on the Bell company's behalf as to the "invincible strength" of the Bell patent. He now testified that during the Dowd case he had become

> convinced that Bell was the first inventor of the telephone and that defendant [Western Union] had infringed said Bell's patent by the use of telephones in which carbon transmitters and microphones were elements, and that none of the defenses which had been set up could prevail against him; and I advised the Western Union Company to that effect, and that the best policy for them was to make some settlement with the complainants.[15]

At best, that testimony would have to be considered as self-serving. At this time, a year after the Dowd settlement, Western Union had nothing to lose and everything to gain by helping defend the Bell patents. In fact, such help was required by the terms of the Dowd agreement. But aside from that, it was simply good business for Western Union to assist the Bell interests. As pointed out earlier, if Bell had competition, Western Union would lose money. Such testimony coming from a former adversary and from someone with the stature of Gifford carried considerable weight. As one of the judges in this case said, "I would attach almost the same weight to an opinion by him, against his own clients, that I would attach to the judgment of a court."[16]

What is especially interesting in Gifford's testimony is his statement that Western Union's carbon transmitters, invented by Edison, had infringed on Bell's patent, which was for a magnetoinduction instrument. Gifford was basing his conclusion on a dubious interpretation of Bell's fourth claim, a claim which was later charged to have been purloined from Gray's caveat and fraudulently inserted into Bell's patent application. The groundwork for this charge actually originated with evidence gathered during the Dowd case, which was never used at that time. This is discussed more fully in chapter 15.

There are those who maintain that the Dowd case was never a true contest in the sense that it was a bitterly fought legal battle. It is argued that, almost from the beginning, there was never any serious thought of going to trial, that it was mainly an exercise to test the relative strengths and weaknesses of the participants and to jockey for position. Based on the mutually agreeable settlement, there is certainly a lot of credibility to the charge, although there is little hard evidence to support it. In filing the suit, the Bell interests may have perceived it initially as their best course of action. But with Orton's death in April 1878, Western Union's attitude toward Hubbard and the Bell Telephone Company became less personal and more pragmatic. It is interesting to speculate what the Dowd outcome might have been if Orton had lived, and what effect it would have had on the nascent telephone industry.

Decree

On April 4, 1881, in U.S. Circuit Court for the District of Massachusetts, the final decree in the Dowd case, approved by Judge Lowell, was handed down. In essence, it states that Alexander Graham Bell is the original and first inventor of the device specified in the fifth claim of Patent No. 174,465 and that the patent is valid. This is the incredibly broad claim that supposedly covered every conceivable form of electrically operated telephone. Although Bell's other patent, No. 186,787, is mentioned, it is the March 7, 1876, patent that would claim the whole art for Bell. That consent decree, although it was binding only on the parties involved, formed the cornerstone for all of the patent infringement litigation that would follow. The courts would interpret Bell's patent to mean that anyone could produce telephones as long as they didn't work by electricity.

The Dowd case record would become part of all future infringement trials. Although at the time the Western Union Telegraph Company believed that it had scored a commercial victory, and for a long time that was certainly the case, the victory ultimately went to the Bell interests. For Alexander Bell it was a victory of vindication: A court of law had decreed that he was the original inventor of the telephone. But the court of public opinion had yet to hand down its decision.

Dowd Case: Final Decree

In this cause, upon the bill, answer and replication, and the proofs taken and filed, and settlement having thereupon been made between the parties upon considerations accepted by the plaintiffs, it is now, to wit, April 4, 1881, with the consent of the counsel of the parties respectively, order, adjudged and decreed that Alexander Graham Bell is the original and first inventor of the inventions specified in the fifth claim of the patent numbered 174,465, granted to said Bell March 7, 1876, and the third, sixth, seventh and eighth claims of the patent number 186,787, granted to said Bell January 30, 1877, being the claims in respect of which the proofs were taken; that the said patents are good and valid patents therefor; that the defendant has infringed the same; that he pay to the plaintiffs the sum of one dollar in full satisfaction of profits, damages and costs, and that he be enjoined from further infringing the said patents.[17]

Notes

1. Robert Conot, *Thomas A. Edison: A Streak of Luck*, Da Capo, New York, 1979, p. 105.
2. G. Hubbard to AGB, February 1, 1878.
3. Thomas A. Watson, *Exploring Life*, D. Appleton, New York, 1926, p. 139.
4. Ibid., p. 146.
5. Ibid.
6. AGB to Mabel Bell, January 21, 1879.
7. AGB to Mabel Bell, January 24, 1879.
8. Dowd case, pp. 18–48, pp. 190–269.
9. AGB to Mabel Bell, January 26, 1879.
10. AGB to Mabel Bell, January 24, 1879.
11. Hubbard's report to the Board of Directors, 1879, Bell Collection, Library of Congress.
12. "The American Bell and Western Union Agreement of 1879," *Electrical Engineer*, August 28, 1895, pp. 208–214.
13. Ibid., p. 212.
14. Watson, p. 140.
15. George D. Smith, *The Anatomy of a Business Strategy*, Johns Hopkins University Press, Baltimore, 1985, p. 76.
16. Robert V. Bruce, *Alexander Graham Bell and the Conquest of Solitude*, Cornell University Press, Ithaca and London, 1990, p. 271.
17. *Bell Telephone Co., et al. v. Peter A. Dowd*, Circuit Court of the United States, Dist. of Mass., April 4, 1881, Final Decree. Gray Collection, Archive Center, National Museum of American History.

Chapter 12

Other Challengers

Two Notable Cases and Their Decisions

Of all the challenges to the Bell patent, two stand out above all others. The first case didn't take place in a courtroom but instead played out in the U.S. Patent Office. It involved a patent application for a telephone filed by an inventor named James McDonough, and it was ruled by the Patent Office to have anticipated the Bell patent, a devastating blow to the Bell Telephone Company.

James W. McDonough of Chicago, Illinois, a wealthy furniture manufacturer with an inventive streak, held several business-related patents. But his creativity wasn't limited to furniture; he was also intrigued with the idea of creating and transmitting sounds by electricity. As early as 1867, he claimed, he had been experimenting with an electromagnetic device for the reproduction of sounds.[1] Like most of the devices we now call "receivers," it consisted of an electromagnet closely positioned to a small piece of iron, which was attached to a flexible membrane. When a pulse of electricity passed through the electromagnet, the armature was attracted, the membrane momentarily flexed, and a noise was heard. By rapidly making and breaking the electrical connection, McDonough demonstrated that he could create various sounds.

McDonough's receiver design was, theoretically at least, the same as the electromagnetic receivers devised by Bell, Gray, Pickering, and others.

Edward Pickering's receiver had been published as early as 1870.[2] Yet, the receiver portion of McDonough's application, not the transmitter design, sank Bell's patent. But just as Acting Commissioner Ellis Spear had come to Bell's rescue earlier, another commissioner, Benjamin Butterworth, again salvaged Bell's patent.

After satisfying himself that he could generate sounds electrically, starting in 1871, McDonough began conceiving of a device that might transmit the human voice. By late 1875, after a number of attempts and design modifications, he had finally devised an instrument that he claimed would transmit speech. On April 10, 1876, he filed his patent application, just one month after Bell made his now-famous, but then-secret, telephone call. But unlike the model waiver that Patent Examiner Wilber gave to Bell, McDonough was required to submit a working instrument.[3] As he said in his patent application; "The object of my invention is to provide a means for transmitting articulate sounds from one place to another through the medium of electricity."

He named his invention the *teleloge*. It is interesting to note that he, like Gray, was quite specific in claiming the transmission of speech (articulate sounds), a claim that was strangely missing from Bell's patent of March 7, 1876. However, it was what he subsequently said in his application, concerning the manner in which his instrument worked, which would ultimately prove fatal to his claims: "My invention also consists in the novel construction of the *circuit breaker*, as hereinafter more fully described." It was the phrase *circuit breaker* that killed his chance for a patent.

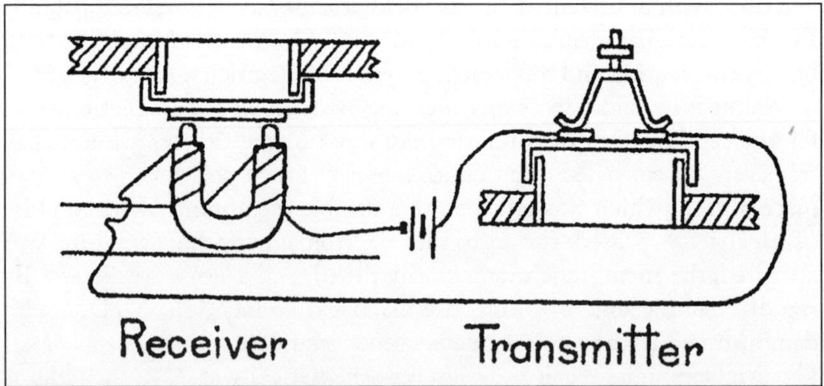

Figure 12–1. Schematic view of the McDonough receiver and transmitter. Note the adjusting nut on top of the Reis-type transmitter.

McDonough's transmitter was essentially a Reis telephone. In other words, it was what we now call, variously, a loose contact transmitter, a variable pressure contact transmitter, or simply a variable resistance transmitter. Regardless of what label we apply, they all belong to that class of telephone transmitters known collectively as *microphones*. McDonough referred to it, as Reis had done many years before, as a make-and-break contact system (i.e., a circuit breaker). We know now that this was an erroneous description. And because it was an erroneous description, it proved just as lethal to McDonough's claims as it had to those of Reis.

McDonough had his witnesses, too, who attested to the fact that his teleloge could, indeed, transmit the human voice. McDonough's brother, J. E. McDonough, testified:

> It was at 72 Warren Avenue, in the later part of June or near the first of July, 1875. I was called in to listen to my brother one evening while my mother was singing in the parlor of the house, and I heard the singing; and slapping my brother on the back and saying "By George, Jimmie, you've got it after all!" I heard "Down come uncle and aunt, down come sister Caturah."[4]

Unfortunately, the examiner of interferences and, later, the commissioner of patents did not put much credence in McDonough's witnesses. They were, as the commissioner later explained, "all his relatives and near friends."[5] This was an unusual objection, and rather unfair at that, since inventors will tell you that they almost never demonstrate their unpatented inventions to strangers.

In attempting to dismiss the witnesses' testimony that they had actually heard speech transmitted, the commissioner also pointed out, "The only inference that can be drawn from the record is that the witnesses are either mistaken or he [McDonough] operated the device in a manner different from that set forth in his application, and unknown to him."[6] The commissioner was merely reiterating what the examiner of interferences had said earlier. It is interesting to note, however, that the examiner concluded that, if the witnesses were not mistaken and had truly heard speech, it was because McDonough's device operated in a manner "different from that set forth." And that is exactly what had happened.

True to the prejudice that had followed the Reis telephone throughout all the court trials, judicial intolerance doomed McDonough's teleloge as it foundered in the Patent Office. The commissioner rejected the witnesses' testimony solely on the grounds that they must have been mistaken. They really hadn't heard speech transmitted, they merely thought they had. The opinion of the Patent Office was that the teleloge couldn't have transmitted speech because it operated on a false theory or in contradiction to "known" scientific principles.

How much did McDonough know of Bell's invention? Since McDonough filed his application a month after Bell's patent was issued and published, he could have had full knowledge of its contents. But this is rather doubtful. The only way he would have known about Bell's patent would have been from the Patent Office's weekly publication, the *Official Gazette*, where it was listed as "Improvements in Telegraphy." It was not a title that would have piqued his interest. There was little if anything in Bell's patent that would have influenced McDonough.

McDonough never did receive a patent for his application of April 10, 1876. Shortly after it was filed, it was denied because the transmitter was based on a "false theory." McDonough later, on March 4, 1878, filed an amendment, and his application was then judged by the patent examiner, based only on the receiver portion, to be in interference with Bell's patent of March 7, 1876. Following standard practice, it was turned over to the examiner of interferences. Even though a patent has already been issued, as was Bell's, it can still be involved in an interference action with an application filed later.

As it turned out, a number of applications from various telephone inventors would all be embroiled in interference actions among themselves and with Bell. This legal tangle would later become known as the Telephone Patent Interferences. There were so many inventors and patent applications involved that they had to be grouped into a number of different cases. Some, such as Edison, Bell, and Gray, were involved in multiple cases. McDonough was assigned to Case G: *Edison v. Gray v. McDonough v. Bell.*

As we have already established, an interference was something to be avoided if at all possible. We saw to what lengths Bell's attorneys went to avoid this situation when he was threatened back in February 1876. A patent interference could be a long, drawn-out affair. In McDonough's case, it would drag out for an incredible nine years before it was completely resolved.

The examiner of interferences did not hold hearings on the matter until late in 1882, almost four and a half years after McDonough filed his amendment. And after that, it took another year and a half before the examiner rendered decisions on all those involved in the Telephone Patent Interferences. But in the end, McDonough emerged victorious; the examiner of interferences found that his receiver had indeed anticipated Bell's receiver, the one depicted in figure 7 of his March 7, 1876, patent. This finding, in effect, gave the basic telephone invention to McDonough.[7]

One can only imagine the impact this devastating decision had on the American Bell Telephone Company—and on Alexander Bell himself.

Obviously, this was no quick, off-the-cuff decision. The examiner's printed decision formed a volume of over 300 pages. Every facet of every application involved was examined and testimony offered. In all decisions except three, Bell was the winner and was awarded priority. In two of those cases, priority was awarded to Edison. But since Edison's patents were assigned to the Bell company, they presented no problems.[8] However, it was the McDonough victory that created a dilemma for the Bell interests. Their patent monopoly was in grave danger.

The decision of the examiner of interferences was appealed by the Bell interests, as well as the other parties, to the examiners in chief, the next level of appeal. This board heard arguments and testimony again, and six months later it affirmed all the decisions of the examiner of interferences—all except the one pertaining to McDonough. McDonough's earlier victory was reversed, and priority was once again awarded to Bell. McDonough's attorneys immediately appealed to the commissioner of patents, Benjamin Butterworth. This was the court of final appeal.

Again testimony was offered, including the testimony of the expert witnesses who testified during the *Overland Telephone Company v. American Bell Telephone Company* case. Two professors of physics, Professor Young and Professor Brackett, testified to explain the concept of the variable pressure contact microphone, the one that formed the basis of McDonough's telephone. This concept was also the basis of all the telephone transmitters then in use. This was to be the crucial, and only, issue in McDonough's appeal. The strategy was to prove that McDonough had, in fact, achieved electrical transmission of speech prior to Bell.[9]

Commissioner Butterworth accepted the finding of the examiner of interferences that McDonough had demonstrated priority of conception over Bell's March 7 patent. As he said, Bell was "junior in date of conception." Nor did Butterworth claim that McDonough's telephone failed to work. As he grudgingly admitted, it "did occasionally talk, as asserted," which was more than Bell's patented figure 7 instrument had done. The big argument was centered on McDonough's explanation, or theory of operation, as expressed in his application. McDonough knew that he had achieved the electrical transmission of the human voice, and he had the witnesses to verify it, but he made the fatal mistake of attempting to explain it in the only terms that made sense to him—the making and breaking of an electrical circuit.

The expert witnesses, Young and Brackett, attempted to explain the true nature of McDonough's transmitter, that it was a make-and-break instrument only in the sense that the circuit was never fully "made" nor fully "broken." As they pointed out, it did not employ a "palpable or perceptible" make-and-break action. But Butterworth would have none of it. As far as he was concerned, McDonough had clearly written that his transmitter operated by a make-and-break set of contacts. And since it was generally held by the scientific community that articulate speech could not be transmitted by this method, it followed that McDonough's transmitter could not possibly transmit such speech *based on his description of the make-and-break mode*. In other words, even though his transmitter worked, as his witnesses testified, it couldn't have worked since it was based on a "false theory." So, with logic that would have appealed to the Mad Hatter, Butterworth had found a reason to sustain the findings of the examiners in chief.

The Patent Office interference actions had tied up McDonough's application for almost nine years. In that time, the Bell Telephone Company had grown from nonexistence to a major industrial monopoly, a monopoly guaranteed solely by a court-sanctioned patent. Bell telephone stock was widely held, and like all stock, its value rose and fell on good and bad news. As Commissioner Butterworth saw it, there was a much bigger issue than merely priority of conception. The Bell Telephone Company, with its multitude of investors, had become an important element of society, and the Bell patent was now extremely valuable. Factoring these concerns into his decision made it easier for him to reject McDonough's claims of priority and functionality. In his decision, Commissioner Benjamin Butterworth said:

> In reaching a right decision in a case like this, where the interests involved are great, as well as the honor of inventing an instrument so wonderful ... as the telephone, certain probabilities ... have great influence.
>
> When an applicant seeks to overthrow a patent granted to one who, though junior in date of conception, has yet shown diligence in filing his application and reducing his invention to practice, the former must, in view of the importance, not merely to the patentee but to the general public, show entire freedom from laches [in law; a delay in asserting a right]. Nothing could sooner bring the patent system into disfavor than to permit a patent granted for a valuable invention in which thousands have become interested to be overthrown by a competitor in the same field of invention on evidence which fails fully to establish the superior claims of the junior applicant to be adjudged the prior inventor. And it is in view of this fact that doubts are resolved in favor of the patentee [Bell].[10]

Once again, Bell was restored to the position of first inventor of the telephone. That decision, and the logic behind it, was as curious as that of former Acting Commissioner Ellis Spear in February 1876, and once again the Patent Office came through for Alexander Bell. Commissioner Butterworth filed his intriguing, but strangely biased, decision on March 3, 1885, the same day he resigned from the Patent Office.

Claims of Daniel Drawbaugh

Of all the stories related to the telephone challengers, that of Daniel F. Drawbaugh is perhaps the most provocative. It is also the most credible as well as the most questionable. This paradox will become more apparent as we review the events that led up to the second closest call the Bell Telephone Company ever had in court. The legal challenge began on November 22, 1880, when the American Bell Telephone Company got an injunction against the People's Telephone Company for patent infringement.

The People's Telephone Company responded to the charges by claiming that Bell's two telephone patents had been anticipated by inventions they presently controlled. One of their inventors was Daniel Drawbaugh of Eberly's Mills, Pennsylvania. This tiny hamlet was located at the confluence of Cedar Run and Yellow Britches Creek and boasted a gristmill, a sawmill, and various other small facilities. Daniel Drawbaugh operated a small machine shop and manufactory.

Drawbaugh was known throughout the area as a skilled machinist and a most clever inventor. Over his lifetime, he would receive a total of 70 patents and later the sobriquet the "Edison of the Cumberland Valley."[11] He died November 3, 1911, at the age of 84. In his obituary notices he was hailed as the "Wizard of Eberly's Mills." He seemed to live well but at the same time was constantly in debt and frequently pleaded poverty. His lifestyle and fortunes were as paradoxical as was his role in the People's Telephone Company's patent conflict.

Drawbaugh has been much maligned by popular history, first by George Prescott in his 1884 edition of *Bell's Electric Speaking Telephone* and then by just about every biographer and historian since. Prescott, it could be argued, had a valid reason to denigrate Drawbaugh, but those who echoed Prescott had none. Because of the Dowd agreement of 1879, Prescott had reversed his earlier position (essentially by court decree) and was now a staunch and ardent supporter of the Bell patent. This, of course, meant that he had to oppose the claims of Drawbaugh. Later historians simply reiterated Prescott's demeaning comments and accepted them as fact. The only biography to come to Drawbaugh's defense is Warren Harder's *Daniel Drawbaugh: The Edison of the Cumberland Valley* (1960).

Much of the biographical background for this section has been drawn from that source. As clever as Drawbaugh was with his hands and perceptive mind, verbally he came across as an inarticulate country bumpkin—a rustic, as his more kindly detractors called him. He was one of those self-taught engineer/inventors who could do but couldn't explain.

Drawbaugh became involved in the People's Telephone Company sometime late in 1879 when he showed the principals of that company the telephonic devices he had been working on since 1867. If what he showed them actually dated from that time—and if it could be proven—those devices could defang the invincible Bell patents. There would be no shortage of witnesses to testify that Drawbaugh's telephones did, indeed, work. Over 50 witnesses would testify that they heard, at various times between 1867 and 1876, these "talking machines" actually transmit the human voice. This was vitally important because it would demonstrate Drawbaugh's priority of conception and reduction to practice, two major points in patent litigation.

In all, some 500 witnesses, for both the plaintiff and the defendant, would eventually testify on various facets of the case, generating a printed record of over 6,000 pages. Many of the plaintiff's witnesses would refute the testimony of those claiming to have heard Drawbaugh's instruments at certain times. Considering that much of the testimony covered events that had taken place some 10 to 12 years earlier, it is easy to see that a witness might have been a little confused on matters of chronology. Some witnesses were much more credible than others and could establish the dates by associating them with easily verifiable events.

But despite the throng of eyewitnesses supporting Drawbaugh's claims of telephone priority, Judge Wallace was able to explain it all away and inject enough doubt on other issues to find in favor of Bell. For one thing, the judge questioned whether Drawbaugh had the academic background to enable him to develop a working telephone. As he explained:

> Drawbaugh, on the other hand, was not only untutored, but he was isolated by his associations and occupations from men of advanced science; he had narrow opportunities for instruction, and few incentives for profound research [22FR329].[12]

Judge Wallace was attempting to show that Drawbaugh didn't have the knowledge to develop a telephone through "scientific" methods, that if he achieved anything it was purely by accident. This elitist view belies the backgrounds of many other inventors. Edison's sketchy academic history was never a problem. Charles Goodyear, perhaps America's most untutored inventor, managed to discover the process for curing raw rubber.

Although he was fervently searching for it, he stumbled upon it purely by accident.[13] Bell himself, when he visited Joseph Henry at the Smithsonian Institution, admitted that he lacked the necessary electrical knowledge to perfect his telephone ideas. As history has so abundantly proven, there is no correlation between academic achievement and the inventive process. Unschooled tinkerers forge hopefully toward success, while academics theorize that it can't be done.

Apparently Judge Wallace believed that a true invention was one that had never existed before, one that had no precedent. Anything less than this, he held, was a mere improvement over an existing device and barely qualified as an invention. As he said in his decision:

> That he was a skillful and ingenious mechanic is undoubtedly true. Invention was his hobby and his vocation. But that he was an inventor in a large sense is disproved by the nature and results of his work. Every patent that he obtained was for some improvement on existing devices, which involve mechanical skill rather than any high degree of inventive faculty. This showed to some extent on the face of his patents, the list of which is as follows: ...*for improvement in stave jointing-machines* ... *for improvement in mill-stones* ... *for improvement in faucets* [22FR329].

But the simple fact is that virtually *all* inventions are considered *improvements* over the existing art. Even Bell's own patents attest to this: "Improvements in Telegraphy," issued March 7, 1876, and his subsequent "Improvements in Telephony." For a member of a court that was charged to adjudicate patent matters, Wallace was woefully ignorant as to the real nature of a patent. This mindset has too often been one of the major difficulties in patent litigation.

One of the issues advanced by Judge Wallace was that Drawbaugh did not apply for any telephone patents until 1880, and his first telephone patent wasn't issued until 1882. Drawbaugh pleaded poverty as his excuse for failing to apply for a patent or even a caveat. Judge Wallace refused to except this explanation, and concluded that Drawbaugh didn't apply for a telephone patent simply because he hadn't invented one. Wallace made the naive assumption, typical among those outside of the engineering society, that if an inventor conceives of an invention, he immediately applies for a patent. It's not always that simple. Nor is it unusual for inventors to spend years between conception and patent application, particularly if they feel that the invention is not sufficiently developed.

Admittedly, Drawbaugh's poverty excuse does not exactly have the ring of sincerity and ultimately proved to be his downfall. It was most likely an ill-conceived alibi concocted by his attorneys to explain his puzzling lack of telephone patents. There were times when he received large chunks of money, but there were also lean periods, not unusual for one who was primarily self-employed. Over the years, he did achieve a small measure of financial success. But he was frequently in debt, and there were long intervals of financial famine between his bountiful harvests. Judge Wallace enumerated some of Drawbaugh's harvests:

> But it is clear from a few plain facts that the theory of extreme poverty is unfounded, and that Drawbaugh is dishonest in putting it forward. In 1867 and 1869, besides what he received for his wages, he received $5,000 from the pump company for his faucet invention, besides $1,000 in the stock of the concern. On the first day of April, 1869, he received $1,000 from one Gardner for the sale of a half interest in a faucet invention.... The pretense that he could not raise the fees to caveat or patent his invention is transparently absurd [22FR321].

On average, after factoring in the proceeds from his inventions, he probably did a little better than the typical skilled machinist, who would earn perhaps $15–18 per week. When he did occasionally receive a large sum, for whatever reason, a major portion of it went to pay off debts incurred during the lean periods. This seemed to be a recurring cycle.

A patent at that time cost $35. With attorney's fees and models, the total cost could easily be triple that or more. The actual, out-of-pocket cost of a patent, in terms of Drawbaugh's labor, could represent over a month's earnings—not exactly a trivial investment. Interestingly, this cost comparison still holds today for the typical individual inventor. This is one reason why an inventor, even now, does not impetuously apply for a patent upon the first flash of inspiration.

Drawbaugh was forever looking for financial backers for his various inventions and schemes. Like most smart businesspeople, he avoided investing his own money if he could find an "angel." There was nothing unusual in this. This was the way both Bell and Gray operated—Bell with the backing of Hubbard and Sanders, and Gray with the assistance of White. Although Drawbaugh was frequently successful in obtaining backing for his other inventions, he was never able to induce investors to finance his telephone devices. The reasons were twofold.

First, his telephones, although functional enough to transmit some speech, were far from being practical or marketable devices. Most investors look for a quick return on their investment. They look for products that can be marketed within a relatively short period of time and are not generally interested in backing research projects. All those who heard speech over Drawbaugh's telephones, even if they were not technically inclined, knew that they were in need of considerable development work. And nobody was more aware of that than Drawbaugh himself.

Second, although the market potential for his other inventions was fairly obvious, no one had the faintest idea as to the commercial application of a "speaking telegraph." We have seen in previous chapters how the telegraph experts looked upon the telephone. The average citizen had even less imagination. Those who witnessed Drawbaugh's demonstrations looked upon them as little more than scientific diversions. They seemed more in the nature of a conjurer's trick, intriguing and mystifying, but for what real purpose? When Bell took his telephone show on the road in late 1876 and early 1877, after his lecture ended everyone politely applauded the entertainment—and then went home. They still had no idea as to the telephone's potential or practicality.

Judge Wallace, who at that time had witnessed eight years of spectacular telephone growth, assumed that Drawbaugh should have been immediately aware of the great value of his telephonic invention:

> Drawbaugh was well aware of the merit and of the great pecuniary value of his invention. He had obtained patents for several inventions of minor value; yet, from 1870 until July 1880, he did not apply for a patent for the telephone [22FR320].

Judge Wallace now had the penetrating vision of hindsight. He was looking back from December 1884, a time when the value of the telephone was firmly established. Prior to 1877, no one had the slightest hint of the telephone's true worth, least of all Daniel Drawbaugh. Judge Wallace was attempting to prove that anyone inventing a telephone would have realized immediately its great value and commercial potential. And once it was realized, he reasoned, the inventor would be a fool not to protect such a valuable invention with a patent. Although Judge Wallace believed Drawbaugh to be a charlatan, he did not consider him a fool. This would be one of the arguments upon which Judge Wallace would conclude that Drawbaugh was not the inventor of the telephone.

Judge Wallace made much of the fact that Drawbaugh had obtained nine patents prior to 1880. He used this as the basis for his argument that if Drawbaugh had really invented the telephone when he claimed he did, around 1870, he would have then filed for a patent. Drawbaugh, he claimed, did not hesitate to get patents on his other inventions and could obviously afford to get them. Judge Wallace therefore concluded that since Drawbaugh's first telephone patent was not issued until 1882, six years after Bell's patent, he didn't "invent" his device until after telephones were commercially and readily available.

That argument, one of several Judge Wallace used to reach his decision, sounds reasonable enough until we look more closely at Drawbaugh's inventing record. He received his first patent in 1851 for a stave-jointing machine and another one four years later for a stave machine. Then followed an eight year period with no inventions. But from 1863 to 1867, he had a burst of creative activity and patented six inventions. For the next 12 years, his inventive mind lay fallow. Unlike Edison, who maintained a more or less steady flow of inventions, Drawbaugh was a sporadic inventor with long periods of inactivity.

Then in 1879, his inventive spirit awakened, and he applied for a patent on an ingenious electric clock, one that got its motive power from an "earth battery." This was a device that, when buried in the ground, produces an electrical current by the chemical action of the soil. Some half dozen of these clocks were built and from all indications gave satisfactory results.

However, the overwhelming mass of evidence supporting Drawbaugh's priority claim came from approximately 60 witnesses. They all testified that they had heard speech transmitted over one or another of Drawbaugh's telephones. Like most witnesses in a court trial, some were more credible than others. It wasn't a question of whether or not they actually heard speech transmitted, but when they heard it. The defendant claimed that these witnesses had heard electrical speech transmitted as early as 1870 and before. Many claimed to have heard it between 1874 and 1876. Some later retracted their earlier testimony and then claimed a later time period.

The plaintiffs never denied that Drawbaugh had actually built telephones and that people had heard voice transmissions. They claimed, however, that this happened only after Bell received his March 7, 1876 patent. In attempting to prove this, the plaintiffs produced witnesses that disputed the times testified to by the defendant's witnesses. Many of the dates testified to were tied to a particular event that could be more or less documented.

Judge Wallace did not consider the defendant's "cloud of witnesses" all that creditable. As he pointed out:

> Without stopping at this point to consider the credibility and probative force of their testimony, it suffices to state that, although some of the witnesses seem to have been reckless and unscrupulous in their statements, the great body of them are undoubtedly honest witnesses.
>
> ...Of necessity, the testimony of most of the defendant's witnesses can only be attacked by showing that the witnesses are mistaken as to the time when they saw Drawbaugh's talking-machine, or as to what they really saw on the occasions they refer to [22FR320, 325].

Although he professed doubts concerning the veracity of the defendant's witnesses, Judge Wallace seemed to accept without question the complainant's witnesses, who refuted the defense's testimony. In short, he simply felt that the defendant's witnesses, although basically honest, were simply confused on the times or on what they heard. In the end, Judge Wallace decided the case in favor of the American Bell Telephone Company. His main argument supporting his decision was that Drawbaugh was not telling the truth when he claimed that poverty prevented him from applying for a telephone patent. Drawbaugh had stated in his testimony, "For more than ten years prior to 1880 he was miserably poor, and utterly unable to patent his invention or *caveat* it." In retrospect Drawbaugh should have simply admitted a reluctance to spend his own money on patents; pleading poverty was probably a rather poor legal strategy—a tactic that doomed his case. As Judge Wallace maintained: "Where a witness falsifies a fact in respect to which he cannot be presumed liable to mistake, courts are bound, upon principles of law, morality, and justice, to apply the maxim, *falsus in uno, falsus in omnibus*." [22FR324]

The Drawbaugh case, actually the *People's Telephone Company v. American Bell Telephone Company*, along with five other cases collectively known as the Telephone Cases, was appealed to the U.S. Supreme Court in 1887. When all of the arguments from the various cases were presented, it was the testimony from the Drawbaugh case that seemed to carry the most weight and that gave the American Bell Telephone Company their second closest call. By a one-vote margin, the court split 4–3 in favor of the Bell patent.

The three dissenting judges were Justices Joseph Bradley, Stephen Field, and John Harlan. Unlike the majority, they felt that the defendant's witnesses were fully credible. In their opinion as to Drawbaugh's priority over Bell, they said:

> We think that the evidence on this point is so overwhelming, with regard to both the number and the character of the witnesses, that it cannot be overcome.... We are satisfied from a very great preponderance of evidence, that Drawbaugh produced, and exhibited in his shop, as early as 1869, an electrical instrument by which he transmitted speech, so as to be distinctly heard and understood [8SCT802].[14]

The dissenting justices did not have a problem with the credibility of the witnesses. Nor did they have a problem understanding why Drawbaugh didn't immediately patent his invention. They observed:

> On the question of time and result, there is such a cloud of witnesses in both cases, that it seems almost impossible not to give credence to them.

> The evidence of some of them may have been shaken with regard to the time they had in mind; but that the great majority was not shaken at all, but corroborated by circumstances which render the proof irrefragable. Many of them, it is true, were plain country people; but they heard the words through the instrument; and that is a matter about which they could not be mistaken.... A number of them were people of position in society, official, professional, and literary—all, however, like the inventor, regarding the matter more as one of curiosity than of public importance.
>
> ...But he looked upon what he had made more as a curiosity than as a matter of financial, scientific, or public importance. This explains why he did not take more pains to bring it forward to public notice [8SCT803].

And so ended a decade of patent litigation. The defendants in the Telephone Cases requested a rehearing, which was denied. Although nine justices sat on the court, only seven participated in the decision. One justice, Lucius Quintus Cincinnatus Lamar, declined to participate because he had just recently joined the Supreme Court and was unfamiliar with the case. Another justice, Horace Gray, also declined to take part. Judge Gray is discussed further in chapter 16.

Notes

1. William Aitken, *Who Invented the Telephone?* Blackie and Son, London and Glasgow, 1939, p. 55.
2. "Professor Pickering's Telephone," *Popular Science Monthly*, May–October 1886, p. 281.
3. Aitken, pp. 55–56.
4. "A Review of Certain Claims to the Art of Telephony," *Electrical World*, December 3, 1887, p. 297.
5. Ibid., p. 296.
6. "Decisions of the Commissioner of Patents," *Official Gazette*, March 17, 1885.
7. *Electrical World*, p. 297.
8. Ibid., p. 297.
9. "Decisions of the Commissioner of Patents," *Official Gazette*, March 17, 1885, p. 1091.
10. Ibid.
11. Warren J. Harder, *Daniel Drawbaugh: The Edison of the Cumberland Valley*, University of Pennsylvania Press, 1960.
12. *American Bell Telephone Co. v. People's Telephone Co.*, 22FR309 (Vol. 22, Federal Reporter), December 1884.
13. Mitchell Wilson, *American Science and Invention*, Bonanza, New York, 1960, pp. 124–125.
14. *People's Telephone Co. et al. v. American Bell Telephone Co.*, 8SCT778 (Vol. 8, Supreme Court Reporter), October 1887.

Chapter 13

THE REIS QUESTION

Reis Telephone in the Courtroom—
It Could Sing, but Could It Talk?

During one of the early infringement trials (*American Bell Telephone Co. v. Spencer et al.*) the defense attempted to show the court that Philipp Reis of Germany had designed a speaking telephone as far back as 1862. Clearly, Reis had antedated Bell, the attorneys claimed, and to prove it they set up a courtroom demonstration of the Reis telephone. This was vital to the defense's contention that Bell had merely invented a particular type of telephone and had not discovered *the art* of telephonic communication, which if true would give Bell the whole field of telephony.

Everyone—except the defense team—was quite amused by the demonstration. Try as they might, neither the defense lawyers nor their experts could coax a word out of the recalcitrant instrument. As later reported, "It would squeak, but not speak." The embarrassed lawyers tried to explain, "It can speak, but it won't."[1] But it was to no avail, and in handing down his decision in favor of the Bell company, Judge John Lowell made his oft-quoted statement: "A century of Reis would never have produced a speaking telephone by mere improvement in construction."[2]

From that moment on, the Reis telephone was a much-maligned device, and even though highly respected scientists rallied to its defense, the courts consistently held that it was not a speaking telephone because it was based on a "false theory."[3] So what was the story behind the Reis telephone? Was it a nontelephone as the courts proclaimed, or was it just a telephone with a bad reputation?

Philipp Reis, an instructor in natural philosophy in Friedrichsdorf, Germany, in about 1860, began experimenting with a device for transmitting speech over a wire. He may have been inspired in this matter by an article written in 1854 by Charles Bourseul of France, who suggested how this might be accomplished (see app. F). So successful was Reis in this pursuit that Germany erected a monument to him in his home town and proclaimed him the Inventor of the Telephone (Germany celebrated the 100th anniversary of the telephone in 1962).[4] However, those telephonic honors went no further than the German border.

The Reis experience in America was another matter. To see why, we need to look briefly at how the Reis instruments were made. His telephone consisted of two devices: a transmitter and a receiver (see fig. 13-1). The main elements of the transmitter were the parchment membrane, or diaphragm, in the center of which was a platinum contact, and, resting by gravity directly above that contact was another platinum contact. Sounds impinging on the membrane would cause it to flex in step with the sound, which would then vary the pressure on the contacts and thus their resistance.

Now this is where the deadly false theory comes in. The Reis transmitter was actually a microphone, no different in principle from all the other telephone transmitters that were built over the next 100 years—but nobody knew it because the microphone principle had not yet been discovered. That wouldn't be announced until after Bell received his famous

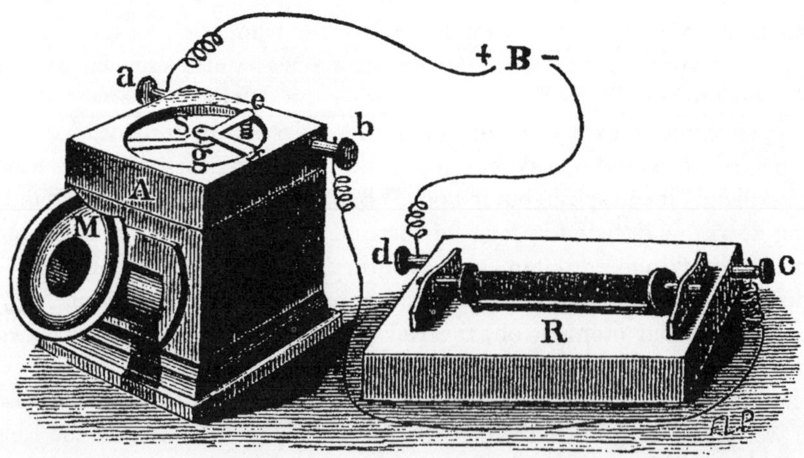

Figure 13-1. A later model Reis transmitter (note contacts above the membrane) and the magnetostriction receiver.

patent. Reis attempted to explain his telephone in the only way that made sense to him, based on the electrical knowledge of his day. Unfortunately, that knowledge said that electrical contacts are either open or closed with nothing in between (which, in reality, was the microphone mode). Reis, therefore, said his transmitter worked in the make-and-break mode, which was not the way a microphone actually works. As a result, Reis's explanation was labeled a false theory. And although his telephone was capable of working, in the logic of the courts it couldn't work because it was based on a false theory.

Reis's receiver was a resonant box on which an iron rod (originally a knitting needle) rested, its ends clamped firmly to the box. Around the iron rod was a coil of wire (or helix, as it was called). The transmitter contacts were connected to the helix and a battery, forming a simple series circuit. The receiver was unique in telephone history; Reis was the only one known to have used it. Based on its appearance, one might assume that it was nothing more than a form of electromagnetic receiver similar to those used by all the other telephone inventors. But it didn't work by magnetism or magnetic attraction. It worked by magnetostriction, a phenomenon that would cause the iron rod to physically change its length in proportion to the current through the helix. These minute changes in length would cause a sound to issue from the box, faithfully mimicking the current fluctuations in the helix. It was probably the first loud speaker. (An original Reis receiver connected to a modern sound system can be heard throughout an average-sized living room.)

A Reis telephone system, properly set up and used, was perfectly capable of transmitting articulate speech. But all Reis transmitters were not created equal. Some were much better than others and could truly transmit speech. Others, though, performed badly. The problem was that nobody, not even Reis himself, really understood the mechanics and dynamics of transmitter or microphone design. We know Reis had no conception of the loose contact operating mode, which defined the microphone. If he had, he would never have used his make-and-break explanation. He merely said that (as McDonough did later) because it was the only explanation he knew of that made sense. Unfortunately for Reis (and all those inventors who repeated Reis's theory), his explanation proved fatal to his claim that he had produced a "speaking" telephone, as contrasted to a telephone that merely transmitted musical tones.

The main problem with the Reis telephone was that it could operate in either of two modes: (1) as a make-and-break transmitter, or (2) as a true microphone, or non–make-and-break instrument. Whereas the former mode could transmit sounds, such as musical notes, its speech-transmitting ability was quite limited because the opening and closing of the contacts would distort or remove the voice's vocal inflections. It gave a monotone quality to the reproduced sound. However, the microphonic mode, which soon became the only telephone transmitter mode, could transmit the voice in all its tones and inflections. In microphone mode, the contacts are neither fully closed nor fully open.

Although the microphone mode, or loose contact mode, had been around since Bourseul first proposed a speaking telephone, no one had identified it as such. The microphone mode was discovered (or identified) by various experimenters (i.e., David Hughes and Thomas Edison) just about the same time that Bell received his second patent. But unfortunately, Reis, who died in 1874, never learned of this. If he had, it's possible that history might have followed a somewhat different path.

There is no question that a Reis transmitter, even a good one, was a delicate instrument and had to be used rather carefully. The major problem was with the parchment membrane; it had to be quite stiff to give microphonic performance. Therefore, a tightly stretched one, like a drumhead, would tend to give the best results. However, this condition was not always appreciated, nor was the fact that loud shouting would force the contacts into make-and-break mode. Oddly enough, that mode seemed to work for singing or when playing a coronet or similar instrument. Although the intensity of the sound would tend to remain the same, the melody usually came through, enough so that tunes could be recognized. But the longer you sang or shouted into a Reis transmitter, the worse it got; the moisture in the breath would soon soften the parchment membrane until it became too soggy to work.

It's easy to belittle Reis's telephonic endeavors in light of later developments. But we must remember that back in 1860 he had no model to follow; he was starting from square one. He was attempting to do what the experts said was impossible. We know now, for instance, that his original receiver was acoustically unsuited for telephonic work and quite insensitive to the subtle current variations needed. Because it operated on the magnetostriction principle, it required a high level of operating current, which a make-and-break operating mode could easily supply. But even in this mode it could often transmit understandable voice messages. When the transmitter was connected to the more sensitive electromagnetic receivers and operated in the microphone mode, the articulation was much improved. And when a carbon electrode was substituted for one of the platinum contacts, the results were spectacular. Had Reis not died so early, he might even have tried it himself. (The fact that a Reis transmitter using carbon electrodes works like any other carbon transmitter tends to refute the notion that it always operates as a make-and-break instrument.)

One of the more ardent supporters of Reis was the English scientist and writer Silvanus Phillip Thompson. He made an extensive analysis of the Reis telephone and published his findings in the book *Philipp Reis: Inventor of the Telephone* (1883). The written testimony collected by Thompson some 20 years after Reis's work, from persons who actually witnessed Reis's early demonstrations, tends to confirm that possibly a combination of microphonic and make-and-break mode was used. The following are excerpts from letters received by Thompson (pp. 112–125):

> Dear Sir,
>
> I was present at the Assembly of the German Naturalists' Association held in the year 1864 in Gieseen, when Mr. Philipp Reis ... showed and explained to the assembly the Telephone which he had invented.
>
> ...I listened at the latter part of the apparatus, and heard distinctly both singing and talking. I distinctly remember having heard the words of the German poem "Ach! du lieber Augustin, Alles ist hin!/ &c.
>
> The members of the Association were astonished and delighted, and heartily congratulated Mr. Reis upon the success of his researches in Telephony.
>
> Dr. G. Quincke, Professor
> Heidelberg, 10th March 1883

> Most Esteemed Sir,
>
> I willingly answer, as well as I am able to do so, the questions put by you.
>
> ...It was known to me (in 1863–64) that Reis intended to transmit words, and certainly spoken words as well as those sung. My interest in the matter was, however, a purely scientific one, not directed to the application as a means of profit.
>
> With great attention the sense of the words was understood. I have understood such myself, without knowing previously what would be the nature of the communication through the telephone. Words sung, especially well accentuated and peculiarly intoned, were somewhat better (or rather less incompletely) understood than those spoken in the ordinary manner.
>
> ...The ear was sometimes laid upon the box of the apparatus, also upon the table which supported the telephone. Then it was attempted to hear at a distance, with the ear in the air; in this respect, when singing, with good result....
>
> Hochachtungsvoll ergebenster,
> Dr. C. Bohn
> Aschaffenburg,
> 10th September, 1882

I knew Philipp Reis, now deceased, during his lifetime.... About the year 1859, he was employed by my father, then proprietor and director of the Friedrichsdorf Garnier Institute, as a teacher of mathematics and natural sciences. He employed his hours of leisure in experimenting for himself in a house occupied by himself, and in which he had established a physical laboratory with a view mainly of realizing an idea which he had conceived sometime before of transmitting the human voice over divers metallic conductors by means of a galvanic current.... I remember especially, that, standing at the end of the wire or conductor, Mr. Reis speaking through his instrument, I distinctly heard the words: "Guten Morgen, Herr Fisher/ (Good morning, Mr. Fisher); /Ich komme gleich/ (I am coming directly); /Passe auf!" (Pay attention!); "Wie viel Uhr ist es?" (what o'clock is it?); "Wie heisst du?" (What's your name?). We often spoke for an hour at a time. The distance was about 150 feet.

Leon Garnier
36, Mark Lane, London, 30th April, 1883

Dear Professor Thompson,

...My knowledge of Philipp Reis dates from 1860, when I was a pupil at Professor Garnier's School at Friedrichsdorf, of which school Reis was one of the undermasters.... Reis insisted that his transmitter (which he called the "ear") should be capable of performing the functions of that organ, and he never tired of drawing diagrams of the numerous curves of sounds to explain how necessary it was that the transmitter should follow these curves before perfect speaking could be attained, and which kind of curves the instrument so far could reproduce.

...One form of transmitter was at that time constructed which I miss amongst the various woodcuts you were good enough to send me, and one which Reis based great hopes upon.... The favorite "Hammerchen" was replaced by a straight wire, fixed in the usual way with sealing wax, and the apparatus stood within a sort of tripod, membrane downwards, the pin just touching the surface of a drop of mercury contained in a small cup forming one of the terminals of the circuit. The apparatus started off with splendid results, but may probably have been abandoned on account of its great uncertainty, thus sharing the fate of other of his earlier instruments.

...[On using the standard Reis transmitter] The wire was stretched from Reis's house, in the main road, through the yard to a hayloft, near the garden or field. We transmitted musical sounds (organs, &c.), singing popular songs ("Wer will unter die Soldaten," "Ich hatt' einen Kameraden," &c.) and speaking, or more correctly, reading. We had a book, and were to find out what part of the page the reader was just transmitting.... I have a distinct recollection of electromagnetic receivers being used, but not of their construction, except that one of them was accompanied by a rattling and disturbing noise. The knitting needle put in the *f* hole of a violin was, however, the more favored receiver, but at this time, in Reis's mind, all seemed to hinge on the electromagnet, as it had before, and, I dare say, did again

> afterwards on the transmitter. I left Friedrichsdorf in '62, and rarely saw Reis after that.
>
> ...Reis's views of the telephone may, of course, have changed after I knew him, and looking at his later instruments, one of which I possess, I cannot help thinking they did; at any rate, I do not see how, in these instruments, the current got interrupted at all, and the instruments must have acted like microphones, whether known or unknown to him....
>
> Yours truly
> Rudolph Messel

The last writer's recollections are particularly revealing. The fact that he recalls the knitting needle receiver being used with a violin for a sound box shows that the experiments took place at a very early date. It wasn't until later versions that this receiver was built using a cigar box–type of sound enhancer. Although Reis experimented with a kind of electromagnetic receiver, for some unexplained reason he seemed to prefer the magnetostriction-based knitting needle receiver. Perhaps, like Bell's first attempt, he just didn't have much luck making an effective electromagnetic receiver.

In evaluating the opinions of those who actually heard voice transmission over a Reis transmitter in the early 1860s and the court officials who heard it during the Bell patent trials in the 1880s, we must consider the 20-year time interval. In the 1860s, no one had ever heard the human voice reproduced in any form whatsoever. There were no standards or benchmarks by which to compare. We can tell by the testimony of those who witnessed Reis's early experiments that the articulation was not the greatest; in fact, it was sometimes quite poor. However, Reis did succeed in transmitting speech that was largely understandable, albeit with some repetitions and with careful enunciations. But we must remember, this was also about the same quality that Bell achieved with his early instruments (see chap. 10).

We know now, based on the work of Thompson, Houston, and others, that Reis actually did anticipate Bell, Gray, and many of the others who also claimed the telephone as their own. Reis, however, never applied for a patent. And Gray was the first to file for a variable resistance transmitter that claimed to reproduce articulate speech. Reis's main contribution was the demonstration that understandable speech could be transmitted by electrical current modulation. What makes the court's rejection of Reis doubly ironic in Bell's case is that it appears that Bell relied on some of Reis's work. Whether this reliance was intentional or subconscious is unimportant, although Bell did claim only scant knowledge of Reis's work. The striking parallels between Reis's explanation of acoustical theory and that found in Bell's patent (No. 174,465) was illustrated by Thompson.[5] These parallels are to be found in Reis's memoir, "On Telephony," as well as in V. Legat's report on the Reis telephone. It has been argued that Bell had only an imperfect knowledge of German and, therefore, could not have fully understood Reis's or Legat's writings. However, there were also some 50 articles, in various languages, including English, that discussed the Reis instrument. In addition, his instrument was described in various physics textbooks, such as Ferguson's, during that era. Reis's work was well known in the scientific community, and Bell was in contact with various members of this group [Thompson, p. 171–2].

Thompson's Reis-Bell Comparison

Reis	*Bell*
That which is perceived by the auditory nerve ... may be **represented graphically**, according to its duration and magnitude by a **curve**.	Electrical undulations, induced by a body capable of inductive action, can be **represented graphically**, without error by the same sinusoidal **curve** which expresses the vibration of the inducing body itself.
The greater the condensation of the sound-conducting medium at any given moment, the greater will be the **amplitude** of the vibration of the membrane.	The intensity of the current varies with the **amplitude** of the vibration—that is, with the loudness of the sound.
Each tone is dependent not only on the number of vibrations of the medium, but also on the **condensation or rarefaction** of the same.	The polarity of the current corresponds to the direction of the vibrating body—that is, to the **condensations and rarefactions** of air produced by the vibration.
Let us exhibit the condensation curves for three tones—each singly: then by adding together the ordinates corresponding to the equal abscissas, we can determine new ordinates and develop a new curve which we may call the **combination curve**. Now this gives us just exactly what our ears perceive from the **three simultaneous tones**.	The combined effect of A and B, when induced simultaneously on the same circuit, is expressed by the curve A + B, Fig. 4, which is the algebraical sum of the sinusoidal curves A and B. This curve A + B also indicates the actual motion of the air when **two musical notes** considered are sounded **simultaneously**.

These are a few of the similarities between the writings of Reis and the descriptions in Bell's patent application. It should not be inferred that Bell purposely copied from Reis's, or Legat's, writings. However, the fact that Reis, in some manner, influenced Bell cannot be denied. The most significant point to be drawn from this is that Bell, in specifying the requirements for articulate speech, described exactly the same type of undulating sound signal as did Reis. Reis knew precisely the nature of the current needed to transmit so-called articulate speech. His big mistake was in saying that his telephone worked by a make-and-break action. True, it could easily be forced to operate in this mode, usually by playing a coronet or shouting into the mouthpiece, and Reis no doubt did operate it this way at times. But it would also operate in the loose contact, or microphone, mode and transmit true articulate speech.

Chief Justice Waite of the Supreme Court, during the appeals of a number of telephone infringement cases, in a decision handed down in the October term of 1887, said, "To follow Reis is to fail, but to follow Bell is to succeed."[6] While that pronouncement simply reflected the court's long-standing and baseless prejudice against Reis's work, it was ironically reversed. In reality, it was Bell's electromagnetic transmitter (Patent Nos. 174,465 and 186,787) that failed in the marketplace, and it was the variable resistance, or microphonic, transmitters devised by Gray, Francis Blake, McDonough, Emile Berliner, and Edison—and originally by Reis and Bourseul—that ultimately succeeded. The variable resistance, or microphonic, transmitter prevailed for the next 100 years.

Once the speaking telephone became a commercial reality, hardly a week would go by without an announcement of some new telephonic invention. Many of these were quite ingenious, although for one reason or another, they never achieved commercial success. As designers know, mere novelty and ingenuity alone do not guarantee success. Just to list and describe all of these devices would take a volume in itself. The novel telephone invented by Theodore F. Taylor in 1885 is typical of these instruments. It is included here because of the inventor's comments on the Reis telephone.

On April 22, 1885, Taylor gave a lecture on his new telephone before the New York Electrical Society. In his opening remarks, he jokingly commented on the horde of people claiming to be the real inventor of the telephone:

> Before going any further, however, I wish to make an announcement which may startle you all and relieve the minds of some. *I do not claim to be the original inventor of the telephone.*

> While half of the States of the Union claim that honor for one of their sons, my native State of Delaware makes no such claim. I am only a gleaner in a field already harvested.

Inasmuch as he was addressing an audience of electrical engineers, his facetious comments were well understood. After describing some of his early experiments in the field of telephony, Taylor went on to explain how he got involved in the present device:

> I will remark that at the time I began this investigation I was but slightly acquainted with the history of the telephone and the claims of rival inventors. But such knowledge as I had led me to suppose that the inventions and publications of Reis had but little relation to the invention of the modern telephone.
>
> I constructed all the forms of transmitters and receivers described by Reis and succeeded in making them all transmit and receive articulate speech. The lectures and papers of Reis prove him to be the original inventor of the telephone.... My feelings are strong on this subject, because I am not only indebted to Reis for instruction in the art, but it was one of his transmitters that first made my receiver talk. It has been the fashion to belittle the inventions of Reis.... I never heard the great discoveries of Newton belittled.[7]

We saw previously that Bell's assistant, Thomas Watson, successfully experimented with Reis-type transmitters when he was searching for an answer to the Edison carbon transmitter. James McDonough's teleloge, essentially a Reis-type transmitter, was able to transmit speech. Why the courts persistently and consistently rejected the works of Reis is still a mystery. No doubt, the prejudice was inspired by the use of the term *make-and-break* to describe one of its operating modes. It was an unfortunate description, but once applied, a bad label is hard to remove.

Notes

1. John Brooks, *Telephone: The First Hundred Years*, Harper & Row, New York, 1975, p. 76.
2. 8FR512. *Spencer et al. v. American Bell Telephone Co.,* June 1881.
3. Ibid.
4. *Encyclopædia Britannica*, 11th ed., vol. 11, p. 217.
5. Silvanus P. Thompson, *Phillip Reis: Inventor of the Telephone*, E. & F. N. Spon, London, 1883, p. 70.
6. 8 S.Ct.787. *People's Telephone Co. et al. v. American Bell Telephone Co.*
7. "Taylor's Electric Telephone," *Electrical World*, April 25, 1885, p. 164.

Chapter 14

The Affidavit

Confessions of Former Patent Examiner Wilber

During the congressional investigation of the Pan-Electric affair, 1886, Colonel Casey Young, a director of that company, offered into evidence the sworn affidavit of Zenas F. Wilber. Wilber, of course, was the patent examiner who handled all of Bell's patents issued between 1875 and 1877. This was not the first affidavit Wilber had made, but it was the one most damning to Bell and the Bell Telephone Company. He had made a brief affidavit earlier, on October 21, 1885, at the request of the Bell Telephone Company, which contradicted this last one. However, as he explained, that affidavit, which sounds as if it were written by a lawyer, was made when his alcoholism had reduced him to desperate measures. He had readily accepted the Bell company's offer of $100 for his statement that he had not shown Gray's caveat to Bell.

Although the chair of the investigating committee, Charles Boyle, agreed to accept the affidavit, he was overruled by a majority of the nine-man committee. This was a rather odd rejection considering that they had previously accepted an affidavit that attested to Wilber's lack of sobriety (see the end of this chapter). They also declined to call any of the witnesses mentioned in Wilber's affidavit, claiming that they had previously agreed not to bring in any more witnesses. The fact that Wilber specifically listed witnesses who could corroborate his affidavit lends further credence to its truthfulness. It is doubtful that he would specify those who would not support his allegations.

As a result of the committee's rejection, the affidavit was withdrawn.

At this point, Young made the decision that if he couldn't get the investigators to accept the affidavit as evidence, he would at least make them aware of its contents. He promptly sent copies to the major Washington newspapers, in particular the *Washington Post*, where it was printed on May 22, 1886.

Needless to say, this was not well received by the Bell faction. We have seen from his 1877 telegram to Elisha Gray just how upset Alexander Graham Bell could get with so-called libels against him. Ignoring the advice of his lawyers, who pleaded to let them handle the matter, he immediately fired off a letter to the chair of the investigating committee protesting and denying Wilber's affidavit, and he then sent his own sworn affidavit to the *Washington Post*. Both the letter and the affidavit are reproduced after Wilber's affidavit later in this chapter.

Wilber's history does not confer a high degree of credibility on him. He was a known alcoholic, a bribe taker, a petty embezzler, and a man of many faults. In short, he was a rather disreputable character. However, in fairness to Wilber, we must state that these were not separate faults; most of them were the direct result of his alcoholism, now generally considered a form of illness. But illness or not, the question is: can Wilber be believed?

Wilber maintained throughout the rest of his life (he died in August 1889) that this affidavit, his last one, was completely true. The document, and its associated map, does have the ring of truth to it, and many of the events he mentions, as we have seen, agree with known facts in the case. Aside from the objections and denials of Bell and the Bell interests, nothing has ever surfaced to disprove what is claimed in Wilber's last affidavit.

The major fact supporting Wilber's affidavit is this: three days after receiving his famous patent, Bell built a working model of a liquid variable resistance transmitter, using water, essentially the same as the one depicted in Gray's caveat. There was nothing in Bell's patent, except the disputed variable resistance clause and claim, that would have inspired such a device. Furthermore, the membrane telephones that Bell built for the Centennial Exposition in June and July 1876 were essentially copies of the receiver shown in Gray's caveat. In Gray's receiver, the armature was glued directly to the membrane and was not hinged. In figure 7 of Bell's patent, the armature was connected by a hinge pin to the frame of the electromagnet. It was, to a certain degree, the inefficiency of that construction that contributed to the failure of Bell's 1875 instruments to transmit articulate speech. Gray's caveat had given Bell the one design clue that enabled him to achieve the success that had so far eluded him.

A secondary fact is this: in a March 2, 1877, letter to Gray, Bell professed ignorance of Gray's caveat but yet wrote (not too prudently) that all he knew was that the caveat involved a "wire vibrating in water." The only way Bell could have known about a wire in *water* was to have read Gray's caveat. In Bell's own patent, there was no mention of water, only mercury. In later testimony, Bell would claim that he couldn't remember what made him think that it was water.

Perhaps the one item that is *not* in Wilber's affidavit does the most to establish its credibility. Nowhere does Wilber state that Bell's application, after it was received on February 14, was ever removed from the Patent Office. This point is more fully explored in the following chapter, which discusses the charges of patent fraud brought to the Supreme Court.

Wilber's Affidavit

Zenas Fisk Wilber, being duly sworn, deposes and says: I am the same Zenas Fisk Wilber who was the principal examiner in the United States Patent Office in charge of a division embracing all applications for patents relating to electrical inventions during the years 1875, 1876 and till May 1, 1877, about which latter date I was promoted to be examiner of interferences; that as such examiner the application of Alexander Graham Bell—upon which was granted to him letters of patent of the United States, No. 174,465, dated March 7, 1876, for multiple telegraphy—was referred to me and was by me personally examined and passed to issue.

And I am the same Zenas Fisk Wilber who has given affidavits in the telephone controversy commonly called the "Bell controversy" in which a bill has been filed and suit brought in the Southern District of Ohio, by the United States, for the voidance of letters patent No. 174,465, issued March 7, 1876, and No. 186,787, issued January 30, 1877, both to Alexander Graham Bell, which affidavits so given by me were used at the hearing before the Commissioner in the Interior Department, consisting of Secretary Lamar, Assistant Secretaries Muldrow and Jenks, and Commissioner of Patents Montgomery; which commission sent for the purpose of advising the Department of Justice as to the advisability and propriety of the general government to bring the suit supra. In none of such affidavits heretofore made by me and referred to in this affidavit have the exact facts and the entire truth been told by me in relation to the circumstances connected with the issuance of the said patent No. 174,465. These affidavits were made by me under circumstances which I propose to relate herein and obtained from me to serve the ends and purposes of the parties who influenced me.

In order that parties may be vindicated and injustice rectified, I have concluded to tell the whole truth, and nothing but the truth. It will be impossible for the courts of the country to mete out exact justice without a knowledge of the influence brought to bear upon me while examiner in the Patent Office in 1875, 1876 and 1877, which caused me to show Professor Bell Elisha Gray's caveat then under my charge and control, as by law provided, and which caused me to favor Bell in various ways in acting on several applications for patents by him made.

This conclusion has not come upon me suddenly, but after due and delicate consideration, and after having carefully weighed the consequences which must result from this disclosure. I am fully aware that it may place me in an awkward position with some of my friends and, possibly, before the public; that it may even alienate some of my friends from me; nevertheless, I have concluded to do as above stated, regardless of consequences, without the hope or promise of reward or favor on the one hand, and without fear of results on the other hand.

The affidavits hereinbefore referred to were executed July 30 and August 3, 1885 (these being duplicated); October 10, 1885; November 7, 1885; and October 21, 1885—given at the request of the Bell Company by Mr. Swan, of its counsel, was given when I was afflicted with and suffering from alcoholism, and was obtained from me when I was so suffering; and after it had been obtained from me, I was vilified and attacked before the commission referred to.

Under such conditions my faculties were not in their normal condition, and I was, in effect, duped to sign it, not fully realizing then, as I do now, the statements therein contained. I had been drinking, and was mentally depressed, nervous and not in a fit condition for so important a matter. As stated, I did not realize (I could not in my then condition) the effect or scope of the affidavit, the data for which were supplied by Mr. Swan, who paid me $100 therefor, for the Bell Company. In this instance, and at this time, I am entirely and absolutely free from any alcoholic taint whatever; I am perfectly sober and a conscious master of myself mentally and physically. This affidavit is, consequently, the outcome of a changed mode of life and a desire on my part to aid in righting a great wrong done to an innocent man. I am convinced by my action while Examiner of Patents that Elisha Gray was deprived of proper opportunity to establish his right to the invention of the telephone, and I now propose to tell how it was done.

The attorneys for Professor Bell in the matter of the application, which became patent No. 174,465, were Messrs. Pollok & Bailey, then a leading firm of patent practitioners in Washington City (since dissolved and each in business for himself). Major Bailey, of that firm, had the active management of the case, and several times appeared before me during the pendency in relation thereto. Major Bailey and I had been acquainted for almost thirteen years. We had for a time been officers in the same regiment, and staff officers upon the staff of the same brigade commander. Upon my appointment to the Patent Office in 1870 our old acquaintance was renewed, and for years we were exceedingly friendly, and still are so to this day. I was poor when I became examiner, and consequently was in constant and great straits for the lack of ready money. In such straits I had several times borrowed money from Major Bailey, not withstanding the fact that Commissioner Legget had in 1871 or 1872 issued an order prohibiting employees of the Patent Office from borrowing, in any way or under any subterfuge, from attorneys practicing before the office or from inventors, which order was then and is still in force.

I was, consequently, in debt to Major Bailey at the time the application of Bell was filed in the office; in addition, I was under obligations to him for a present to my wife—a very handsome and expensive gold hunting-case lady's watch, which, I understood, he procured from George P. Reed & Co., of Boston, Mass. I, consequently, felt under many and lasting obligations to him, and, necessarily, felt like requiting him, in some degree at least, by favoring him in his practice whenever and however I could.

As I recollect, I borrowed $100 from him about the time the Bell application was filed. He was known as a liberal man, and gave expensive presents and loaned money to others in the office. Feeling thus in his power from the obligations noted, surrounded by such environments, I was called upon to act officially upon the applications of Alexander Graham Bell.

When I suspended Bell's application because of Gray's caveat I did not, in the official letter to Bell, give the name of the inventor nor his date of filing. Major Bailey appearing before me in regard to such suspension, I allowed him to become acquainted with both facts, telling him personally the same, so that he immediately knew the exact facts upon which to base the protest he subsequently filed against such suspension, and which was referred by me to the Commissioner, in person, for instructions.

The Commissioner directed me to investigate and determine, if possible, which (the application of Bell or the caveat of Gray) was filed the earlier on Feb. 14, 1876, and be governed by such finding of fact as to the maintenance or dissolution of such suspension.

From the circumstances hereinbefore detailed, I was anxious to please Major Bailey, keep on the best and most friendly terms with him, and, hence, was desirous of finding that the Bell application was the earlier filed, and I did not make as thorough an examination as I have done in justice to all concerned. So, when I found in the cash blotter the entry of the receipt of Bell's ahead of the entry of the receipt of Gray's fee, I closed the examination and determined that Bell was the earlier, whereas I should have called for proofs from both Bell and Gray, and have investigated in other directions, instead of being controlled by the entries alluded to and the statement of Major Bailey to me. The effect of this was to throw Gray out of court, without his having an opportunity to be heard or of having his rights protected, and the issuance of the patent hurriedly, and in advance of its turn, to Bell. Immediately thereafter I again borrowed some money from Major Bailey, which has never been repaid. We have never had a settlement, and for years I was constantly in debt to him, and still am. He has yet demanded no settlement or repayment from me.

After the suspension of Bell's application had been revoked, Professor Bell called upon me in person at the office, and I showed him the original drawing of Gray's caveat, and I fully explained Gray's method of transmitting and receiving. Professor Bell was with me quite a time on this occasion, probably upwards of an hour, when I showed him the drawing and explained Gray's method to him. This visit was either the next day or the second day after the revocation of the suspension.

There were several clerks and assistants in the room at the time who might have heard the conversation when I showed Professor Bell the drawing and verbally explained to him the methods of Professor Gray. Bell had been in the office before this and on several occasions in relation to other cases, so we were then acquainted. On this visit he was alone, and the visit occurred in the forenoon. About 2 P.M. of the same day he [Bell] returned to the office for a short time. On his leaving I accompanied him into the hall and around the corner into a cross-hall leading into the court-yard, where Professor Bell presented me with a hundred dollar bill. I am fully aware that this statement will be denied by Professor Bell, and that probably the statements I have made as to my relations with Major Bailey and his influence will be denied, but nevertheless they are true, and they are stated, subscribed and sworn to by me while my mind is clear and my conscience active and bent on rectifying, as far as possible, any wrong I may have done.

Gray's caveat was a secret, confidential document under the law, and I should not have been influenced to divulge the same, but I did so, as hereinbefore related.

Upon the following page I make a diagram of the room (No. 118), the hall and the cross-hall where Professor Bell handed me the one hundred dollar bill.

The assistants and clerks had free access to the archives and records in the room. They could go in and out, outside of regular office hours. The caveat was for some weeks in a file box on my desk, and could have been taken therefrom and from the office and kept overnight without my knowledge, either by a watchman, a messenger, a clerk, or an assistant, or by a clerk or assistants from other divisions. At that time examiner's rooms were not locked, and the key was kept at the desk of the captain of the watch when the rooms were not occupied, outside of office hours, as is now the case, nor were passes then required for employees to enter the building outside of regular office hours.

The Force then on duty in my division and room was:

H. C. Townsend	1st Asst. Examiner
J. H. McDonald	2nd Asst. Examiner
Miss S. R. Noyes	3rd Asst. Examiner
W. S. Chase	Act. Asst. Examiner
Mrs. S. R. Andrews	Clerk

Professor Bell, in his testimony in the Dowd case, admits having a conversation with me in relation to the caveat, but says, as I remember it, that I declined to show him the caveat, which is not true. I did show him the original drawing, as hereinbefore stated.

In corroboration of the fact stated herein, that Major Bailey had influence over me, I desired to refer to several other applications of Professor Bell's which were acted on and became patents in remarkably quick order, as will be shown by the records of the Patent Office.

The application for this patent, 174,465, was filed February 14, 1876, became a patent (after the several actions thereon) March 7, 1876.

For No. 161,739, filed March 6, patented April 6, 1875. For No. 181,553 filed August 12, patented August 29, 1876. For No. 186,787, filed January 15, patented January 30, 1877. For No. 178,399, filed April 8, suspended May 18, 1876 on account of a possible interference with another pending application of Professor Gray, was amended, and protest against interference filed May 20; suspension revoked, case passes to issue May 29, and patented June 6, 1876.

Such rapid progress from applications to patents are exceptional, and few such instances, if any, can be found outside of Bell's cases.

For the sake of justice, the easement of my own conscience and to place myself right to this matter, I have concluded to tell the whole truth thereabouts, in so far as I had any connection therewith in an official capacity, and this without regard to whom it aid, help or hurt, and I have thus concluded after full and frank consultation and conversation with my old college mate, comrade-in-arms and long-time friend, Major Marion D. Van Horn, and I shall intrust this document to him, hoping and trusting that I may yet be able to repair, in some degree, the wrong done, and I stand ready, and shall always be ready and willing, to verify this statement before any court or proper tribunal in the land.

Zenas Fisk Wilber

Sworn to and subscribed before me this 6th day of April, 1886
Thomas W. Swan, Notary Public.[1]

Bell's Reply to Wilber's Affidavit

After Wilber's affidavit appeared in the *Washington Post* and other publications on May 22, 1886, Bell fired off a letter to the chair of the committee investigating the Pan-Electric affair and prepared his own affidavit. This affidavit was subsequently printed on May 25, 1886, in the *Washington Post* as a rebuttal to Wilber's affidavit. Bell had been instructed by his attorneys not to reply to Wilber's charges but to let them handle it. Bell, however, was not one to let a challenge to his honor, real or fancied, go unanswered.

Although there had long been suspicions concerning the extraordinary speed with which Bell got his patents, there had never been any supporting evidence of preferential treatment. Now, with Wilber's last affidavit, there was substantiation to these suspicions, at least to the extent of Wilber's credibility. Although Wilber offered to testify in court and even offered to name others who might confirm his allegations, he was never called as a witness. His testimony went no further than the court of public opinion.

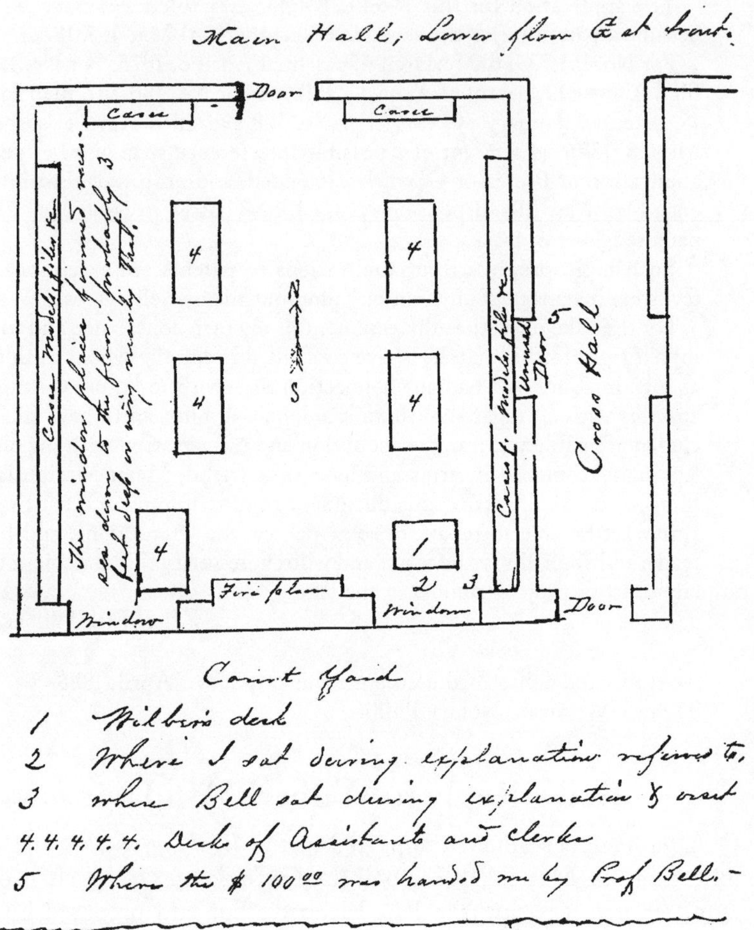

Figure 14–1. ***Wilber's hand-drawn map of his office and his explanations: (1) Wilber's desk; (2) Where I sat during explanation referred to; (3) Where Bell sat during explanation & visit; (4,4,4,4,4,) Desks of assistants and clerks; and (5) Where the $100 was handed me by Prof. Bell.***

Washington, D.C., May 24, 1886
The Hon. Charles E. Boyle
Chairman Pan-Electric Telephone Investigating Committee:

Dear Sir: I have read in the Washington Post and other newspapers of May 22, 1886, what purports to be a copy of an affidavit of Zenas F. Wilber, sworn to about seven weeks ago and offered to your committee. The persons who offered this to the committee are now at Baltimore and New Orleans, in the United States courts, defending suits for infringing my patents. I am informed that testimony for final hearing is now being taken in both these cases. If those persons or anyone else associated with those defenses think that any court would believe what Mr. Wilber swears to, it would be their duty and their interest to call him as a witness; he could then be cross-examined and his truthfulness or want of truthfulness established. If they believe him, they will do so. I am not disposed, however, to let his statements wait for denial, and, therefore, inclose with this my affidavit. I also call your attention to his various affidavits made before this one. At the request of Mr. Van Benthuysen and others he made an affidavit at Washington on July 31, 1885, and repeated it on Aug. 3. This was filed before the Secretary of the Interior by the petitioners for the government suit. In that his only ground of attack on my patent rested on an official written communication of Feb. 19, 1876, and on his present opinion of the rules of law on the subject. He did not suggest any other communication nor any fraud. On Oct. 10, 1885, before I or anyone interested with me had communicated with him, my opponents took another affidavit from him and filed it before the Secretary of the Interior, and it is printed on page 342 of the printed record of the testimony then used. In that he states in terms that he gave no information about the Gray caveat beyond what appears in the official communications in the files. Subsequently, Mr. Wilber made an affidavit, Oct. 21, 1885, which was used on behalf of my patent before the Secretary of the Interior. It contains the following:

"In the conduct of such application there was no fraud of any kind whatever, nor anything, any transaction, any communication, oral or written, which would support any such allegation in the least manner whatsoever, either on the part of Prof. Bell, his attorney, myself, or any other person whatsoever."

I call your attention to the fact which appeared before the Secretary of the Interior, that the whole of the affidavit, covering more than twelve pages of foolscap, is in Mr. Wilber's handwriting. Subsequently, and on Nov. 10, 1885, Mr. Wilber made another affidavit for my opponents, which they used before the Secretary of the Interior. It contained no allusion to the topic now referred to. It is printed on page 377 of the record of petitioners' proof before the Secretary. I request that you will kindly communicate this letter and the enclosed affidavit to your committee. Yours respectfully,

Alexander Graham Bell[2]

Affidavit of A. G. Bell

Washington, May 24, 1886

I, Alexander Graham Bell, being duly sworn on oath depose and say: I reside in Washington, District of Columbia, I am the inventor to whom were issued letters patent of the United States, No. 174,465, dated March 7, 1876. I have read in the *Washington Post* of May 22, 1886, what purports to be an affidavit of Zenas Fisk Wilber, sworn to April 6, 1886. I never presented, paid, gave, or handed to Zenas Fisk Wilber a one-hundred dollar bill or any other bill, or any other money, or any valuable consideration or thing at the place he mentions or any other place for any purpose whatsoever. I never promised to, or undertook to, or attempted to, or expressed any willingness to, pay him any money or any valuable consideration or thing whatever for any purpose. I never knew or believed or heard that Mr. Bailey or Pollok or anyone else undertook to influence said Wilber or made any attempts so to do, or employed or endeavored to employ any corrupt practices to obtain my letters patent, and do not believe so now. So far as my personal acts and knowledge are concerned I know that all proceedings in the filing and prosecution of the application for my patent and in the grant of it were free from fraud and trickery and honest in all respects, and I believe that all the acts of others concerned were also in all respects honest. I make these statements in the fullest and broadest sense.

Mr. Wilber did not show me Gray's caveat or the drawing of it or any portion of either. I have never seen the original papers of that caveat, and I did not even see a copy of them until after the Dowd suit was brought, which was in the fall of 1878. When I saw Mr. Wilber about my application in 1876 he took up my original papers and pointed out a paragraph which was in them when the application was originally filed, Feb. 14, 1876, and has not been changed since, and which contained the following passage:

> "The external resistance may also be varied. For instance, let mercury or some other liquid form part of a voltaic circuit; then the more deeply the conducting wire is immersed in the mercury or other liquid the less resistance does the liquid offer to the passage of the current. Hence the vibration of the conducting wire in mercury or other liquid included in the circuit occasions undulations in the current."

Mr. Wilber said that the caveat I had been put in interference with interfered with that. I did not have any other knowledge of the contents of Gray's caveat, specification or drawing, or either of them until after Gray had published the caveat in 1878, except what Mr. Gray wrote me himself about his caveat Feb. 21, 1877, in a letter which is in the record of proofs for my patent before the Secretary of the Interior, page –. I testified to this in 1879.

Alexander Graham Bell

City of Washington, District of Columbia, ss.:

Subscribed and sworn to before me, a notary public, in and for the city and district aforesaid, this 24th day of May, A.D. 1886.

Robert R. Shellabarger
Notary Public [3]

As stated earlier, the congressional investigating committee refused to accept Wilber's affidavit; however, they had no hesitation in allowing the following one:

Affidavit of John F. Guy

County of Washington
District of Columbia, ss.:
John F. Guy, being duly sworn, deposes and says:

My name is John F. Guy; I am forty-one years of age; reside at Washington, and am lieutenant of the Metropolitan police force of the District of Columbia, and in charge of the fourth precinct.

I have known Wilber for about a year; have frequently seen him intoxicated on the street, and from frequent complaints from the people with whom he boards, and from my observations during that time, I believe him to be a man of dissolute habits. I don't think twenty times would cover the number of times we have been bothered with him.

John F. Guy[4]

Notes

1. "The Latest Wilber Affidavit," *Electrical World*, May 29, 1886, pp. 252–253.
2. Ibid., p. 254.
3. Ibid.
4. Elisha Gray Collection, National Museum of American History, Washington, D.C.

Chapter 15

Revelation of Patent Fraud

Uncovering the "Lost Copy" of Bell's Patent Application

It took over ten years, but finally a piece of evidence emerged that, had it been investigated from the beginning, would most likely have changed the course of telephone history. On January 18, 1887, Lysander Hill, the former law partner of former Acting Patent Commissioner Ellis Spear, filed a brief with the Supreme Court charging the American Bell Telephone Company with patent fraud. Hill was then representing the People's Telephone Company (known as the Drawbaugh case, discussed previously), which was appealing Judge Wallace's 1884 decision. This was one of a group of five cases, known collectively as the Telephone Cases, being appealed to the Supreme Court.

The patent in question was Bell's famous telephone patent, No. 174,465, issued on March 7, 1876. The brief stated that the crucial description of the variable resistance method and the present fourth claim were not in Bell's patent application when it was filed on February 14, 1876. This information, Hill charged, was appropriated from Gray's caveat filed that same day and illegally inserted into Bell's application a few days later. Hill alleged that Bell's attorneys, Pollok and Bailey, had an "underground railroad" to the patent examiner, from whom they received illicit knowledge of the variable resistance method described in Gray's caveat. The examiner, Zenas Wilber, then allowed them to secretly withdraw Bell's application, in violation of Patent Office regulations, just long enough to add the purloined resistance clause and related fourth claim.

Supporting evidence for this came from a copy of the patent specification that George Brown received from Bell just before Brown sailed for England on January 26, 1876. As we learned earlier, Brown was to obtain British patents on Bell's harmonic telegraph, based on the same specifications Bell was submitting to the U.S. Patent Office. Hill, apparently, had obtained Brown's original copy from the files of the old Dowd case, where, supposedly, it had rested undisturbed ever since Bell retrieved it from Brown in November 1878. Why this copy went unnoticed, or rather unscrutinized, for over eight years is rather puzzling. Possibly, it was looked upon as just another preliminary copy and of no particular probative value. At the time of the Dowd case, there were no hints of patent irregularities, much less fraud. And, of course, at that time the defendants had no idea that Brown's copy even existed. Although Bell and his attorneys were obviously aware of its existence, it was never entered into evidence in this case, and there was never any testimony concerning it. In fact, during his deposition for the Dowd case, Bell even denied the existence of such a copy:

> *Int.* 102. Have you any of the sheets on which your rough draft of that specification was made in October, 1875? And if so, please produce them.
> *Ans.* I have, and I now produce them.
>
> [Seven sheets of note paper were produced and described, showing various preliminary portions.]
>
> *Int.* 110. Are these all the original drafts made in preparing that specification which you now have?
> *Ans.* They are.
>
> *Int.* 111. Are they all that you made?
> *Ans.* By no means.
>
> *Int.* 112. Have you made search for the others, and have you been able to find them?
> *Ans.* I have made search, but have been unable to find any others than those produced.[1]

The seven sheets referred to did not form a complete copy but were simply remnants—preliminary notations and paragraphs exhibiting many erasures and modifications. Nowhere in the Dowd case records or evidence inventory nor in any of the depositions was there any mention of the Brown copy. Yet it had been retrieved a mere six months earlier.

Now, some eight years later, the patent litigation scene had changed. Perhaps People's attorney Hill was looking for a new angle or a different line of attack, but whatever inspired him, he decided to compare the now-discovered Brown copy with Bell's patent of March 7, 1876. That's apparently when he made the curious discovery: the variable resistance clause and supporting fourth claim were missing from the Brown copy. And the evidence showed that Brown received this copy *five days after* Bell's patent was notarized (January 20, 1876) and sent to Washington. However, Bell would later testify that he might have given Brown the copy prior to January 20 and that "by some oversight" failed to notice that it was missing the variable resistance clause.[2]

All those years of litigation, all those thousands of pages of court testimony, and no one had noticed this discrepancy or, if they had, never mentioned it. Even the Supreme Court voiced surprise: "During the whole course of the protracted litigation upon the Bell patent, no argument was ever presented based on this discrepancy."[3] In addition to the missing variable resistance clause and associated claim, Hill discovered also that the Brown copy specifically stated that the famous "undulatory currents," the essence of Bell's patent claims, could be produced *only* by inductive action. In the issued patent, it stated that those currents could be produced by *both* induction and variable resistance.

Just how Brown's copy got into the Dowd files is also somewhat of a mystery. Although it was never listed in the original evidence inventory of the Dowd case, Bell and Watson retrieved it from George Brown near the beginning of the case in November 1878. It was, however, among some other evidence collected from Brown that was introduced and inventoried. If the evidence disclosed in the Brown copy were as incriminating as it seemed, it is easy to see why it was never inventoried. At the time Watson retrieved Brown's copy, Brown wrote the following notation:

> These papers were received by me from Prof. Alex. G. Bell in the winter of 1875–6, shortly before I left for England. I can fix the date by reference to my books and papers, but have not them at hand now.
>
> George Brown, Toronto, 12 November, '78[4]

As we saw earlier, Bell had been busily engaged during early January in making various copies of his specifications:

> I have so much copy work to do that I have employed a copyist but must still do a good deal myself—as I require three copies of each of my four

> specifications. One for the U.S. Patent Office, one for George Brown, and one for myself.[5]

This is a fairly significant statement, since it implies that all of the copies were prepared at essentially the same time. The Bell company attorneys would later claim that Brown's copy had been written long before this time. The now-unaccounted-for copy was one of the three original copies Bell made just prior to submitting the first one to Pollok and Bailey, on or about January 12. The first copy was used to prepare the final notarized *fair copy*, which would be submitted to the Patent Office. The second copy Bell supposedly gave to Brown on January 25. And on February 12, 1876, he sent the third copy to his father:

> I thought you would like to see the specification that has cost me so many sleepless nights—so I forward you my only copy.[6]

Shortly after this letter, Bell telegraphed his father instructing him to forward that copy of the application to Gordon Brown so that he could apply for Canadian patents. Near the end of February 1876 the Browns canceled their agreement with Bell, and Gordon Brown never filed the application.[7]

As the Dowd case progressed, Bell remembered that a third copy, apparently the same as the Brown copy, was unaccounted for. Now, three years after it was prepared, Bell's attorneys became concerned about the whereabouts of this particular copy. As we saw earlier, Bell had Watson retrieve George Brown's copy in November 1878. Now, in June 1879, Bell and the attorneys were anxious to retrieve Gordon Brown's copy. Bell wrote to his father inquiring about this particular copy:

> It is probable that this was my original copy and it is important that we should find out where it is. I have written to Gordon Brown and we should like to know if you can help us with any recollections concerning this point.[8]

Whether Gordon Brown's copy was ever retrieved is unknown. But the question is: why was it so important to locate this copy? If it were essentially the same as the copy in the Patent Office, there would be no point in retrieving it. It would have been just another copy of no particular interest. And in June 1879, no one had raised any doubt as to the validity of the patent. However, if, like the George Brown copy, it differed substantially from the official Patent Office copy, there would be every reason to retrieve it. If this were the case, it could be a potential problem if it fell into the wrong hands. But in January 1887, it was the George Brown copy that caught the court's attention.

When Bell's attorneys were confronted with the evidence of this substantial difference between the Brown copy and the Patent Office copy, they offered only one explanation. They contended that Brown must have inadvertently received an earlier, incomplete copy. Most likely, they claimed, it was given to Brown when he concluded his agreement with Bell on December 29, 1875, in Toronto. Although they admitted that Brown's copy did not contain the variable resistance clause nor the related fourth claim, they insisted that Bell had written them into his Patent Office copy sometime during the first two weeks of January 1876. On January 12, Bell's handwritten copy was sent to Hubbard, who then turned it over to Pollok and Bailey for final processing. On or about January 18, the attorneys returned to Bell a neatly rewritten fair copy to be signed, witnessed, and notarized. This was done on January 20 and the copy returned to Pollok and Bailey. The course of this document from this point (except for a brief period discussed in the next chapter) has been fully covered in the previous chapters. Brown's copy is reproduced in full in appendix G.

One section of the text of the Supreme Court's decision on Hill's charge of patent fraud, as delivered by Justice Waite, is shown here:

> Another objection to Bell's patent, put forth in the oral argument of Mr. Hill, and in the printed brief signed by him, and in that signed by Mr. Dixon, is that his application as originally filed in the Patent Office did not contain his present fourth claim, or any description of the variable resistance method, and that all which now appears in the specification on that subject, including the fourth claim, was surreptitiously interpolated afterwards. Bell's application was filed February 14, 1876, and afterwards, during the same day, Elisha Gray filed a *caveat*, in which he claimed as his invention "the art of transmitting vocal sounds or conversations telegraphically through an electric circuit," and in his specification described the variable resistance method. The precise charge now made in the printed brief of Mr. Hill is that "Mr. Bell's attorneys had an underground railroad in operation between their office and Examiner Wilber's room in the patent-office, by which they were enabled to have unlawful and guilty knowledge of Gray's papers as soon as they were filed in the patent-office," and "that an important invention, and a claim therefore, were bodily interpolated into Bell's specification, between February 14, 1876, and February 19, 1876, by Pollok, in consequence of the guilty knowledge which the latter already had of the contents of Gray's *caveat* before the declaration of interference with Gray on February 19th." So grave a charge, made in so formal a manner, is entitled to careful consideration. It involves the professional integrity and moral character of eminent attorneys, and requires us to find from the evidence that after Bell swore to his application on January 20th of 1876, and after the application thus sworn to had been formally filed in the

> patent-office, an examiner, who got knowledge of the Gray *caveat* put in afterwards, disclosed its contents to Bell's attorneys; that they were then allowed to withdraw the application, change it so as to include Gray's variable resistance method over Bell's signature, and over the jurat, and then restore it to the files, thus materially altered, as if it were the original; and all this between February 14th and February 19th.[9]

This was the essence of Hill's charge. His only tangible evidence was the George Brown copy of Bell's patent specification. By this time, Wilber's incriminating affidavit had been published, detailing his misconduct in handling Gray's caveat and his collusion with Bell's attorney Marcellus Bailey. Oddly, Hill never mentioned Wilber's affidavit. With such nefarious activities going on at the Patent Office, Hill offered what he felt was a reasonable explanation of how Gray's variable resistance method ended up in Bell's patent. It is interesting to note, as shown above, that even a Supreme Court justice had accepted without question the myth that Bell had filed before Gray. Pollok had done a masterful job in perpetuating this bit of fiction. A minor issue, which had no direct bearing on Hill's main charge, is shown below:

> Although much stress was laid in argument of the fact that what purported to be a certified copy of the specification of Bell, as found in the file-wrapper and contents printed in the Dowd case, differed materially from the patent, the cause of these has been explained in the most satisfactory manner; and we entertain no doubt whatever that the specification as now found in the patent is precisely as it was when the order for the patent was granted. Not a shadow of suspicion can rest on anyone growing out of the misprint of the specification in the Dowd case.[10]

Apparently, a certified copy of the original patent application had been prepared for the attorneys in the Dowd case. In those days, a Patent Office certified copy was just that—a copy duplicating as closely as possible the original, even to such details as pencil notations, erasures, cross-outs, and interlineations. A well-done copy would be almost indistinguishable from the original.

Bell's attorneys, as they later admitted, had made certain notations on this copy, which were inadvertently included in the official printed record of the Dowd case. Hill had maintained that those notations were further evidence of tampering and other irregularities, charges that were argued at length by the opposing Bell counsel. They were able to offer an explanation reasonable enough to be accepted by the court. This discrepancy was obviously an innocent error on someone's part and had little bearing on the main issue. Hill's pursuit of this relatively minor issue did little to help his argument and probably contributed to the court's ultimate rejection. The more serious charge, however, was that the variable resistance clause and claim could not be found in Brown's copy. The critical part of the decision comes next:

> All that remains, therefore, on which to rest this serious charge is that in a paper handed by Bell to George Brown, of Toronto, describing his invention, and which was intended to be used in England to secure a British patent, what is now claimed to be an interpolation in the American application is not to be found. It is but right to say that, during the whole course of the protracted litigation upon the Bell patent, no argument was ever presented based on this discrepancy until the brief of Mr. Hill was filed in this court on the 18th of January, 1887, six days before the argument in these appeals was begun. So far as we are advised, nothing had ever before occurred in the cases that seemed to make it necessary to prove when the variable resistance method or the fourth claim was put into the American application, or why it was left out of the paper handed to Brown. It seems always to have been assumed, until the case got here, that, because it was in the American patent, it was rightfully there. Certainly, there is nothing in the pleadings in any of the cases to direct attention to the materiality of this fact.[11]

The court was correct in saying that in all the previous patent suits nothing of this nature had ever been raised (charges of fraud had been leveled before, but never for patent tampering). But now, in 1887, the legal arguments had been dramatically changed. Previously, the patent suits had revolved around the issues of infringement and the validity of claims. When the Bell interests charged a defendant with infringement, the defendant would counter by claiming either that his particular device did not infringe or that the Bell patent was invalid because it had been anticipated by an earlier inventor. This was the first time that the patent was challenged on the basis that it had been obtained fraudulently. (This should not be confused with the government's contention of fraud in its suit to annul Bell's patents. The fraud claimed in that case was that Bell was not the first inventor and that he withheld knowledge of Reis's telephone.)

What makes this charge unusually puzzling is the fact that the document that demonstrates it had been found in the Dowd case file, where it had supposedly been since its retrieval in November 1878. However, it is also possible that it had been placed in the case file after the Dowd settlement and simply left in storage at the courthouse. The Dowd case testimony was introduced into subsequent court cases; but, apparently, no one had bothered to wade through all the documents that had been accumulated at that time—not until Lysander Hill decided to dig into it. The Supreme Court's decision continues:

> A comparison of the paper handed Brown with the American application show that they differ in more than 30 different places, besides those which relate to the variable resistance method and the fourth claim. The differences are generally in forms of expression; thus indicating that one was written after the other, and evidently for the purpose of securing greater accuracy. The paper handed Brown was clearly a rough draft, and not a fair copy, for the record shows that it bore on its face the evidence of many erasures and interlineations. Bell says in his testimony that he began writing his specification in September or October, 1875, and wrote and rewrote it a number of times, finally adopting that mode of expression which seemed to him the best to explain his invention, and the relation which one portion bore to another. He visited Brown in September, and again in December, of 1875. The arrangement was made between them on the 29th of December, at his last interview, by which Brown was to interest himself in getting out British patents. Other inventions besides the telephone were included in the contract entered into for that purpose. Bell returned to Boston on the 1st of January, and immediately set himself to work to complete his specification. He had it done so that it was taken to Washington by Mr. Hubbard about the 10th of that month, and delivered to Pollok and Bailey, the attorneys. It was then examined by the attorneys, found correct, and a fair copy made, and returned on the 18th to Bell in Boston for his signature and oath. It was signed and sworn to in Suffolk county, Mass., January 20th, and immediately returned to the attorneys. Afterwards Pollok met Bell in New York, and it was again gone over with care by the two together. No change whatever was made in it at that time, and Pollok took it back with him to Washington. On the 25th of January, 1876, Bell met Brown, who was then on his way to England, in New York. It is now assumed that the paper which Brown took to England was handed to him then; and, because the variable resistance method and the fourth claim were not in that, it is argued that they could not have been in the American specification at that time. But no one has said when the paper was actually handed to Brown. Bell says he cannot tell, but it must have been after he made his contract with Brown on the 29th of December. As the American specification was signed and sworn to five days before the interview with Brown on the 25th of January, and the paper of Brown differs from it in so many particulars besides that now in question, it would seem to be clear that the paper was a copy of some earlier draft which Bell had made—possibly one taken to Canada in December—and not of that which was perfected afterwards. As the specification which had been prepared and sworn to was a fair copy, without erasures or interlineations, the fact that the paper handed Brown was not a fair copy would imply that it was not intended to be an exact transcript of the other.[12]

Despite the magnitude of evidence, the court minimized the charges and simply refused to consider the possibility that "eminent attorneys" and "officers of the Patent Office" could possibly be guilty of wrongdoing. The fact that one of the officers of the Patent Office, Zenas Wilber, had previously made a most incriminating affidavit carried no weight with the Supreme Court. Although Wilber's affidavit was never introduced, its contents were widely known. As weak as the court's counterarguments were, the court never had to explain why they rejected the obvious. Their decisions were final, with no appeals. Justice Waite continued:

> At any rate, the bare fact that the difference exists, under such circumstances, is not sufficient to brand Bell and his attorneys, and the officers of the patent-office, with the infamy which the charges made against them imply. We therefore have no hesitation in rejecting the argument. The variable resistance method is introduced only as showing another mode of creating electrical undulations. That Bell had his mind upon the effect of such a method is conclusively established by a letter which he had addressed to Mr. Hubbard on the 4th of May, 1875, and which is found in the Dowd record, introduced into the Overland case by stipulation. Its insertion in his final draft of his specification is another proof of the care with which his work had been done.[13]

Incredibly, the court failed to see any significant difference between the two documents. They dismissed the variable resistance method by saying that, in any event, it was just another operating mode and, furthermore, that Bell had been thinking about it since his May 4, 1875, letter to Hubbard. This was the letter that the Bell lawyers had used in the previous cases to support their claim that Bell conceived of a variable resistance transmitter before Gray did. As Bell explained to Hubbard:

> I have read somewhere that the resistance offered by a wire … is affected by the *tension of the wire*. If this is so, a *continuous current of electricity* passed through a vibrating wire should meet with a varying resistance, and hence a pulsatory action should be induced in the current.[14]

What Bell said was true, but he was merely reciting Ohm's Law (current varies inversely with resistance). To say that this (a wire under tension) inspired his variable resistance clause (a wire vibrating in mercury) is to strain credibility to the breaking point. Yet, the courts accepted it as his proof of priority of invention. But this stretch of the imagination was nothing compared to Bell's explanation of why his patent showed no illustration of a variable resistance transmitter. During the government's suit to annul his patents, Bell testified:

Cross-Int. 823. Is any apparatus illustrated in the drawings of your patent in which the vibration of a conducting wire in mercury or other liquid included in the circuit, is shown, or is there any description of such an apparatus in the specification?

Ans. I think that a careful reading of the specification would enable anyone skilled in the art to construct such an apparatus ... in the case of Fig. 7, I presumed it would be understood that the conducting wire to be vibrated might be attached to the center of a stretched membrane, *a*; and that the mercury or other liquid should be included in the circuit in place of the electro-magnet *b*.

Of course, in this case, as the surface of the mercury or other liquid would necessarily be horizontal, the membrane *a* would be required to be substantially horizontal in order to allow the wire to dip into the liquid. I presumed that this would be understood by anyone skilled in the art, without further description that is contained in the patent itself.[15]

And so, despite rather convincing evidence of patent fraud, the court, this time the Supreme Court, once again ruled in favor of the American Bell Telephone Company. The margin of victory, though, was slim—a mere 4–3 majority. Although there were nine justices on the court, only seven participated. Justice Lamar, who was new and not familiar with the cases, took no part. Justice Gray, whom we will meet in the next chapter, sat as a circuit court judge and had rendered a favorable decision for the Bell company during the 1883 Dolbear infringement trial. But at the same time he was deciding the Dolbear case, he was also a Supreme Court justice and was thus entitled to take part in the Dolbear appeal at the Supreme Court. For reasons we'll cover later, he wisely declined. Until near the end of the nineteenth century, Supreme Court justices were required to "ride the circuit" (literally on horseback at one time) and hear cases at the circuit court level.[16] If the cases were appealed to the Supreme Court, they would also render a decision on the appeal. The idea of a judicial conflict of interest was not an issue in those days. With the exception of the government's cases to annul the Bell patents (which eventually just withered away) and the Berliner patent, this brought to an end a decade of undefeated patent litigation for the Bell interests. But none of the court decisions ever solved the mystery of the missing variable resistance claim.

Berliner Case

With the appeals of the Telephone Cases settled in favor of the American Bell Telephone Company, the infringement lawsuits seemed to be over. The government, although still trying to annul the Bell patents, now focused on another issue: a "submarine patent." As the name implies, such a patent, actually a patent application, lurks below the surface for a long time (i.e., within the confidential files of the Patent Office) unknown to the public until it suddenly surfaces (the patent is issued). Sometimes, a submarine patent can work to the patent holder's advantage, which is the whole point. The Bell company knew that its monopoly would end when the 17-year life of their original patents ran out, starting in 1893.

However, back in 1877, the Bell company had acquired the telephone patent application of a young German immigrant, Emile Berliner. They had filed the application on June 4, 1877, but it didn't surface (issue) until November 17, 1891—14 years later. This new patent, which covered the basic telephone transmitter, would run until 1908, and the Bell company could extend its monopoly for another 17 years, or so it hoped. But to the U.S. government, the whole deal looked a little suspect, and the government filed suit against the American Bell Telephone Company to annul the Berliner patent. Judge Carpenter, the trial judge, suspected some collusion between the Bell company and the Patent Office, and there no doubt was. Various excuses for the delay were offered—pending interferences, waiting for trial verdicts, and so on—with most of them being quite lame. The judge came down especially hard on the telephone company, saying: "Their acts were so gross as to forbid any inference except that they dishonestly delayed the issue of the patent."[17] On December 18, 1894, Carpenter voided the Berliner patent, and, for the first time, the American Bell Telephone Company lost a case—but not for long. The company appealed the case and won. However, the patent was interpreted quite narrowly and had little impact.

The Berliner patent itself was something of a mystery. It was nothing more than a Reis-type transmitter, the very instrument that the Bell company, throughout the various trials, had said could not transmit articulate speech because it was based on a false theory. It supposedly operated on a make-and-break principle, because that's how Bourseul, Reis, McDonough, and others said it worked. But they didn't know any better, and simply saying that it worked by make-and-break was fatal to their cause. Berliner never said that, because he knew at the time of filing that all Reis-type transmitters worked by the microphone principle, as most of the variable resistance transmitters did. The irony is that using an incorrect theory to explain how an invention works shouldn't have invalidated the invention. If it works, it works, regardless of how the inventor thinks it works.

Notes

1. Dowd case, pp. 486–490. *Bell Telephone Co. et al. v. Peter A. Dowd,* filed Sept. 1878.
2. American Bell Telephone Company, *Deposition of Alexander Graham Bell*, 1908, p. 88.
3. 126US568, *People's Telephone Co. et al. v. American Bell Telephone Co.*, Vol. 126, United States Supreme Court Reports, p. 568, Oct. 1887.
4. *Petition of Elisha Gray to Re-open Interference Hearings*, 1888, p. 117.
5. AGB to M. Hubbard, January 19, 1876.
6. AGB to AMB, February 12, 1876.
7. AGB to AMB, March 3, 1876.
8. AGB to AMB, June 25, 1879.
9. 126US567.
10. 126US568.
11. 126US568–569.
12. 126US569–570.
13. 126US570.
14. AGB to G. Hubbard, May 4, 1875.
15. *Deposition of Alexander Graham Bell*, p. 416.
16. Supreme Court Historical Society, Washington, D.C.
17. 65FR90, *United States v. American Bell Telephone Co. et al.*, vol. 65, Federal Reporter, p. 90, Dec. 1894.

Chapter 16

Charges of Collusion Are All Moonshine

Claim Defenders of Judges Lowell and Gray

How did Bell's patent manage to survive so many court trials? One would think that out of a dozen such battles, the Bell interests might have lost one or two. However, the laws of probability do not apply in patent litigation. In games of chance, the longer your streak of luck, the more likely it will end. But in patent litigation, it's just the opposite; the more often you win, the more likely you are to win again—and again. If you win your first contest, your chance of winning the second is not just good, it's very good, because you now have a precedent, and the legal industry thrives on precedents. This is the way it worked for the Bell Telephone Company, although it might have had some help along the way.

The company's first victory came, as we have seen, when the Dowd case was settled out of court, by negotiation, to the mutual financial benefit of Western Union and the Bell Telephone Company. In 1881, Judge John Lowell of Boston signed the final consent decree, which stated that Western Union had infringed on the Bell patent, that Bell was the original inventor, and that his patents were valid. Because of the extensive depositions taken during this case, the Dowd record was introduced into the trials that followed by stipulation. The next major infringement challenge was the Spencer case, which was argued on June 14, 1881, before the same Judge John Lowell in the U.S. Circuit Court in Boston, headquarters for the American Bell Telephone Company. On June 27, just 12 days after arguments, he handed down a decision in Bell's favor. This was the one that interpreted Bell's patent in the broadest possible terms:

> But Bell discovered a new art,—that of transmitting speech by electricity,—and has a right to hold the broadest claim for it which can be permitted in any case; not to the abstract right of sending sounds by telegraph, without any regard to means, but to all means and process[es] which he has both invented and claimed.[1]

Judge Lowell's decision was not only good news for the Bell company principals but very good news for Bell stockholders—in just several days, the stock jumped 24 points, from 146 to 170. Had the decision been reversed, Bell stock would have plummeted.[2]

The next big infringement suit is known as the Dolbear case. Amos Dolbear, a physics professor at Tufts College, came to the attention of Bell and Hubbard around the beginning of 1877 when they learned, through a mutual friend, that Dolbear had made two significant improvements on Bell's telephone. Dolbear had proposed using permanent magnets, thus eliminating the batteries, and replaced the parchment membrane and attached disk with a full-sized iron disk. This would become the basic receiver design for the next 100 years. Dolbear didn't patent his telephone improvement because, he claimed later, he had been told by the mutual friend that Bell already had a patent on it. However, this wasn't the case. Although Bell, too, had been experimenting with permanent magnets, he had yet to apply for a patent. Shortly after he heard of Dolbear's design, he got together with Pollok and, on January 15, 1877, filed an application covering the use of permanent magnets and metallic disks. This would become the so-called Second Telephone Patent. Patent Examiner Wilber, in his most expeditious feat yet, approved it ten days later, and it was issued on January 30, 1877.[3]

Oddly enough, Dolbear's infringement suit had nothing to do with permanent magnets. In fact, it was quite the opposite. He had designed an electrostatic receiver that did not rely on the magnetic attraction required for all other telephone receivers, Bell's included. He reasonably believed that this would not infringe on Bell's electromagnetic instruments. But he was wrong; he had not reckoned on Judge Lowell's, now aided by Judge Horace Gray's, unique interpretation of electricity. As they said in their joint decision sustaining Bell's patent:

> It does not appear to us to be important to determine whether, in scientific exactness, the varying influences of static electricity may properly be called currents; or whether the two properties of electricity differ in kind and in substance, or only in degree, or in the form of manifestation.... Whatever name may be given to the property, or the manifestation, of the electricity in the defendants' receiver, the facts remain that they avail themselves of Bell's discovery.[4]

In other words, according to Judges Lowell and Gray, electricity was electricity, no matter what you called it. And if electricity was involved, it infringed on Bell's patent. Between this decision and previous ones, Bell's patent was now essentially bulletproof. The Bell company so far had acquired three incredible victories: three valuable court precedents. On the morning of January 23, 1883, the day the Dolbear decision was handed down, Bell stock was at 200. That evening, it shot up to 228 and soon climbed to 290.[5] It was now becoming clear that perhaps the only way the Bell patent could be defeated would be to have it annulled by the federal government.

About the 1st of December 1886, the New York *Herald* published a story by an investigative reporter revealing the surprising financial connection between the American Bell Telephone Company and Judges Lowell and Gray. It turned out that the judges' families, but not the judges themselves, held substantial blocks of American Bell Telephone Company stock. But not surprisingly, Judges Lowell and Gray claimed they knew nothing about this. As Judge Lowell said later:

> I never knew that my brother had any Bell Telephone stock until the present year, when the fact came out through some chance conversation which we had concerning the Pan-Electric investigation. Of course, had I known that he or any relatives of mine were interested in the stock, I should have been most glad to decline hearing the case.[6]

As it turned out, not only did Judge Lowell's brother own Bell stock, but during the previous Spencer trial, his father had held 1,300 shares of the stock as collateral for a loan he had made.[7] It was also revealed that the judge's nephew owned Bell stock, as did many of his other relatives. In the case of Judge Gray, no fewer than 17 relatives and friends held Bell stock, including two brothers, two sisters, and ten cousins. Altogether, they held over 1,700 shares—at the time, valued at just over a half million dollars. Judge Gray simply stonewalled the issue. According to published accounts, "Judge Gray has taken no notice of the matter." Although Judge Gray refused to make any public comment, spokespeople for the American Bell Telephone Company rushed to the judges' defense. The company's treasurer said, "I don't think there is any need to reply to the *Herald* article. The judges are too well-known as men of unimpeachable character to need any defense." Another company representative said, "The charges of collusion are all moonshine."[8]

Predictably, nothing came of the charges, and the Bell company now had, with the three favorable decisions of Judges Lowell and Gray, enough precedents to fight off any would-be infringers—which it did. But these revelations did little to reassure the public about the Bell monopoly and no doubt raised questions as to what degree the company's court victories were based on financial as well as judicial considerations.

Pan-Electric Affair

In 1883 another telephone company appeared, the Pan-Electric Company, which pursued a different approach to getting around the Bell patents. Rather than fighting the inevitable infringement suit in court, it attempted to have the federal government annul the patents on the grounds that they had been obtained by fraud. Unlike the other would-be telephone companies, many of those involved in the Pan-Electric Company were at the highest levels of government, including some congressmen and, eventually, an attorney general. They all held large blocks of Pan-Electric stock. Using their political clout, they attempted to get a bill passed in 1884 allowing the government to annul any patents obtained illegally. Although it passed the House, it failed in the Senate.[9]

In 1885, newly elected President Grover Cleveland appointed Senator Augustus Garland, a major Pan-Electric stockholder, as attorney general. Shortly afterward, Pan-Electric officials asked the new attorney general to bring a suit to annul Bell's patents on the grounds that they were obtained fraudulently and that Bell was not the first inventor. For one reason or another, Garland declined to do this, then left town briefly, and during his absence the matter ended up in the hands of Garland's solicitor general, who then ordered that the suit should proceed. The Department of the Interior, which was then overseer of the Patent Office, launched an investigation and held hearings to determine if the suit had merit and, because of allegations of wrongdoing in the Patent Office, concluded that it did. Pan-Electric then tried to use the pending government annulment suit to prevent the Bell company from obtaining an injunction against Pan-Electric until after the suit had been settled, which could take quite a long time. The ploy failed. Because so many of those involved in the Pan-Electric affair were public figures, a congressional committee was formed to investigate.[10] This committee refused to consider Wilber's affidavit; and in the end, it split along party lines, five Democrats versus four Republicans, and concluded that no wrongdoing had occurred.

The government's case dragged on, incredibly even after the Bell patents expired, until 1896, when it slowly ground to a halt, apparently for lack of interest. It was never adjudicated, despite the mass of evidence compiled by the secretary of the Interior. The only legacy left by the Pan-Electric affair was a titillating scandal and much editorializing and political posturing.[11]

Two Tin Cans and a String

The Bell company might ignore, at least for awhile, a small-time competitor in a remote area if it thought the upstart not profitable enough. But this was not its normal practice. Not only was the company quick to sue any perceived infringer (if it couldn't settle otherwise), it didn't hesitate to file lawsuits occasionally against the infringer's customers, if Bell felt it was to its advantage. Customers of the Central Union Telephone Company of LaPort, Indiana (users of Cushman telephones), found out about this the hard way when they were all hit with lawsuits.[12] This was not so much out of meanness as it was a way of sending a not-so-subtle message to the general public: beware of signing up with a non-Bell company—you could be in trouble. No doubt some small telephone companies were formed with the expectation that they would eventually become licensees of the Bell company or be bought out by it. However, there were a couple of telephone companies that figuratively thumbed their noses at the Bell patent and operated openly without any threat of an infringement suit.

Although Bell's patent effectively covered all telephones that worked by electricity, it did not apply to non-electric telephones—known at the time as mechanical, or vibrating telephones. In principle, they were no different from a child's tin-can-and-string toy, or what was once called a lover's telephone. However, they were far from toys. They were sophisticated communication systems that could transmit remarkably clear conversations for over a half mile. One manufacturer, the American Molecular Telephone Company, claimed to have a model that would work satisfactorily on a line four miles long. They were inherently simple, essentially maintenance-free, and relatively inexpensive.[13]

The market for these mechanical telephones was, of course, limited. They were primarily intended for commercial or industrial use in factories, such as between a front office and a warehouse or other outbuilding. Farmers could use them between the house and the barn. One manufacturer, the

Elgin Telephone Company of Elgin, Illinois, even offered an acoustic switchboard that could route calls to various locations. Unfortunately, few of these unusual telephones have survived, and most people are unaware that they even existed.[14]

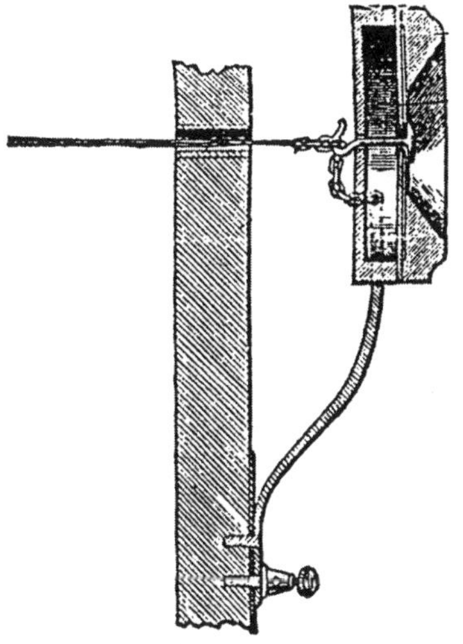

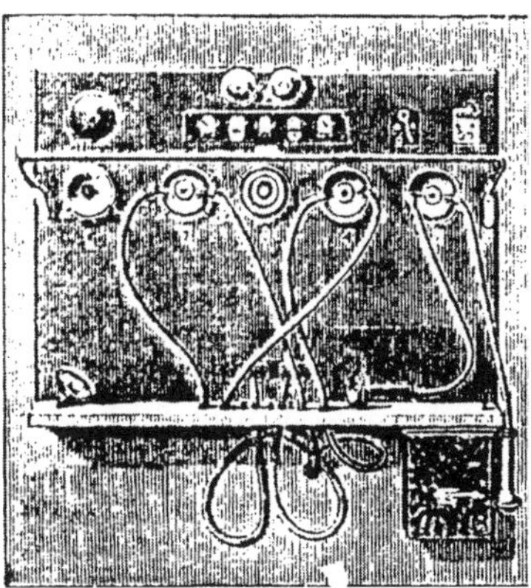

Top: ***Figure 16-1. Cross-section of typical mechanical telephone. The spinglike mounting bracket maintained tension on the wire.*** **Bottom:** ***Figure 16-2. An acoustic switchboard for routing calls to various locations.***

Unanswered Questions

Three enigmas have always surrounded that famous patent filed on Valentine's Day 1876: (1) What precipitated its sudden filing? (2) Why was a legitimate interference action between Bell and Gray canceled and Bell's patent quickly issued? and (3) How did the variable resistance claim get into Bell's patent application?

Popular history treats the first question as though there were no unusual circumstances: it was merely a coincidence that Bell's attorneys happened to go to the Patent Office the same day that Gray did, and they just happened to get there a little before he did. However, as we have seen, there was a lot more to it than mere coincidence—Bell's attorneys had advance warning that there was going to be trouble with Gray at the Patent Office. As to the second question: again, popular history tells us that Bell was granted his patent simply because he got to the Patent Office first. We know now that Gray almost certainly arrived first, but that arrival time was completely irrelevant. So there is still an element of mystery surrounding the second question, and it is still partly unsolved. Why did Acting Commissioner of Patents Spear ignore established office procedure, reverse a decision he had made just three weeks earlier in the equivalent Essex case, and allow Bell's patent to be granted? Although we know what Spear did, we'll probably never know why he did it.

Final Question

As to the third question, though, we have a more difficult problem because there is little documented evidence to support a conclusion. However, this much is established: Brown's copy of Bell's application contains no mention of the variable resistance that is found in Bell's published patent, although the two copies should have been essentially the same. In addition, Brown's copy contains only four claims; Bell's published patent contains five claims, one of which incorporates variable resistance. In chapter 15, we saw that attorney Lysander Hill charged that sometime between February 14 and February 19, Patent Examiner Wilber allowed Bell's attorneys to illegally remove Bell's application, along with Gray's caveat, copy Gray's variable resistance method into Bell's application, and then return the documents to the Patent Office.

As shown in the previous chapter, the court rejected Hill's explanation. It was just too much of a conspiracy for the justices to accept, and perhaps Hill made one accusation too many. He might have shot himself in the foot when he accused the Bell lawyers of smuggling an altered copy of Bell's application into the Patent Office files. But the fact that the court didn't accept Hill's argument doesn't mean that it didn't happen. Perhaps it didn't happen quite the way Hill said it did.

Somehow, a variable resistance claim, strangely similar to that in Gray's caveat, got into Bell's patent. But when? The most convincing argument that Hill's version is inaccurate can be found in Zenas Wilber's affidavit. It's not so much what Wilber said, as what he *didn't* say. In Wilber's tell-all, soul-baring confession, he makes no mention of Hill's allegation. If Wilber had done what Hill claimed, there would be no reason for him not to say so. After all, Wilber was making a full confession, and that particular transgression would have been no worse than others to which he confessed. This being so, the only logical conclusion we can come to is that the variable resistance claim was already in Bell's application when it was filed on February 14, 1876.

This gives some credence to Bell's later testimony that he inserted the variable resistance statement and claim at the last minute, just before he mailed the application to Hubbard on or about January 12. Pollok then mailed back a final draft, which Bell signed and had notarized on January 20 and then returned to Pollok. Accordingly, the variable resistance claim was supposedly in this notarized patent application. But countering this is the question of why the claim wasn't in the copy Brown took to England on January 26. Bell dismissed this as a mere oversight, saying that he may have given Brown an earlier copy, one made before January 12.[15] However, on January 25, just five days after mailing the notarized application back to Pollok, Bell met Brown in New York for a final briefing. Hubbard and Pollok also came up from Washington to attend, with the latter bringing copies of Bell's latest application.[16] When Watson retrieved Brown's copy in November 1878, Brown wrote on it:

> These papers were received by me from Prof. Alex. G. Bell in the winter of 1875–6, shortly before I left for England. I can fix the date by reference to my books and papers, but have not them at hand now.
>
> George Brown, Toronto, 12 November, '78[17]

It's remarkable that neither Bell, Hubbard, nor Pollok bothered to look at Brown's copy to make sure it was the latest version, especially if Bell had just added a new claim. This was one of the purposes of the New York meeting. Brown's trip was a major undertaking, and the patent application was paramount. If Brown's copy had only four claims and Bell's copy had five, wouldn't a question have been raised? The only logical conclusion is that both copies had only four claims; there was no variable resistance claim on January 25, 1876.

Later, sometime between January 26 and March 3, 1876, Bell's copy acquired a fifth claim, the variable resistance claim. Wilber's affidavit makes it unlikely that this acquisition occurred after February 14, therefore, it had to have happened prior to that date. Because of the uncanny similarity between Gray's variable resistance method and Bell's method, we can reasonably infer that it could only have come from Gray's caveat. Since the caveat wasn't finished until February 12,[18] the variable resistance claim would have to have been added between then and February 14. And at that time, Bell's application was still in Pollok and Bailey's office, waiting for word from Brown.

We can be quite certain that Bell had nothing to do with adding this fifth claim. In the first place, he was in Boston and the application was in Pollok and Bailey's Washington, D.C., office. And in the second place, it is extremely doubtful, based on his electrical knowledge, that he would have specified mercury. Mercury, because of its low resistance, is the worst possible liquid for this purpose. A wire vibrating in mercury simply doesn't work, as Bell himself later proved.[19] (Substituting a high-resistance carbon rod for the wire does work to a degree, but that's not what the specifications state.) So why would the person who added this new claim have specified such an unworkable substance? Perhaps he simply wasn't that knowledgeable, or perhaps he wanted to cover up the fact that he was borrowing from another inventor.

When Pollok and Bailey discovered the nature of Gray's caveat that weekend, they realized that Bell had overlooked an important method of producing undulating currents, as he called them. Those currents could also be created, as they learned from Gray's caveat, by varying the resistance of a circuit by a wire vibrating in water (a source of high resistance). But they couldn't say that. It would appear highly unlikely that there would be two inventions, filed on the same day, both specifying the same wire vibrating in water. By specifying a wire vibrating in mercury, they hoped it would not look like a case of theft, only like a remarkable coincidence.

During later court trials, this strange use of mercury didn't go unnoticed, and so to preempt any challenge by opposing counsel, Bell company lawyers questioned Bell on this point. Bell, who was considered by his attorneys to be a dream witness, was never at a loss for an explanation. At the time he was writing his specification, he testified, he was also working on a spark suppressor, which used a wire immersed in water as a high-resistance shunt to replace the usual arc-suppressing condenser. (As Bell later discovered, this was an old idea and not a very good one at that.) When asked to explain the use of mercury in his patent application, he testified, "It occurred to me that water was not a good illustrative substance to be specified in this connection, on account of its decomposability by the action of the current. I therefore preferred to use as a typical example a liquid that could not be decomposed by the current, and specified mercury as the best example of such a liquid known to me."[20] He never mentioned that it didn't work.

As we saw, the court rejected Hill's argument. However, his argument was still valid: the variable resistance method that so closely paralleled Gray's was added after January 25. Based on all the available evidence, it was most likely added over the weekend of February 12–14, while the application was still in the office of Pollok and Bailey.

Gray and Prescott's Curious Reversal

Of interest is the attitude of Western Union's chief engineer, George B. Prescott, with respect to his initial views on the telephone and his later, post-Dowd views. In addition to his position as electrician and an officer of that company, Prescott was also an accomplished writer and science historian.[21] It was Prescott's engineering background in telegraphy that made him eminently qualified to write on the emerging field of telephony. One of his best known works is titled *The Speaking Telephone, Electric Light, and Other Recent Electrical Inventions*, copyrighted 1878 and published 1879. The electric light mentioned in the title is not the one that Edison developed (Edison did not receive his famous patent until January 27, 1880) but rather the carbon arc lamp, of which there were many variations. In the preface to this book, Prescott states:

> No effort has been spared in our investigation to obtain all the facts as they are; and these are now given as we have found them, without favor or prejudice. The reader will thus be enabled to judge for himself just what measure of credit to accord to each of the different experimenters who have been engaged with the problem of electrical transmission of articulate speech, and whose labors have been crowned with such abundant success.[22]

Because of his engineering background, Prescott was able to describe in full technical detail all of the electrical devices that pertained to the budding telephone industry. Because of Prescott's ability to judge these devices through the eyes of an engineer, we have the best record of how they were made and how they functioned. After evaluating both Gray's and Bell's telephone apparatuses, Prescott made the observation:

> Whether or not Prof. Bell invented the apparatus independently of Mr. Gray, we have no means of judging; but that he was not the first inventor, we think the facts conclusively show. Had he been the first to invent it, is there any reason why he should not have described it in his application, filed simultaneously with Mr. Gray, on the 14th of February, 1876?[23]

Prescott went about as far as he could, or as far as he dared, in questioning Bell's priority as to the invention of the telephone. Prescott raised the same question raised by so many challengers to the Bell patent: "Had he [Bell] been the first to invent it, is there any reason why he should not have described it in his application?" Prescott was comparing Bell's skimpy and vague telephone patent description to the specific disclosures of Gray, McDonough, and others. While this was a valid concern among the scientific community, it was totally rejected by the courts. There is little doubt that Prescott did not support Bell's claim of being the true inventor of the telephone. In fact, Prescott publicly stated that Gray was the inventor of the telephone in a telegram he sent on November 15, 1878. The occasion was a testimonial banquet and reception, given in Gray's honor as the true inventor of the telephone, by the citizens of Highland Park, Illinois, Gray's home town. Among the many testimonials given that night and the multitude of congratulatory telegrams received, was this one:

> From G. B. Prescott, Chief Electrician W. U. Telegraph:
> Master Ceremonies:
>
> To Elisha Gray, the inventor of the telephone and solver of the problem of the ages, thanks to whose genius Job can not only affirmatively answer the query: "Canst thou send lightnings, that they may go and say unto thee, here we are?" but can add that he can deliver the message in the vernacular.[24]

However, when Prescott published the second edition of his book in 1884, he did a curious about-face. In this edition, he not only supported Bell's telephone priority claim but refuted some of the claims of Gray and others.

Had Prescott finally realized the errors of his previous belief and now knew the truth? While this is a remote possibility, we must also take into account the following fact: George Prescott, in 1884, in addition to his other duties, was also a vice president of the Gold and Stock Company, a subsidiary of Western Union. When Western Union and Bell Telephone settled the Dowd suit in November 1879, one of the stipulations was that Alexander Bell be acknowledged as the inventor of the telephone and that his patents be considered valid. This was a contractual agreement and spelled out in a court decree. Prescott, a good company man, despite originally championing Gray as the inventor of the telephone, now had no choice but to agree to this stipulation. And so, in 1884, he dedicated the second edition of his book to Bell. *The Speaking Telephone* of 1879 had become *Bell's Electric Speaking Telephone* in 1884.

Summary

It took ten years, but finally most of the pieces to the telephone puzzle fell into place. There are still a few pieces missing, but now, more than a century later, if we step back and look at the overall picture, we can more or less fill in those blanks. In attempting to evaluate that remarkable chain of events that defined the telephone's first turbulent decade, we find that there was no master plan. Each scene in that continuing drama was a separate event, and, although there were many supporting players, the roles of Alexander Bell and Elisha Gray predominate, and their paths will forever be entwined. While Bell got most of the headlines, Gray's presence was always there, from the time Bell's first patent application was filed until the fraud charges some ten years later. If we seem to know more about Bell's thoughts and actions, it's only because he was a more prolific letter writer—and letter saver. As to the conclusion of this story—we leave that to the reader.

Notes

1. *Federal Reporter*, 8FR511. *American Bell Telephone Co. v. Spencer.*
2. "A New York Paper's Charges Against a Judge," *Chicago Tribune*, December 3, 1886, p. 1.
3. Robert V. Bruce, *Alexander Graham Bell and the Conquest of Solitude*, Cornell University Press, Ithaca and London, 1990, p. 264.
4. *Federal Reporter*, 15FR454. *American Bell Telephone Co. v. Dolbear et al.*
5. "Bell Telephone and the Bench," *Electrical World*, December 11, 1886, p. 281.
6. Ibid., p. 282.
7. "A New York Paper's Charges against a Judge," *Chicago Tribune*, December 3, 1886, p. 1.
8. "Bell Telephone and the Bench," p. 282.
9. Frederick L. Rhodes, *The Beginnings of Telegraphy*, Harper, New York, 1929, p. 72.
10. "Telephone Scandal," *Chicago Tribune*, January 31, 1886, p. 20.
11. John Brooks, *Telephone: The First Hundred Years*, Harper & Row, New York, 1975, pp. 88–89.
12. "The Telephone," *Electrical World*, August 21, 1886, p. 120.
13. "Some Novel Forms of Mechanical or Vibrating Telephones," *The Electrical World*, July 10, 1886, p. 16.
14. "Elgin Mechanical Telephones," *Electrical World*, March 5, 1887, p. 121.
15. American Bell Telephone Company, *Deposition of Alexander Graham Bell*, 1908, p. 81.
16. U.S. 126, *Telephone Cases*, October 1887, p. 231.
17. *Petition of Elisha Gray to Re-open Interference Hearings*, 1888, p. 117.
18. Appendix B.
19. Bernard S. Finn, "Alexander Graham Bell's Experiments with the Variable-Resistance Transmitter," *Smithsonian Journal of History* 1, no. 4 (Winter 1966), p. 10.
20. *Deposition of Alexander Graham Bell*, p. 87.
21. The term *electrician* is equivalent to today's electrical engineer.
22. George B. Prescott, *The Speaking Telephone, Electric Light,* D. Appleton, New York, 187, Preface.
23. Ibid., p. 217.
24. *Reception and Banquet to Elisha Gray*, November 15, 1878, Highland Park Historical Society.

Appendix A

The following article by John Paul Bocock, entitled "The Romance of the Telephone," appeared in Munsey's Magazine *in November 1900:*

The Strange History of a Great Modern Invention, and the Long Struggle, with a Huge Fortune as the Stakes, Between the Men Who Have Claimed It as Their Own

The toy of a quarter century ago has come to be the key to a treasure chest whose gold has grown past all precedent; grown overnight, from the air and the water, the curiosity of men, the laws of nature. It is not the vulgar accumulation of toil, but the joint product of luck and pluck, of opportunity improved and advantage mercilessly pressed, fostered always by the Patent Office and the courts of the United States.

Interwoven in this story of the golden growth of the Bell Telephone Company, which has so long controlled the latest and most useful gift of science to mankind, are such marvelous oaths, such charges of corruption and treachery, such tales of ruin and oppression, such accusations against men high in the public esteem, such sacrifices of truth and honor, such disappointments and defeats of the many who have sought to share the reward of the one, that the bare relation of them all, were that possible, would surpass any romance ever written.

A Memorable Day in Telephone History

On a stormy Monday in the month of February, 1876, a patent lawyer in Washington sat in his office at work. There was nothing in the air, in the morning papers, or in the formal caveat over which he bent at his desk to hint to him that this 14th of February was to be a red letter day, a day to be remembered for all time in the history of American patents. The lawyer worked patiently away until lunch time, and then rested and refreshed himself. After a while, an office boy came to the private office and announced Professor Elisha Gray, who was at once shown in. The papers, now ready for signature, were carefully examined by Professor Gray, whose discovery of "a new art of transmitting vocal sounds telegraphically" they were to announce to the world—not for the world's benefit, but for Professor Gray's, after he should have applied for and obtained a patent. Some time before the Patent Office was closed for business that afternoon, this caveat was duly filed, according to law, in the department of electricity. The fees incidental to this filing were paid in, and entered as paid on the blotter in the chief clerk's room. Had the chief clerk also entered on his blotter the hour of filing, millions of dollars since spent in litigation would probably have been saved.

For this same blotter showed, at the close of business hours on that same day, that some time between the opening and closing of the office one Alexander Graham Bell had paid the fees incidental to the filing of an application for a patent "for the electric transmission of noises or sounds of any kind"—not mentioning vocal sounds or human speech. But whether the caveat was filed before the application, or vice versa, the records do not show, nor do they show to this day.

Now, if the filing of these two papers, the legal effect of which was quite different, as we shall presently see, indicated that two inventors were honestly striving to patent—each for his own benefit—a valuable discovery, and to obtain that precedence which in patent law is so vital by filing each his own papers at the earliest possible moment, there was one plain duty incumbent on the examiner in the electrical department. That duty was to give each of the inventors the same opportunity to perfect his claims, and to stand by impartially until the law should declare which one was entitled to priority.

What did happen? Out of the tangled web of contention which at once began to be woven about the telephone, what undisputed facts stand out? First, the fact that Alexander Graham Bell was notified in writing, in care of his patent lawyers, that his application for a patent was suspended in consequence of the filing of Professor Gray's caveat. Second, that Bell was subsequently notified, under date of February 25, that this suspension, "having been declared under a misapprehension of applicant's rights," was "withdrawn." Both these notices were signed "Z. F. Wilber, Examiner." The same day, the 25th of February, Examiner Wilber made a formal entry that "the cash blotter in the chief clerk's room shows conclusively that the application was filed some time earlier on the 14th than the caveat."

On the other hand, it has been charged under oath that Gray's caveat was actually filed before Bell's application, but having been first, *was entered last*, being at the bottom of the pile of papers accumulated for entry by the close of the day. It has also been suggested that while the fees for filing were paid in by Bell's attorneys before Gray's caveat was filed, the actual Bell papers were not filed until later. Such surmises are not profitable; they have already proven expensive—for the Bell Telephone Company has paid out as much as four hundred thousand dollars in one year for the quieting of the legal curiosity outsiders have felt about these and similar questions. "Not one cent for tribute, millions for defence," is a costly motto when lavishly followed out.

On March 7, 1876, eleven days later still, a patent, number 174,465 was duly issued to Bell in accordance with his application. Such alacrity of action on an application filed only three weeks before must have been extremely gratifying to Mr. Bell. It is quite unusual in the Patent Office. For example, the famous Berliner patent, now in litigation in the United States courts (the last patent, by the way, that stands between the public and the unrestricted use of the telephone), was not issued until fourteen years after the application was filed. Before passing on to the next telephone tragedy, it should be remembered that Mr. Bell has consistently denied that he took or tried to take any unfair advantage of Professor Gray. It is said for Mr. Bell, also, that if Professor Gray had sent in an application for a patent instead of a simple caveat, he, Gray, would have received the same notice as Bell, an application being a paper requiring official action, while a caveat was simply a private paper not requiring official action—so private, the anti-Bell add, that it ought not to be shown, or its contents made known to any one, especially not to a rival. The anti-Bell people have the daring to state that Mr. Bell was allowed to see the caveat, which contained the first written description of a speaking telephone, and that he profited by this to such an extent that he constructed a talking instrument which apparently corresponded to the description in his patent of March 7. More, they charge that Bell was thus enabled, having at last realized that a speaking telephone, a thing of enormous commercial value, would soon be patented by somebody, to go on and apply for another patent, this time describing it in no ambiguous terms, which second and conclusive patent was issued on the 30th of January following, and numbered 186,787. Mr. Bell denies any such inspiration from either the Gray caveat or the Reis telephone, then on exhibition in the Smithsonian Institute.

These two patents, No. 174,465, of March 7, 1876, and No. 186,787 of January 30, 1877, have been the famous Bell telephone patents which have made more than a hundred million dollars for their owners. The life of a patent being seventeen years, both are now defunct; but they served their purpose.

The next scene in the telephone melodrama is more comic than tragic. It takes place on a hot Sunday in June, in this same centennial year, which, curiously enough, brought to a head the struggle to construct the telephone. The Emperor of Brazil and a number of other distinguished visitors to the World's Fair were invited by Professor Barker, of the University of Pennsylvania, to attend, in one of the Exposition buildings, an exhibition of a novel apparatus. This was a "harmonic multiple telegraph," by which a number of messages could be sent over a single wire by means of musical notes. The exhibition was an interesting one; the inventor, Professor Gray, was superintendent of the Western Electric Manufacturing Company, Professor Barker was a well known scientist, and, besides Dom Pedro, the eminent electrician Sir William Thompson, now Lord Kelvin, was among the auditors. So was Alexander Graham Bell, comparatively an unknown man, who was then exhibiting, on week days, at the Centennial, the interesting scientific toy known as the Bell telephone. This instrument Mr. Bell had completed that spring. He had not been required to comply with the usual regulation that a practical model should be filed with his application for a patent. The obliging Mr. Wilber had been kind enough to pencil on the "jacket" or envelope of the Bell papers, "Model not required."

The Telephone at the Centennial

This gave plenty of time for the construction of the speaking telephone which Mr. Bell now, on this Sunday morning in June, 1876, humbly requested that he might have the privilege of showing to the distinguished gathered to hear Professor Gray's musical telegraph. There was some disinclination to waste time over a "toy" which, however interesting, could not share in scientific importance with Professor Gray's apparatus; but Mr. Bell got the chance he sought. He had taken chances all his life, and improved every opportunity. He knew that the telephone would be a gold mine, no matter who called it a toy.

Speaking into the transmitter, he asked one of the gentlemen to go to the other end of the long hall and listen at the receiver—which, by the way, was a duplicate of the transmitter, and not an entirely distinct part of the apparatus, as it is in the telephone of today. Various tests were made, and everybody was pleased. Finally Sir William Thompson spoke into the telephone Hamlet's soliloquy, and Professor Gray, of all men in the world, went to the receiver to hear the prophetic words, "To be or not to be." It was not to be, for Professor Gray. He said that he could hear only a confused jumble of sounds, and at last these words, "Aye, there's the rub!"

So the company dispersed. Some of them, of a surety, knew that at that moment there was in the Smithsonian Institute, not a hundred miles away, another telephone, so named and made by Philip Reis, who had died in Germany two years before, believing himself the inventor of the telephone, and supposing that he had given his invention to the world.

Bell and Gray separated that June Sunday, not suspecting how soon and how often they were to meet in the press, in the courts, in the tribunals of public opinion. Nobody else thought much about the speaking telephone. Gray himself never took the trouble to make one until November, 1877. But Bell never flagged in his energies. He believed in himself and in the invention, though he knew that much remained to be done before it would be useful. His transmitter bothered him above all things. He did not realize the far reaching importance of the undulatory electric current he used in his telephone instead of the "make and break" current used in telegraphing. That was what his lawyers say he had attained and patented—the use of an undulating current to take up the sound waves in his transmitter, to transform them into electric waves, to speed them over a telegraph wire, and then to convert them back in the receiver into other sound waves, exact reproductions of the original ones talked into his telephone. He had learned how to project the simulacrum of the human voice over leagues of space, enabling us, with the latest development of his magic instrument, to materialize the vocal spirit at a distance of two thousand miles. He declares he did not learn this from Reis or Gray.

By a strange series of coincidences, as subsequently recorded in the courts and the newspapers, at least a dozen men in different parts of the country were at this very time working at telephone inventions, trying to construct a machine that would reproduce or carry the human voice. The atmosphere seethed with telephone thoughts, according to the claimants who began presently to spring up.

Other Telephone Inventors

Nearly all of those claimants are living today, their modest competence strikingly contrasted with the gilded eminence of Bell. Learned and incorruptible scientists support, as against Bell, the claims of McDonough, Drawbaugh, and Dolbear, which the courts have denied. Edison, Blake, Berliner, and Short, whose telephone inventions passed for a valuable consideration into the control of the Bell company, are also to be named in this category. Antonio Meucci, the veteran of Garibaldi's wars, found, in his last years on Staten Island, many believers in his assertion that he had invented a speaking telephone in 1857. But of them all, perhaps James W. McDonough, of Chicago, can claim precedence as an inventor of the telephone receiver, for, given a Reis transmitter, in the Smithsonian Institute, free to anybody's use, the telephone receiver became at once the all important mechanism. On April 10, 1876, McDonough applied for a patent on a "teleloge, or means of transmitting articulate sound by electricity." His application was formally "placed in interference with"—that is, declared apparently to conflict with—the patent of Bell and the applications of Edison, Gray, Dolbear, Richmond, and Holcombe. The examiner, the first official to pass on the McDonough receiver, awarded him the priority. And there, for a moment, fortune shook her horn of plenty over his head. But the *examiner in chief* promptly reversed the decision, and his reversal has stood unshaken. Yet McDonough, who began experimenting in 1867, before Bell ever thought about a telephone, had by June, 1875, completed, by the help of the Reis transmitter, an apparatus "which was successfully employed for the transmission of articulate speech, on many occasions during the same month," according to Professor E. J. Houston, of the Franklin Institute.

But, say the Patent Office experts and the United States courts, McDonough used a Reis transmitter, he employed a make and break current to transmit speech, instead of the undulating current discovered by Bell, and Bell only; and therefore we cannot recognize McDonough's claims, for the undulating current is *the only one* which will transmit human speech. In other words, you may talk as much as you like through a Reis transmitter into a McDonough receiver, but the courts of the United States will not admit the existence of your talk, or even the possibility of its existence, because they once decided that only the (Bell) undulating current can transmit human speech, and that decision must stand and shall stand.

So what chance had Professor Amos E. Dolbear against the Medes and Persians of Washington? Professor Houston declares that "the experiments of this gentleman in telephony were contemporaneous with those of Bell, and covered a wide field of research." He unquestionably invented the electrostatic telephone, and "did much to give commercial efficiency to the telephone." But he didn't pay enough attention to the Patent Office!

And poor Drawbaugh, the most pathetic figure of them all, what chance had he, a humble mechanic, experimenting for years in his shop at Eberly's Mills, Pennsylvania, knowing nothing of Reis, but telling his neighbors forty years ago that speech could be conveyed by electricity; and then, in the next seven years, according to their sworn evidence, actually constructing an apparatus which did transmit speech electrically, by an undulating current, it was claimed, from a table tumbler transmitter to a tin can receiver? What chance did he have, in his poverty, too poor even to go to Washington—against the world, and the Patent Office.

Philip Reis and His Telephone

Professor Gray's disappointment has been the most bitter of all, in some respects. His rank in the scientific world gave him a great advantage. Such an expert as Houston says of him that "he is clearly entitled at least to share with Bell the honor of the invention." As long as he lives, and his family live, the honors and the enormous wealth that were so nearly in his grasp will not be forgotten. All of which points inevitably to the prologue of the play, the story that the telephone had already been invented in Germany more than twenty years before the centennial year by Philip Reis, who may truthfully be described as a martyr to science, and upon whose tombstone at Friedrichsdorf may be seen to this day the singularly pathetic sentence, "Erfinder des Telephons." The epitaph is pathetic, because the life of John Philip Reis was itself a tragedy. He was born on January 7, 1834, at Gelnhausen, near Frankfort, and his father, a master baker, spared no means at hand for the lad's education. His lungs were weak, his health delicate, his application to his studies incessant. He came across a copy of the French journal *L'Illustration* of August 26, 1854, in which a young French telegrapher, Charles Bourseul, published a plan for the transmission of sound (not speech) by a "make and break" electric current. This emphasized the direction of Reis' mechanical studies. He constructed an electrical apparatus consisting of a transmitter and a receiver connect[ed] by a telegraph wire, in which "each sound wave," as he described it, "caused a breaking and closing of the current."

The whole telephone controversy turns to some extent on what Reis did with his apparatus after he devised it. Bell says that the instrument was a "musical toy"; that it reproduced musical pitch and no more. Professor Paddock, of the Stevens Polytechnic Institute, stated under oath, in the patent suits, that he could and did "talk over the Reis Apparatus." The Bell lawyers, the ablest money could retain in this country, have always insisted that Reis did not aim at inventing a speaking telephone and did not invent one, although they concede that Bell's invention applied to the Reis apparatus makes the latter a speaking telephone. But Professor Silvanus P. Thompson, now holding the chair of experimental physics in University College, Bristol, England, declares deliberately not only that Philip Reis was "the inventor of the telephone," but goes so far as to say that "Reis' telephone was expressly intended to transmit speech; it did transmit speech; it will transmit speech" if made today according to the inventor's instructions. Professor Houston, of the Franklin Institute, says that the Reis telephone could and did transmit articulate speech.

Some Bell advocates say, "Reis did invent a speaking telephone, but he did not know it." Contemporary publications show that Reis "publicly exhibited" his instrument from 1861 to 1864, lectured on it, and practically devoted his life to it. There is no sort of doubt that he originated the name "telephone" and applied it in the year 1860 to the most important part of his apparatus, the transmitter.

Now, the transmitter is still the most important part of the telephone. It was the Blake transmitter that made the Bell telephone commercially valuable. It is the patent on the Berliner transmitter that has held the anti-Bell world at bay since the Bell patents expired. It was the Edison transmitter, patenting the use of carbon, which perfected the discoveries and appliances of Bell and Berliner. Those three—Bell, Berliner, and Edison—are the men whom the electrical world of today, or the vast majority of its representatives, regard as the telephone trinity. What is one to think of Professor Thompson, whose integrity and scientific ability no American expert can deny, when he asserts that "*all* transmitters" utilize Reis' fundamental principles; that "they come back to Reis' fundamental idea" of "setting the voice to vary the degree of contact in a mechanism which he called an interrupter." Reis used a "tympanum," or drum, like the ear drum, in his transmitter. Gray speaks of a "tympanum" in his caveat. Bell describes the same thing as "stretched membrane" in his application. They simply followed in Reis' footsteps, according to Professor Thompson, who has already been quoted. What is more, Professor Thompson affirms that Bell's crowning achievement, his one vital contribution to the composite telephone as we know it today, "the undulatory current," was known to and used by Reis.

Bell's Strange Ignorance of Reis

Of course if the United States courts believed with Professor Thompson and believed that Mr. Bell knew of Reis' discoveries and their publication, the whole telephone situation would be different; the Bell patents would never have been issued. The hundred million dollar chest would have no gold in it.

Reis died January 14, 1874; the Bell patent was applied for February 14, 1876. And what a death this young German enthusiast met, after all! He, the "*Erfinder des Telephons,*" the discoverer, some say, of the art of electrically transmitting speech, to lose his voice and die of the breaking down of the organs of speech!

Bell and Gray were both educated men. Would it not be strange that neither one of them had read or heard of the Reis telephone? The European world of science knew all about it. Bell had even been to Germany, prosecuting his studies in deaf and dumb language, in which he was an expert. His father and grandfather before him had been teachers of languages. As a youth in Edinburgh—where he was born March 3, 1847—he had learned the anatomy of the vocal organs, had built an automaton speaking machine. At this very time Reis was lecturing before the Physical Society of Frankfort on the Main. No. 15 of *Bottger's Polytechnic Notizblatt*, published in 1863, declares that persons using "the Reis telephone could even communicate to each other words, only such, however, as they had already heard frequently."

Bell and Gray must surely have known all about the Reis telephone. But Bell denied it, in court, although he admitted that he had read parts of a German book in which the Reis telephone was described.

In 1870 Mr. Bell emigrated to Canada, in 1871 to Boston, all the while studying and experimenting in the deaf and dumb language and in the transmission of speech, as he says. One would think that the Reis telephone in the Smithsonian Institute might excite the liveliest interest in his mind. His friends say Bell "was not the first who tried to invent a speaking telephone, but he was the first who did." But it was Gray, in his caveat, who made the first claim to this invention—"I have invented a new art of transmitting vocal sounds telegraphically."

The Financial Romance of the Bell Telephone

The Bell telephone, as exhibited in 1876, excited only passing interest among the wonders of the Centennial. The transmitter was not reliable; you never knew whether you were going to hear a buzz, a break, or a word. Mr.

Edward S. Renwick, the well known New York expert, brother of the architect who designed St. Patrick's Cathedral, swore in court in one of the telephone suits whose name is always Bell against somebody or other, and whose pages of evidence are legion—that he, Renwick, made a pair of bell telephones according to Bell specifications, and that they would not transmit speech. As late as the summer of 1878, when the Bell Telephone Company, for convenience' sake, moved from New York to Boston, its future seemed dark and uncertain. The assistant secretaryship of the Bell company was offered to a New York newspaper reporter if he would go to Boston. He did not think well of the proposition, surmising that his pay would be in stock, for the company sadly lacked money. A single share of such stock as he would then have received is now worth from twenty five to thirty thousand dollars. The original stock has been watered over and watered over again, expanded and inflated, paying dividends and extra dividends, with tremendous legal expenses, and still piling up millions besides.

It was in those troublous days, when the Bell transmitter would not work properly, and the Bell company had no money in its treasury, that the manufacturing firm of E. S. Greeley & Co. were asked to make Bell telephones for the owners of the patent. They looked askance at the proposition; they were in the habit of receiving cash, and plenty of it, for their work. So the Bell Telephone Company applied to Charles L. Williams, Jr. of Boston, and when his bill became due, paid him in stock, "the supposed equivalent" of the cash. More bills were paid in stock, and Mr. Williams acquired quite a lot of it; he tried to sell some of it at twenty five cents on the dollar, but nobody wanted to buy it, and so the Williams stock was laid away.

Francis Blake, a bright young man who afterwards entered the service of the Bell company, invented a new kind of transmitter which the Bell concern acquired the exclusive right to make. Bell telephones with Blake transmitters were introduced as if by magic into every big city in the United States. Their value was instantly recognized. The stock went up by long leaps. Mr. Williams, of Boston, was one of those now able to pull a trunk full of stock from under the bed. He got three shares of new stock for each of his original shares, and the dividends on his new stock made him a very rich man. Mr. Blake at once began to reap his reward. He is declared to have "made telephony an art."

What Emile Berliner Accomplished

Here Berliner and Edison come into the story of the telephone. Emile Berliner, born in Hanover in 1851, came to the United States in 1870, friendless, craving knowledge, looking for opportunities. He worked for a German druggist in New York. One day his master gave him an old copy of Muller's "Physik." While he was intent upon this, he found La Cour's "Researches in Phonic Wheels" on an old book stand. The idea of transmitting human speech by electricity began to burn in his brain. In the centennial year he went to Washington, where he became a clerk in a dry goods shop; but he never relaxed his devotion to his electrical and telegraphic studies.

He was standing at the key one day when an operator named Richards said to him, "You'll have to press down harder, or it may happen that the sounder at the other end will not respond well." The thought at once flashed through Berliner's mind that if pressure modified the electrical current, by making this difference in the contact, a vibratory contact would transmit human speech—since sound waves are undulations—by a vibratory current. He at once began experimenting with a transmitter of his own devising and a Bell receiver. In his transmitter he used a metallic diaphragm touching screws tipped with broken lead pencil points. He also conceived the idea of placing his transmitter in the primary of an induction coil, and got a patent for that. The value of his discoveries was at once recognized, and he was invited to join the staff of the Bell Telephone Company. But his invention did not become that company's property as yet.

Berliner is always spoken of as one of the three telephone discoverers. "If," said the Bell company in the brief in support of its complaint against the National Bell Company, in the case heard in Boston in November, 1899—"if Edison and Berliner are to be regarded as rival inventors of the telephone, Berliner is plainly the prior inventor, as he clearly conceived the invention in January, 1877, and completed it in April, 1877, by filing the description of his caveat … Berliner was the first to conceive the microphone principle." This principle, "constant contact, variable pressure," enabling the electric current to transmute the undulations of the voice into electrical undulations, was Berliner's discovery, ranking second in telephone science to Bell's of the undulatory current itself. Reis called his transmitter the "telephone"; that is why Berliner's wonderful improvement over Bell's transmitter justifies Berliner's being called one of the "inventors of the telephone."

Although Berliner applied for his patent in 1877, it was not issued until 1891. The sinister influence of the Bell Telephone Company is declared to have been responsible for this delay. Having the Blake transmitter to use in its business, it was content to allow the Berliner patent to rest in abeyance, since no one else could use a Berliner transmitter under these circumstances. It also owned the patent on a telephone receiver issued to Berliner on November 2, 1880.

Edison's Carbon Transmitter

At this point in the story of the telephone we encounter Thomas Alva Edison. The marvelous Ohioan, then some thirty years of age, had been getting out electrical patents for ten years past. His genius had attracted the attention of the Western Union Telegraph Company, which offered him a high salary to give the company the right to examine and purchase, if [it] chose, any and all of his electric inventions. Among other discoveries made about this time was this: that the microphone, or Berliner transmitter, which produces the variations of current in the telephone, worked much better when one or both of the wire ends, or electrodes, as they were called, were made of carbon. From the universal use of carbon in transmitters since Edison's discovery they are now called "carbon transmitters." This was the third discovery contributing virtually to the telephone of today.

Now the Western Union at once bought Edison's carbon transmitter invention under its contract. An interference on the loose contact principle having been established by the Patent Office between Edison and Berliner, the latter not having yet joined the Bell company, it also bought Berliner's application. The Western Union people were not slow to realize the full value of the telephone and the growing power of the Bell company. Among others they acquired Gray's rights, Gray being at that time the most conspicuous anti-Bell claimant. In a suit brought by the Bell Telephone Company against one Dowd, who really represented Gray, Gray's rights were fully canvassed and considered. It was urged on behalf of Gray that the Patent Office had defrauded him of his lawful rights by not giving him notice of Bell's application as it had given Bell notice of his (Gray's) caveat. It was even charged that "Bell's patent was surreptitiously issued."

Bell's Victory Over Gray

The result of this suit settled forever Gray's claims to the invention of the telephone. He made, through his counsel, a formal admission that "Bell was the first inventor of the telephone." It is said the sum of one hundred thousand dollars was paid to Professor Gray for this admission. The decree, entered by consent of counsel on both sides, not only put Gray on record against the claims of his own caveat—and the claims he has since made again and again—but it had another and even more important effect. It transferred to the Bell Telephone Company absolutely all the Western Union's electrical patents, and rights to have patents issued, including the Berliner patent, the Edison transmitter, the Page patent, covering the induction coil used in the transmitter; the Short transmitter, the patent on which was awarded to Professor Short, now a distinguished electrical engineer, in an interference, over Edison's contemporary claims; and others still. Four thousand shares of Bell telephone stock passed at this time to the Western Union Telegraph Company. The arrangement practically gave over the telephone field to the Bell company—at least, until the expiration of existing patents. The last of these was the Berliner patent, finally—and, the anti-Bell people say, fraudulently—issued in 1891, in order to prolong as much as possible the Bell supremacy. Should the Berliner patent be held effective for seventeen years from 1891, the Bell company will continue to have until 1908 a great advantage over independent companies. The latter aver not only that the Berliner patent of 1891 was fraudulently held back, but that it is invalid anyhow, by reason of the expiration of Berliner's patent of 1880, which covered substantially the same principle.

The next scene in the telephone drama is pathetically farcical. Again Elisha Gray is the hero, and again Alexander Graham Bell is accused of being the villain.

Notwithstanding the settlement in the Dowd case, which was supposed to conclude the Bell-Gray controversy, on December 24, 1886, Gray filed a petition for a reopening of the whole case in the United States courts. This time the charges of fraud, involving Wilber by innuendo, are spread formally on the record as follows:

> That on or about the first day of March, 1876, A. G. Bell, the successful party in said interference proceedings, went to the Patent Office and by undue and unlawful means and influence procured full knowledge of the contents of and drawings attached to a certain caveat accurately describing a speaking telephone then recently (viz., on the 14th day of February, 1876) filed by petitioner ... By the knowledge thus obtained ... the said Bell was enabled to construct an apparatus a few days afterward by which he succeeded in transmitting articulate speech ... and which apparatus the said Bell claimed was the apparatus described in ... an application which he had filed in the Patent Office on the said 14th day of February, 1876.

This suit was decided against Gray. Nor have the courts of the United States, no matter who attacked Bell, failed as yet to decide in Bell's favor. That is why the consensus of expert opinion is that Bell must be regarded as the inventor of the telephone, because he first made it practical and introduced it into general use. This opinion ignores all charges of fraud and innuendoes of bribery and perjury. It is the opinion held by such eminent experts as F. W. Jones, chief engineer of the Postal Telegraph Cable Company.

A Strange Chapter of History

There are many thousands of American citizens who conscientiously believe not only that Gray is a much abused man, but also that Dolbear, McDonough, and Drawbaugh, all of whom have been parties to some of the various litigations, have each and all been cheated of their just dues, cheated by the courts, and in the courts, by perjured testimony, by the admissions of treacherous counsel, by the oppression of the Bell millions, by the precedents fraudulently established.

Professor Gray is now sixty four years of age, a resident of Highland Park, near Chicago, and still an active worker in the electrical field. A patent was issued to him some months ago. He is a professor in Oberlin College, at which he studied in his youth, a raw blacksmith's apprentice. His has been a long and wonderfully interesting life. Professor Dolbear, of Tufts College, was bred, like Gray and Edison and Short, in the telephone school of Ohio. Dolbear was graduated from the Ohio Wesleyan College, at Delaware, in 1866, having already invented a "magneto electric telegraph." Going as professor of physics to Tufts in 1874, Professor Dolbear shortly afterwards began experimenting in telephony and the conversion of sound vibration into electricity. In 1876, the year of Gray's caveat and Bell's application, he actually invented a speaking telephone, but not until September. Bell's first patent had already been issued in March; his second patent had been applied for. Before Dolbear had completed the model of his speaking telephone, to be filed in the Patent Office, he "was informed," the records say, "that Professor A. Graham Bell had declared that he had secured a patent upon the same thing."

That was the Bell-Dolbear encounter, and Professor Dolbear was unhorsed, like all the other anti-Bell champions. In 1881 Professor Dolbear secured a patent upon a new (static) system of telephony. His original rights are believed to have passed to the Bell company by purchase.

Speaking of the Bell telephone exhibits at the Centennial Exposition, Professor Dolbear says in his book on "The Telephone":

> That was the first speaking telephone that was ever constructed so far as the writer is aware, but it was not a practical instrument.

If the original Bell telephone was the "first speaking telephone," then the Bell contention is gained. There is no doubt that it was soon made "practical," and the courts have consistently refused to impeach the means used to reach that result. And once more there is an apparent vindication of the intelligence, energy, and resourcefulness of the man who tried so hard to sell Don Cameron a one third interest in the Bell telephone for ten thousand dollars "that Senator Cameron ordered the 'crazy inventor' to be turned way from his door."

That was in 1878; and a quarter of a century has never in the history of the world seen such marvelous developments from any one product of man's mechanical genius as have crowned what has all that time remained and is yet "the Bell telephone."

Appendix B

Shortly after the death of Elisha Gray, the following article appeared in Electrical World and Engineer *for February 2, 1901. (The G. C. Maynard referred to was affiliated with the Bell Telephone Company. He was also the same Maynard who earlier had owned an electrical supply store and about whom Bell once complained, "was evidently trying to humbug me." See chap. 4.)*

Dr. Elisha Gray and the Invention of the Telephone

An article by Mr. George C. Maynard, which appeared recently in one of our contemporaries, on the early days of the telephone, gave the impression that Dr. Elisha Gray had conceded to Prof. Bell priority in the invention of the telephone, and had consented to the public recognition of such priority. The sudden death of Dr. Gray noted in these columns last week, has led to the republication of Mr. Maynard's statement, and under the circumstances we feel constrained to publish the letter from Dr. Gray, written to us on Jan 14 from Boston. From this letter it will be seen that whatever may have been his earlier attitude on the subject, Dr. Gray died fighting strenuously against any idea that Prof. Bell was entitled to priority. We feel that, while in no sense committing ourselves to any approval or endorsement of what Dr. Gray asserts, we must, as a matter of duty, let his letter appear as part of the history of the invention of the telephone, as regarded by one of the leading participators. The paragraph from Mr. Maynard's article is as follows:

"Early on the morning of Feb. 14, 1876, Bell's application for a patent on his invention, which had been carefully prepared months before, was filed in the United States Patent Office. On the afternoon of that day the attorney for Elisha Gray sent to the Patent Office, the amount of money required as a fee for filing a caveat, which, at that time, had not even been written. The document was hastily prepared and rushed to the Patent Office just before the department closed on that day. Gray's caveat did not describe an invention, but gave an indefinite explanation of what he hoped to invent. In the ensuing controversy, growing out of interference proceedings and culminating in bitter legal battles and much newspaper discussion, it has often been stated that Prof. Bell's was granted through some irregular or dishonest action on the part of Major Z. F. Wilbur, the principal examiner, who had charge of the telephone cases. The statement is not true. Wilbur was then, and thereafter continued to be, hostile to Bell, whose patent was issued in March 1876. It is much to the credit of Mr. Gray that he recognized and publicly declared that Bell, and not himself, was the first inventor of the telephone."

Dr. Gray's letter is as follows:

I have been reading George C. Maynard's article, that stirs me up a little. "On the afternoon of that day," etc., is a fine touch of romance. I was there—had been for a number of days. The caveat was prepared deliberately, and completed the day before it was filed; and my recollection was that it was filed in the morning of Feb. 14. There was no reason for haste; I did not know or suspect that Bell was working on anything of the kind at that time, so that "hastily prepared and rushed" is a fairy story and a vile insinuation that I had wind of Bell's application, presumably through the accommodating Wilbur. After some years, the Government instituted an investigation as to the habits of the Patent Office, and found that cases as they came in were thrown into a basket till 3 p.m. when they were taken out and entered on the "blotter." My case was near the bottom of the basket and entered near the last. Bell's was near the head of the list. So whatever evidence there is, is in favor of the caveat having been filed first. As to his statement that the caveat was an "indefinite explanation of what he hoped to invent," I will say that not only myself, but others—notably Bell himself—constructed [an] apparatus after the drawings and description of my caveat, and it worked. Bell is on record as saying that it was with the liquid variable resistance transmitter that he obtained the first speech transmission. This he swears to in the Dowd suit. Wilbur swears, as you will see by the affidavit I send you, that he showed Bell my caveat a few days before Bell says he obtained his first articulate speech.

Now, if what Wilbur swears to in this affidavit is true, I showed Bell *how* to make the telephone. He could not mistake it, because the drawings were explicit, as well as the specifications. I am convinced, on testimony independent of the Wilbur affidavit. Wilber declared, so says a friend of his, on his death bed that his last affidavit was true. This document was given in the suit, and afterward sent to me. After the Centennial Exhibition, I did give the right to Bell, in a letter I wrote him, on the ground that he first constructed a machine and obtained results. Two or three letters passed, and in one of them I told him of the caveat. In his answer he said: "*I do not know about* your caveat, except that it had something to do with a wire vibrating in water," or words to that effect. "Vibrating in water" was the whole thing. How would he know that much?

They published garbled statements all over the world from my letter to him, that would have conveyed a different meaning if the whole correspondence had been published. When I wrote him, I believed that he had done all his work up to the time of the Centennial independent of any knowledge of my work; and because he was first to reduce the invention to practice I conceded it to him. And, notwithstanding there were suspicious circumstances early in the history of the telephone, it was not until eight or ten years—at least, a long time after the telephone was in use—that I became convinced, chiefly through Bell's own testimony in the various suits, that I had shown him *how* to construct the telephone with which he obtained his first results.

The statement in *Munsey* that I received $100,000, or any amount, for conceding priority to Bell is a *lie*. It is not true that Wilbur was hostile to Bell at the time of the filing of our cases. I, on the other hand, was but slightly acquainted with him. Some years after, I met Wilbur on the street in New York. He came up to me and said, "Gray, you invented the telephone, and if your damned lawyers had done their duty, you would have had it. But at that time I did not know you very well, and you had never given me any cigars or asked me out to take a drink." Ye Gods! A drink and a cigar might have saved me millions!

I send you a brief marked for your reference. Now, I don't know as all this interests you. You are at liberty to make use of the information contained in these documents if you see fit. You may say that Wilbur's statements are discredited in the fact of his life and character. I answer, that no other kind of man would do such a dastardly thing. The fact that he was the kind of man he makes himself out is strong proof that he did what he says he did.

We don't know what was in the brief that Gray mentioned, but apparently it pertained to Wilber's confession in his affidavit that he had illegally allowed Bell knowledge of Gray's caveat. Wilber had died by the time Gray's letter appeared and, of course, could not reply to the charges. However, as we have seen, other testimony bears out the fact that Wilber did not adhere to the Patent Officc's rule of strict confidentiality. This was not the first time that charges of Patent Office impropriety had occurred. During the challenges to Samuel Morse's telegraph patent, a similar charge was leveled against the Patent Office but apparently was never substantiated.

A few comments on the article by Maynard, who as earlier stated was associated with the Bell Telephone Company, may be in order. The statement that Bell's application (for Patent No. 174,465) "had been carefully prepared months before" does not square with the facts. Where Maynard obtained this information is unknown, as Bell's own court testimony refutes it. Bell didn't finish the final draft until just about a week before the application was notarized and returned to Pollok and Bailey.

In reference to Gray's caveat, Maynard stated that it "did not describe an invention, but gave an indefinite explanation of what he hoped to invent." It would appear that Maynard never saw the caveat, which was so explicit as to leave no doubt as to its purpose. If ever there was an "indefinite explanation," it was in Bell's patent not Gray's caveat.

Despite a long career of design and product development, Gray still found time to become a professor of physics at Oberlin College, his alma mater. He had accumulated scores of patents over his lifetime and was considered one of the foremost engineers of his era. It has been said, but never verified, that Gray made more money from his patents than Bell did from his, but that he spent most of it on research. It's reasonably possible, but very few inventors ever become truly rich. For every Bell or Edison, there are a hundred other inventors who receive little more than the satisfaction of having created something that never existed before. Gray lived well, but there is nothing to indicate that he enjoyed Bell's lifestyle.

Appendix C

Patent Office Copy of Gray's Caveat, Feb. 14, 1876

To whom it may concern: Be it known that I, Elisha Gray, of Chicago, in the county of Cook, and state of Illinois, have invented a new art of transmitting vocal sounds telegraphically, of which the following is a specification:

It is the object of my invention to transmit the tones of the human voice through a telegraphic circuit, and reproduce them at the receiving end of the line, so that actual conversations can be carried on by persons at a long distance apart.

I have invented and patented methods of transmitting musical impressions or sounds telegraphically, and my present invention is based on a modification of the principle of said invention, which is set forth and described in letters patent of the United States, granted to me July 27th, 1875, respectively numbered 166,095 and 166,096, and also in an application for letters patent of the United States, filed by me, February 28, 1875.

To attain the objects of my invention, I devised an instrument capable of vibrating responsively to all the tones of the human voice, and by which they are rendered audible.

In the accompanying drawings I have shown an apparatus embodying my improvements in the best way now known to me, but I contemplate various other applications, and also changes in the details of construction of the apparatus, some of which would obviously suggest

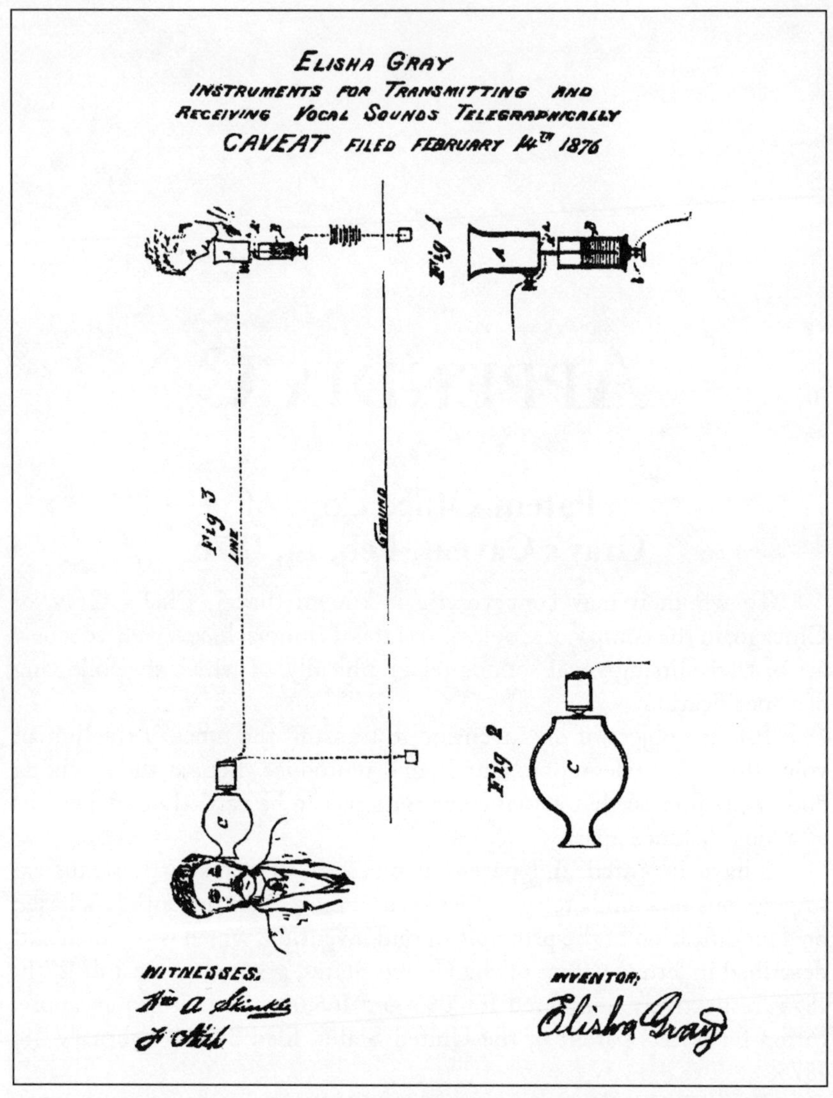

C-1. First page of Gray's caveat.

themselves to a skillful electrician, or a person versed in the science of acoustics, on seeing this application.

Fig. 1 represents a vertical central section through the transmitting instrument;

Fig. 2, a similar section through the receiver; and

Fig. 3, a diagram representing the whole apparatus.

My present belief is that the most effective method of providing an apparatus capable of responding to the various tones of the human voice, is a tympanum, drum or diaphragm, stretched across one end of the chamber, carrying an apparatus for producing fluctuations in the potential of the electric current, and consequently varying its power.

In the drawings, the person transmitting sounds is shown as talking into a box, or chamber, A, across the outer end of which is stretched a diaphragm *a*, of some thin substance, such as parchment or gold-beaters' skin, capable of responding to all of the vibrations of the human voice, whether simple or complex. Attached to this diaphragm is a light metal rod, A', or other suitable conductor of electricity, which extends into vessel B, made of glass or other insulating material, having its lower end closed by a plug, which may be made of metal, or through which passes a conductor *b*, forming part of the circuit.

This vessel is filled with some liquid possessing high resistance, such, for instance, as water, so that the vibrations of the plunger or rod A', which does not quite touch the conductor *b*, will cause variations in resistance, and, consequently, in the potential of the current passing through the rod A'.

Owing to this construction, the resistance varies constantly in response to the variations of the diaphragm, which, although irregular, not only in their amplitude, but in rapidity, are nevertheless transmitted, and can, consequently, be transmitted through the single rod, which could not be done with a positive make and break of the circuit employed, or where contact points are used.

I contemplate, however, the use of a series of diaphragms in a common vocalizing chamber, each diaphragm carrying an independent rod, and responding to a vibration of different rapidity and intensity, in which case contact points mounted on other diaphragms may be employed.

The vibrations thus imparted are transmitted through an electric circuit to the receiving station, in which circuit is included an electro-magnet of ordinary construction, acting upon a diaphragm to which is attached a piece of soft iron, and which diaphragm is stretched across a receiving vocalizing chamber A.

The diaphragm at the receiving end of the line is thus thrown into vibrations corresponding with those at the transmitting end, and audible sounds or words are produced.

The obvious practical application of my improvement will be to enable persons at a distance to converse with each other through a telegraphic circuit, just as they now do in each other's presence, or through a speaking tube.

I claim as my invention the art of transmitting vocal sounds or conversations telegraphically through an electric circuit.

Gray's Comments from Prescott's *The Speaking Telephone* (1879)

"Although it is not my intention, as I said in the beginning, to raise the question of priority of invention as between myself and other parties, I will nevertheless state in this connection, that so far as I am aware, this is the first description on record, of an articulating telephone which transmits the spoken words of the human voice telegraphically by means of electricity" (p. 205).

Appendix D

Patent Office Copy of Bell's Patent No. 174,465 (Filed February 14, 1876; published March 7, 1876)

To all whom it may concern:

Be it known that I, Alexander Graham Bell, of Salem, Massachusetts, have invented certain new and useful improvements in telegraphy, of which the following is a specification.

In letters patent granted to me April 6, 1875, No. 161,739, I have described a method of, and apparatus for, transmitting two or more telegraphic signals simultaneously along a single wire by the employment of transmitting instruments, each of which occasions a succession of electrical impulses differing in rate from the others; and of receiving instruments, each tuned to a pitch at which it will be put in vibration to produce its fundamental note by one only of the transmitting instruments; and of vibratory circuit-breakers operating to convert the vibratory movement of the receiving instrument into a permanent make or break (as the case may be) of a local circuit, in which is placed a Morse sounder, register, or other telegraphic apparatus. I have also therein described a form of autographic telegraph based upon the action of the above mentioned instruments.

In illustration of my method of multiple telegraphy I have shown in the patent aforesaid, as one form of transmitting instrument, an electromagnet having a steel spring armature, which is kept in vibration by the action of a local battery. This armature in vibrating makes and breaks the

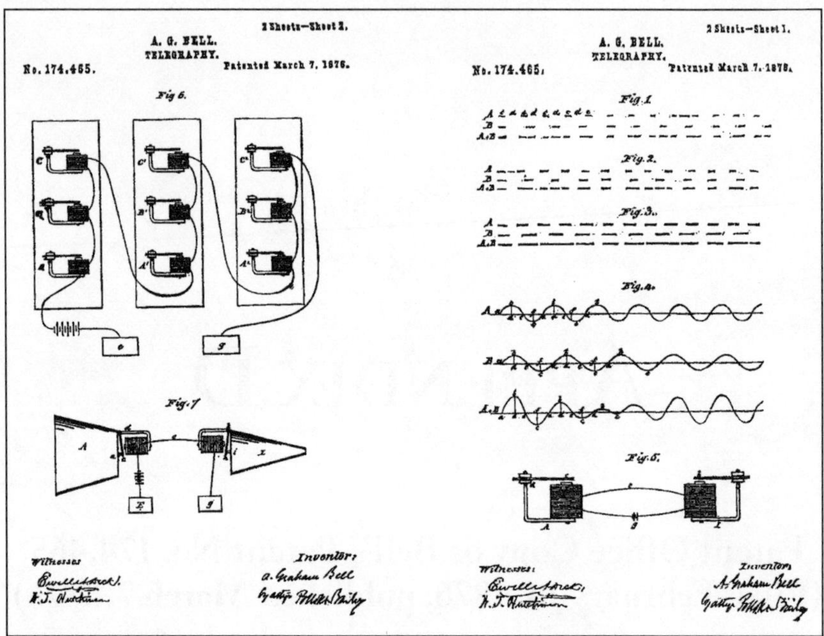

D-1. First page of Bell's Patent No. 174,465.

main circuit, producing an intermittent current upon the line wire. I have found, however, that upon this plan the limit to the number of signals that can be sent simultaneously over the same wire is speedily reached; for, when a number of transmitting instruments, having different rates of vibration, are simultaneously making and breaking the same circuit, the effect upon the main line is practically equivalent to one continuous current.

In a pending application for letters patent, filed in the United States Patent Office February 25, 1875, I have described two ways of producing the intermittent current—the one by actual make and break of contact, the other by alternately increasing and diminishing the intensity of the current without actually breaking the circuit. The current produced by the latter method I shall term, for distinction sake, a pulsatory current.

My present invention consists in the employment of a vibratory or undulatory current of electricity, in contradistinction to a merely intermittent or pulsatory current, and of a method of, and apparatus for, producing electrical undulations upon the line wire.

The distinction between an undulating and a pulsatory current will be understood by considering that electrical pulsations are caused by sudden or instantaneous changes of intensity, and that electrical undulations result from gradual changes of intensity exactly analogous to the changes in the density of air occasioned by simple pendulous vibrations. The electrical movement, like the aerial motion, can be represented by a sinusoidal curve or by the resultant of several sinusoidal curves.

Intermittent or pulsatory and undulatory currents may be of two kinds, according as the successive have all the same polarity or are alternately positive and negative.

The advantages I claim to derive from the use of undulatory current in place of a merely intermittent one are, first, that a very much larger number of signals can be transmitted simultaneously on the same circuit; second, that a closed circuit and single main battery may be used; third, that communication in both directions is established without the necessity of special induction coils; fourth, that cable dispatches may be transmitted more rapidly than by means of an intermittent current or by the methods at present in use; for, as it is unnecessary to discharge the cable before a new signal can be made, the lagging of cable signals is prevented; fifth, and that as the circuit is never broken, a spark-arrester becomes unnecessary.

It has long been known that when a permanent magnet is caused to approach the pole of an electro-magnet a current of electricity is induced in the coils of the latter, and that when it is made to recede a current of opposite polarity to the first appears upon the wire. When, therefore, a permanent magnet is caused to vibrate in front of the pole of an electro-magnet an undulatory current of electricity is induced in the coils of the electro-magnet, the undulations of which correspond, in rapidity of succession, to the vibrations of the magnet, in polarity to the direction of its motion, and in intensity to the amplitude of its vibrations.

That the difference between an undulatory and an intermittent current may be more clearly understood, I shall describe the condition of the electrical current when the attempt is made to transmit two musical notes simultaneously—first upon the one plan and then upon the other. Let the interval between the two sounds be a major third; then their rates of vibration are in the ratio of 4 to 5. Now, when the intermittent current is used, the circuit is made and broken four times by one transmitting instrument in the same time that five makes and breaks are caused by the other. A and B, figs. 1, 2 and 3, represent the intermittent currents produced, four impulses of B being made in the same time as five impulses of A. *c c c*, etc., show where and for how long the circuit is made, and *d d d*, etc., indicate the duration of the breaks of the circuit. The line A and B shows the total effect upon the current when the transmitting instruments for A and

B are caused simultaneously to make and break the same circuit. The resultant effect depends very much upon the duration of the make relative to the break. In fig. 1 the ratio is as 1 to 4; in fig. 2, as 1 to 2; and in fig. 3 the makes and breaks are of equal duration. The combined effect, A and B, fig. 3, is very nearly equivalent to a continuous current.

When many transmitting instruments of different rates of vibration are simultaneously making and breaking the same circuit, the current upon the main lines becomes for all practical purposes continuous.

Next, consider the effect when an undulatory current is employed. Electrical undulations, induced by the vibration of a body capable of inductive action, can be represented graphically, without error, by the same sinusoidal curve which expresses the vibration of the inducing body itself, and the effect of its vibrations upon the air; for, as above stated, the rate of oscillation in the electrical current corresponds to the rate of vibration of the inducing body—that is, to the pitch of the sound produced. The intensity of the current varies with the amplitude of the vibration—that is, to the condensations and rarefactions of air produced by the vibrations, Hence, the sinusoidal curve A or B, fig. 4, represents, graphically, the electrical undulations induced in a circuit by the vibrations of a body capable of inductive action.

The horizontal line *a d e f*, etc., represents the zero current. The elevation *b b b*, etc., indicates the impulses of positive electricity. The depressions *c c c*, etc., show impulses of negative electricity. The vertical distance *b d* or *c f* of any portion of the curve from the zero line expresses the intensity of the positive or negative impulse at the part observed, and the horizontal distance *a a* indicates the duration of the electrical oscillation. The vibrations represented by the sinusoidal curves B and A, fig. 4 are in the ratio aforesaid, of 4 to 5—that is, four oscillations of B are made in the same time as five oscillations of A.

The combined effect of A and B, when induced simultaneously on the same circuit, is expressed by the curve A+B, fig. 4, which is the algebraical sum of the sinusoidal curves A and B. This curve A+B also indicates the actual motion of the air when the two musical notes considered are sounded simultaneously. Thus, when electrical undulations of different rates are simultaneously induced in the same circuit, an effect is produced analogous to that occasioned in the air by the vibration of the inducing bodies. Hence, the coexistence upon a telegraphic circuit of electrical vibrations of different pitch is manifested, not by the obliteration of the vibratory character of the current, but by the peculiarities in the shapes of the electrical undulations, or, in other words, by peculiarities in the shapes of the curves which represent those undulations.

There are many ways of producing undulatory currents of electricity, depending for effect upon the vibrations or motions of bodies capable of inductive action. A few of the methods that may be employed I shall here specify. When a wire, through which a continuous current of electricity is passing, is caused to vibrate in the neighborhood of another wire, an undulatory current of electricity is induced in the latter. When a cylinder, upon which are arranged bar magnets, is made to rotate in front of the pole of an electro-magnet, an undulatory current of electricity is induced in the coils of the electro-magnet.

Undulations are caused in a continuous voltaic current by the vibration or motion of bodies capable of inductive action; or by the vibration of the conducting wire itself in the neighborhood of such bodies. Electrical undulations may also be caused by alternately increasing and diminishing the resistance of the circuit, or by alternately increasing or diminishing the power of the battery. The internal resistance of a battery is diminished by bringing the voltaic elements nearer together, and increased by placing them farther apart. The reciprocal vibration of the elements of a battery, therefore, occasions an undulatory action in the voltaic current. The external resistance may also be varied. For instance, let mercury or some other liquid form part of a voltaic circuit, the more deeply the conducting wire is immersed in the mercury or other liquid, the less resistance does the liquid offer to the passage of the current. Hence, the vibration of the conducting wire in mercury or other liquid included in the circuit occasions undulations in the current. The vertical vibrations of the elements of a battery in the liquid in which they are immersed produces an undulatory action in the current by alternately increasing and diminishing the power of the battery.

In illustration of the method of creating electrical undulations, I shall show and describe one form of apparatus for producing the effect. I prefer to employ for this purpose an electro-magnet A, fig. 5, having a coil upon only one of its legs *b*. A steel spring armature *c* is firmly clamped by one extremity to the uncovered leg *d* of the magnet, and its free end is allowed to project above the pole of the covered leg. The armature *c* can be set in vibration in a variety of ways, one of which is by wind, and, in vibrating, it produces a musical note of a certain definite pitch.

When the instrument A is placed in a voltaic circuit, *g b e f g*, the armature *c* becomes magnetic, and the polarity of its free end is opposed to that of the magnet underneath. So long as the armature *c* remains at rest no effect is produced upon the voltaic current, but the moment it is set in vibration to produce its musical note a powerful inductive action takes place, and electrical undulations traverse the circuit *g b e f g*. The vibratory current passing through the coil of the electro-magnet *f* causes vibration in its armature *h*, when the armature *c h* of the two instruments A I are normally in unison with each other; but the armature *h* is unaffected by the passage of the undulatory current when the pitches of the two instruments are different.

A number of instruments may be placed upon a telegraphic circuit, as in fig. 6. When the armature of any one of the instruments is set in vibration, all the other instruments upon the circuit which are in unison with it respond, but those which have normally a different rate of vibration remain silent. Thus, if A, fig. 6, is set in vibration, the armatures of A^1 and A^2 will vibrate also, but all the others on the circuit will remain still. So if B^1 is caused to emit its musical note, the instruments B B^2 respond. They continue sounding so long as the mechanical vibration on B^1 is continued, but become silent with the cessation of its motion. The duration of the sound may be used to indicate the dot or dash of the Morse alphabet, and thus a telegraphic dispatch may be indicated by alternately interrupting and renewing the sound. When two or more instruments of different pitch are simultaneously caused to vibrate, all the instruments of corresponding pitches upon the circuit are set in vibration, each responding to that one only of the transmitting instruments with which it is in unison. Thus the signals of A, fig. 6, are repeated by A^1 and A^2, but by no other instrument upon the circuit; the signal of B^2 by B and B^1; and the signals of C^1 by C and C^2—whether A, B^2 and C^1 are successively or simultaneously caused to vibrate. Hence by these instruments two or more telegraphic signals or messages may be sent simultaneously over the same circuit without interfering with one another.

I desire here to remark that there are many other uses to which these instruments may be put, such as the simultaneous transmission of musical notes, differing in loudness as well as pitch, and the telegraphic transmission of noises or sounds of any kind.

When the armature *c*, fig. 5, is set in vibration, the armature *h* responds not only in pitch, but in loudness. Thus, when *c* vibrates with little amplitude, a very soft musical note proceeds from *h*; and when *c* vibrates forcibly the amplitude of the vibration of *h* is considerably increased, and the resulting sound becomes louder. So, if A and B, fig. 6, are sounded simultaneously (A loudly and B softly), the instruments A^1 and A^2 repeat loudly the signals of A, and B^1 B^2 repeat softly those of B.

One of the ways in which the armature of *c*, fig. 5, may be set in vibration has been stated before to be by wind. Another mode is shown in Fig. 7, whereby motion can be imparted to the armature by the human voice or by means of a musical instrument.

The armature *c*, fig. 7, is fastened loosely by one extremity to the uncovered leg *d* of the electro-magnet *b*, and its other extremity is attached to the centre of a stretched membrane, *a*. A cone, A, is used to converge sound-vibrations upon the membrane. When a sound is uttered in the cone the membrane *a* is set in the vibration, the armature *c* is forced to partake of the motion, and thus electrical undulations are created upon the circuit E *b e f g*. These undulations are similar in form to the air vibrations caused by the sound—that is, they are represented graphically by similar curves. The undulatory current passing through the electro-magnet *f* influences its armature *h* to copy the motion of the armature *c*. A similar sound to that uttered into A is then heard to proceed from I.

In this specification the three words, "oscillation," "vibration," and "undulation," arc used synonymously, and in contradistinction to the terms "intermittent" and "pulsatory." By the term "body capable of inductive action," I mean a body which, when in motion, produces dynamical electricity. I include in the category of bodies capable of inductive action brass, copper, and other metals, as well as iron and steel.

Having described my invention, what I claim, and desire to secure by letters patent, is as follows:

1. A system of telegraphy in which the receiver is set in vibration by the employment of undulatory currents of electricity, substantially as set forth.
2. The combination, substantially as set forth, of a permanent magnet or other body capable of inductive action, with a closed circuit, so that the vibration of the one shall occasion electrical undulations in the other, or in itself, and this I claim, whether the permanent magnet be set in vibration in the neighborhood of the conducting wire forming the circuit, or whether the conducting wire be set in vibration in the neighborhood of the permanent magnet, or whether the conducting wire and the permanent magnet both simultaneous be set in vibration in each other's neighborhood.
3. The method of producing undulations in a continuous voltaic circuit by the vibration or motion of bodies capable of inductive action, or by the vibration or motion of the conducting wire itself, in the neighborhood of such bodies, as set forth.
4. The method of producing undulations in a continuous voltaic circuit by gradually increasing and diminishing the resistance of the circuit, or by gradually increasing or diminishing the power of the battery, as set forth.

5. The method of, and apparatus for, transmitting vocal or other sounds telegraphically, as herein described, by causing electrical undulations, similar in form to the vibrations of the air accompanying the said vocal or other sounds, substantially as set forth.

Appendix E

Patent Office Copy of Bell's Patent No. 186,787 Filed: January 15, 1877; published January 30, 1877

To all whom it may concern:

Be it known that I, Alexander Graham Bell, of Boston, Massachusetts, have invented certain new and useful improvements in Electric Telephony, of which the following is a specification:

In Letters Patent granted to me on the 6th day of April, 1875, No. 161,739, and in an application for Letters Patent of the United States now pending, I have described a method of an apparatus for producing musical tones by the action of a rapidly-interrupted electrical current, whereby a number of telegraphic signals can be sent simultaneously along a single circuit.

In another application for Letters Patent now pending in the United States Patent Office I have described a method of, and apparatus for, inducing an intermittent current of electricity upon a wire, whereby musical tones can be produced, and a number of telegraphic signals be sent simultaneously over the same circuit, in either one or both directions; and in Letters Patent granted to me March 7, 1876, No. 174,465, I have shown and described a method of an apparatus for producing musical tones by the action of undulatory currents of electricity, whereby a number of telegraphic signals can be sent simultaneously over the same circuit, in either or both directions, and a single battery be used for the whole circuit.

In the applications and patents above referred to, signals are transmitted simultaneously along a single wire by the employment of

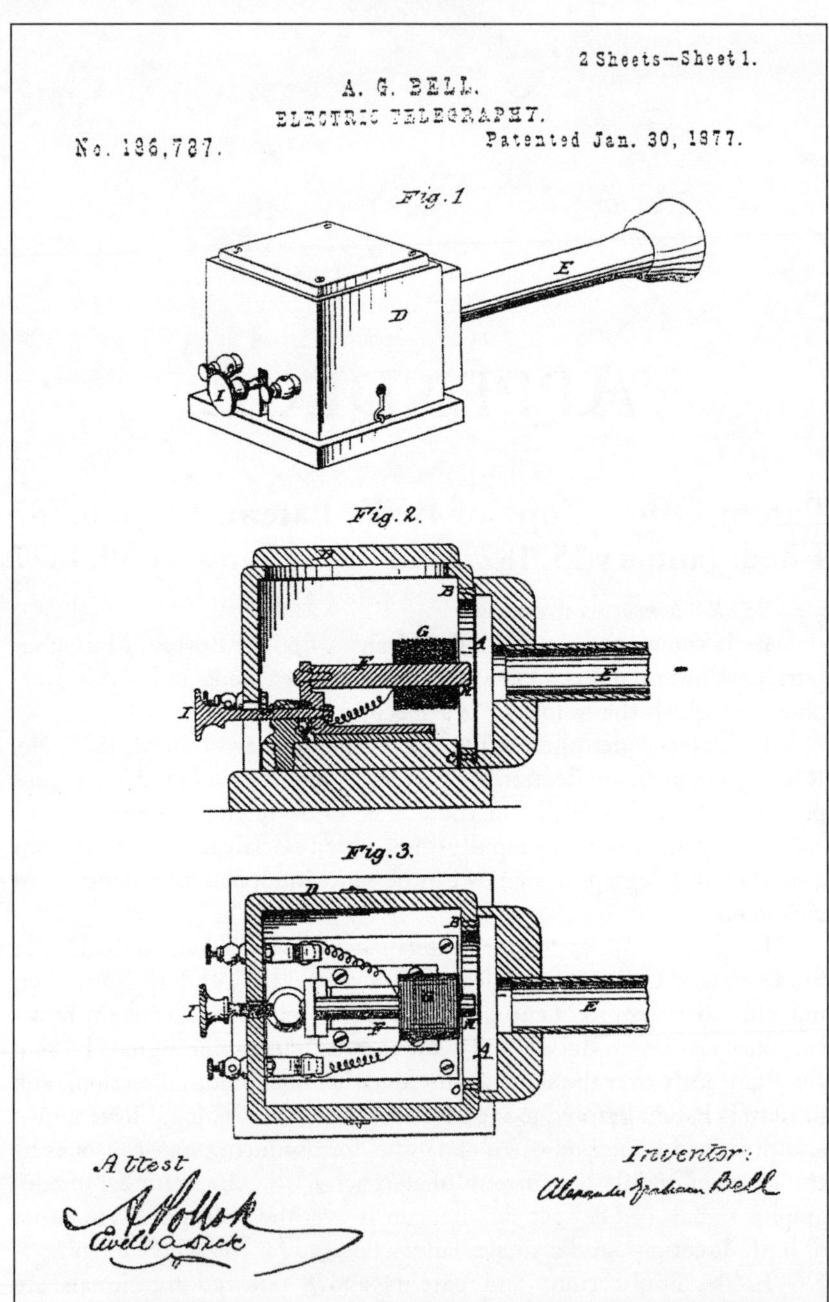

E-1. Page one of Bell's second patent, No. 186,787.

transmitting instruments, each of which occasions a succession of electrical impulses differing in rate from the others, and are received without confusion by means of receiving instruments, each tuned to a pitch at which it will be put in vibration to produce its fundamental note by one only of transmitting instruments. A separate instrument is therefore employed for every pitch, each instrument being capable of transmitting or receiving but a single note, and thus as many separate instruments are required as there are messages or musical notes to be transmitted.

My invention has for its object, first, the transmission simultaneously of two or more musical notes or telegraphic signals along a single wire in either or both directions, and with a single battery for the whole circuit without the use of as many instruments as there are musical notes or telegraphic signals to be transmitted; second, the electrical transmission by the same means of articulate speech and sounds of every kind without the necessity of using a voltaic battery.

In my Patent No. 174,465, dated March 7, 1876, I have shown as one form of transmitting instrument a stretched membrane, to which the armature of an electro-magnet is attached, whereby motion can be imparted to the armature by the human voice, or by means of a musical instrument, or by sounds produced in any way.

In accordance with my present invention I substitute for the membrane and armature shown in the transmitting and receiving instruments alluded to above, a plate of iron or steel capable of being thrown into vibrations by sounds made in its neighborhood.

The nature of my invention and the manner in which the same is or may be carried into effect will be understood by reference to the accompanying drawings, in which—

Figure 1 is a perspective view of one form of my electric telephone. Fig. 2 is a vertical section of the same, and Fig. 3 is a plan view of the apparatus. Fig. 4 is a diagram illustrating the arrangement upon circuit.

Similar letters in the drawings represent corresponding portions of the apparatus.

A, in said drawings, represents a plate of iron or steel, which is fastened at B and C to cover of sounding box D. E represents a speaking-tube, by which sounds may be conveyed to or from the plate A. F is a bar of soft iron. G is a coil of insulated copper wire around the extremity of the end H of the bar F. I is an adjusting-screw, whereby the distance of the end H from the plate A may be regulated.

The electric telephones J, K, L, and M are placed at different stations upon a line, and are arranged upon the circuit with a battery, N, as shown in diagram, Fig. 4.

I have shown the apparatus in one of its simplest forms, it being well understood that the same may be varied in arrangement, combination, general construction, and form, as well as material of which the several parts are composed.

The operation and use of this instrument are as follows:

I would premise by saying that this instrument is and may be used both as a transmitter and as a receiver—that is to say, the sender of the message will use an instrument in every particular identical in construction and operation with that employed by the receiver, so that the same instrument can be used alternately as a receiver and a transmitter.

In order to transmit a telegraphic message by means of these instruments, it is only necessary for the operator at a telephone, (say J) to make a musical sound, in any way, in the neighborhood of the plate A—for convenience of operation through the speaking-tube E—and to let the duration of the sound signify the dot or dash of the Morse alphabet, and for the operator, who receives the message, say at M, to listen to his telephone, preferably through the speaking-tube E. When two or more musical signals are being transmitted over the same circuit all the telephones reproduce the signals for all the messages; but as the signals for each message differ in pitch from those for the other messages it is easy for an operator to fix his attention on one message and ignore the others.

When a large number of dispatches are being simultaneously transmitted it will be advisable for the operator to listen to his telephone through a resonator, which will re-enforce his ear to the signals which he desires to observe. In this way he is enabled to direct his attention to the signals for any given message without being distracted or disturbed by the signals for any other messages that may be passing over the line at the time.

The musical signals, if preferred, can be automatically received by means of a resonator, one end of which is closed by a membrane, which vibrates only when the note with which the resonator is in unison is emitted by the receiving-telephone. The vibrations of the membrane may be made to operate a circuit-breaker, which will operate a Morse sounder or a telegraphic recording or registering apparatus.

One form of vibratory circuit-breaker which may be used for this purpose I have described in Letters Patent No. 178,399, June 6, 1876. Hence by this plan the simultaneous transmission of a number of telegraphic messages over a single circuit in the same or in both directions, with a single main battery for the whole circuit and a single telephone at each station, is rendered practical. This is of great advantage in that, for the conveyance of several messages, or signals, or sounds over a single wire

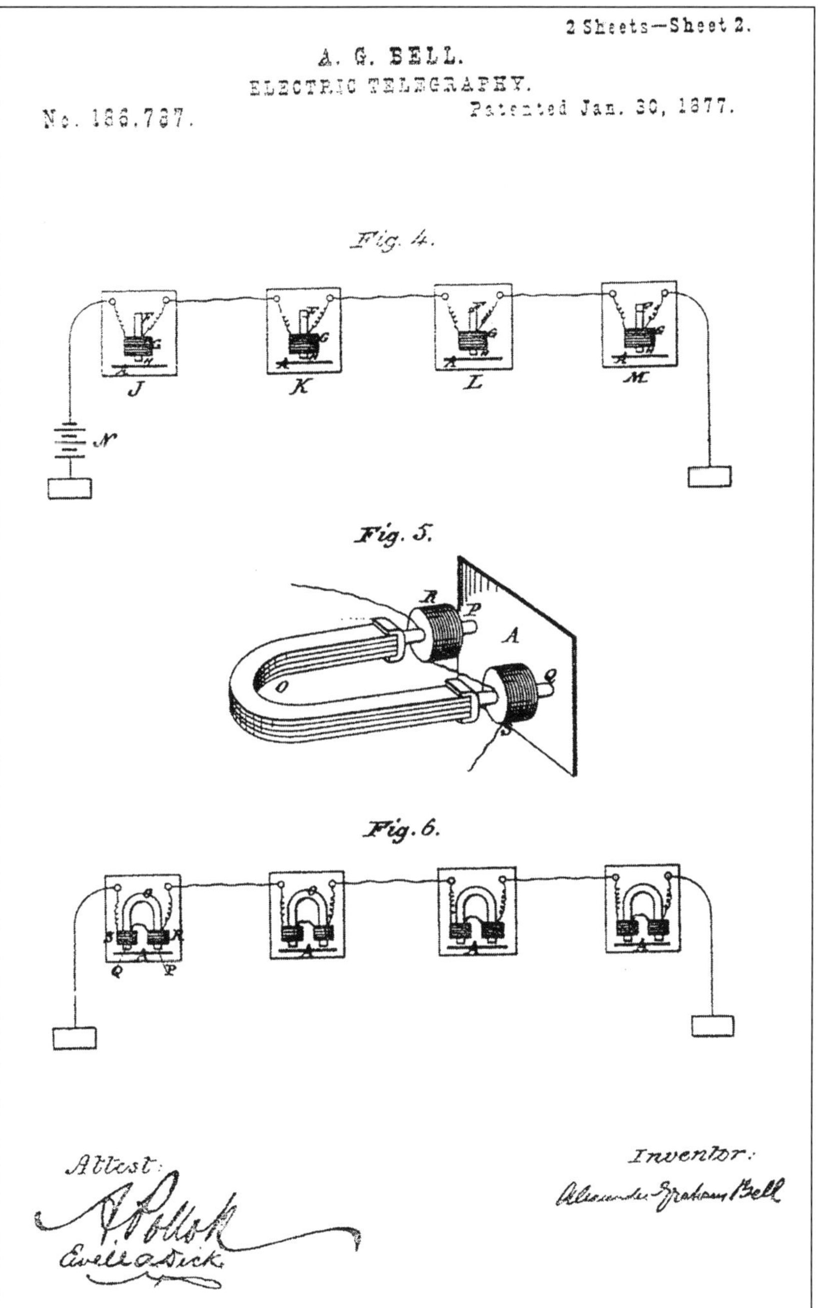

E-2. Page two of Bell's second patent, No. 186,787.

simultaneously, it is no longer necessary to have separate instruments correspondingly tuned for each given sound, which plan requires nice adjustment of the corresponding instruments, while the present improvement admits of a single instrument at each station; or, if for convenience several are employed, they all are alike in construction, and need not be adjusted or tuned to particular pitches.

Whatever sound is made in the neighborhood of any telephone, say at J, Fig. 4, is echoed in facsimile by the telephones of all the other stations upon the circuit; hence, this plan is also adapted for the use of transmitting intelligibly the exact sounds of articulate speech. To convey an articulate message it is only necessary for an operator to speak in the neighborhood of his telephone, preferably through the tube E, and for another operator at a distant station upon the same circuit to listen to the telephone at that station. If two people speak simultaneously in the neighborhood of the same or different telephones, the utterances of the two speakers are reproduced simultaneously by all the other telephones on the same circuit; hence, by this plan a number of vocal messages may be transmitted simultaneously on the same circuit in either or both directions. All the effects noted above may be produced by the same instruments without a battery by rendering the central bar F H permanently magnetic. Another form of telephone for use without a battery is shown in Fig. 5, in which O is a compound magnet, to the poles of which are affixed poll-pieces of soft iron P Q surrounded by helices of insulated wire R S.

Fig. 6 illustrates the arrangement upon circuits of similar instruments to that shown in Fig. 5.

In lieu of the plate A in above figures, iron or steel reeds of definite pitch may be placed in front of the electro-magnet O, and in connection with a series of such instruments of different pitches, an arrangement upon circuit may be employed similar to that shown in my Patent No. 174,465, and illustrated in Fig. 6 of Sheet 2 in said patent. The battery, of course, may be omitted.

This invention is not limited to the use of iron or steel, but includes within its scope any material capable of inductive action.

The essential feature of the invention consists in the armature of the receiving-instrument being vibrated by the varying attraction of the electro-magnet, so as to vibrate the air in the vicinity thereof in the same manner as the air is vibrated at the other end of the production of the sound. It is therefore by no means necessary or essential that the transmitting-instrument should be of the same construction as the receiving-instrument. Any instrument receiving and transmitting the impression of agitated air may be used as the transmitter, although for convenience, and for reciprocal communication, I prefer to use like instruments at either end of an electrical wire. I have heretofore described and exhibited such other means of transmitting sound, as will be seen by reference to the proceedings of the American Academy of Arts and Sciences, Volume XII.

For convenience, I prefer to apply to each instrument a call-bell. This may be arranged so as to ring, first, when the main circuit is opened; second, when the bar F comes into contact with the plate A. The first is done to call attention; the second indicates when it is necessary to readjust the magnet, for it is important that the distance of the magnet from the plate should be as little as possible, without, however, being in contact. I have also found that the electrical undulations produced upon the main line by the vibrations of the plate A are intensified by placing the coil G at the end of the bar F nearest the plate A, and not extend it beyond the middle, or thereabouts.

Having thus described my invention, what I claim, and desire to secure by Letters Patent, is—

1. The union upon, and by means of, an electric current of two or more instruments, constructed for operation substantially as herein shown and described, so that, if motion of any kind or form be produced in any way in the armature of any one of the said instruments, the armatures of all the other instruments upon the same circuit will be moved in like manner and form; and if such motion be produced in the former by sound, like sound will be produced by the motion of the latter.
2. In a system of electric telegraphy or telephony, consisting of transmitting or receiving instruments united upon an electric circuit, the production, in the armature of each receiving instrument, of any given motion, by subjecting said armature to an attraction varying in intensity, however such variation may be produced in the magnet, and hence I claim to production of any given sound or sounds from the armature of the receiving instrument, by subjecting said armature to an attraction varying in intensity, in such manner as to throw the armature into that form of vibration that characterizes the given sound or sounds.
3. The combination, with an electro-magnet, of a plate of iron, or steel, or other material capable of inductive action, which can be thrown into vibration by the movement of the surrounding air, or by the attraction of a magnet.
4. In combination with a plate and an electro-magnet, as before claimed, the means herein described, or their mechanical equivalents,

of adjusting the relative position of the two, so that, without touching, they may be set as closely together as possible.

5. The formation, in an electric telephone, such as herein shown and described, of a magnet with a coil upon the end or ends of the magnet nearest the plate.
6. The combination, with an electric telephone, such as described, of a sounding box, substantially as herein shown and set forth.
7. In combination with an electric telephone, as herein described, the employment of a speaking or hearing tube, for conveying sounds to or from the telephone, substantially as set forth.
8. In a system of electric telephony, the combination of a permanent magnet with a plate of iron or steel, or other material capable of inductive action, with the coils upon the end or ends of said magnet nearest the plate, substantially as set forth.

In testimony whereof I have here unto signed my name this 13th day of January, A.D. 1877.

A. Graham Bell

Appendix F

Charles Bourseul, *L'Illustration*, August 26, 1854

The idea of communicating over vast distances is nothing new. The ancient Jews used a visual telegraph to keep their lunar-solar calendar accurate. Observers stationed on distant mountains would watch for the first, faint glimmer of the new crescent moon after sunset, which signified the start of a new month. The moment it was detected, a bonfire was lit to communicate the event to the priests in the temples. Whether this was the first instance of telecommunications is unimportant; the concept of communicating beyond the range of the human voice is old.

As we have seen, communicating with electricity is also old. But whether the communication was by visual or electrical means, it had always involved a prearranged code. The idea of using electricity to communicate directly by the spoken word was surely contemplated long ago, just as aviation and extraterrestrial travel were once contemplated. But until someone could offer at least a plausible scheme to accomplish it, it would always be dismissed as impractical woolgathering. In 1854 someone did just that.

In the 24th volume of the Parisian magazine *L'Illustration*, on August 26, 1854, Charles Bourseul not only said that electrical voice communication was possible but described in general terms a plan of how it could be accomplished. Other than the experiments he mentions in his article, there is no evidence that he ever reduced to practice the method he described. However, we do know that the basic elements he proposed were capable of transmitting vocal intelligence. In addition to the telephone, Bourseul describes as a fait accompli another instrument everyone today assumes to be a product of "modern" telecommunications: the fax machine.

> The electric telegraph is based on the following principle: An electric current, passing through a metallic wire, circulates through a coil around a piece of soft iron which it converts into a magnet. The moment the current stops, the piece of iron ceases to be a magnet. This magnet, which takes the name of electromagnet, can thus in turn attract and release a moveable plate [*plaque mobile*] which by its to-and-fro movement produces the conventional signals employed in telegraphy. Sometimes this movement is directly utilized, and is made to produce dots or dashes on a strip of paper which is drawn along by clockwork. The conventional signals are thus formed by a combination of those dots and dashes. This is the American telegraph, which bears the name of Morse, its inventor. Sometimes this to-and-fro movement is converted into a movement of rotation. In that way we have either the dial telegraph used on railroads, or the telegraph used in the government system, which by means of two line-wires and two indicating needles, reproduces all the signals of the aerial telegraph or semaphore which was formerly used. Suppose, now, that we arrange upon a moveable horizontal circle letters, figures, signs or pronunciations, &c. One can understand that the principle we have stated can be used to choose at a distance such and such a character, and to determine its movement, and consequently to print it on a sheet of paper appropriately placed for this purpose. This is the printing telegraph.
>
> We have gone still further. By the employment of the same principle, and by means of a mechanism rather complicated, it has been possible to reach a result which at first would seem to be almost a miracle. Handwriting itself is produced at a distance, and not only handwriting, but any line or any curve; so that, being in Paris, you can draw a profile by ordinary means there, and the same profile draws itself at the same time at Frankfurt. Attempts of this sort have succeeded. The apparatus has been exhibited at the London Exhibition. Some details, however, remain to be perfected. It would seem impossible to go beyond this in the region of the marvelous. Let us try, nevertheless, to go a few steps further. I have asked myself, for example, if the spoken word itself could not be transmitted by electricity; in a word, if what was spoken in Vienna may not be heard in Paris? The thing is practicable in this way:
>
> We know that sounds are made by vibrations, and are made sensible to the ear by the same vibrations, which are reproduced by the intervening medium. But the intensity of the vibrations diminishes very rapidly with the distance; so that even with the aid of speaking tubes and trumpets, it is impossible to exceed somewhat narrow limits. Suppose that a man speaks near a moveable disk, sufficiently flexible to lose none of the vibrations of the voice; that this disk alternately makes and breaks the connection with a battery: you may have at a distance another disk which will simultaneously execute the same vibrations.
>
> It is true that the intensity of the sounds produced will be variable at the

point of departure, at which the disk vibrates by means of the voice, and constant at the point of arrival, where it vibrates by means of electricity; but it has been shown that this does not change the sounds. It is, moreover, evident that the sounds will be reproduced at the same pitch.

The present state of acoustic science does not permit us to declare *a priori* if this will be precisely the case with syllables uttered by the human voice. The mode in which these syllables are produced has not yet been sufficiently investigated. It is true that we know that some are uttered by the teeth, others by the lips, &c.; but that is all.

However this may be, observe that the syllables can only reproduce upon the sense of hearing the vibrations of the intervening medium. Reproduce precisely these vibrations, and you will reproduce precisely these syllables.

It is, at all events, impossible, in the present condition of science, to prove the impossibility of transmitting sound by electricity. Everything tends to show, on the contrary, that there is such a possibility. When the application of electro-magnetism to the transmission of messages was first discussed, a man of great scientific attainments treated the idea as Utopian, and yet there is now direct communication between London and Vienna by means of a simple wire. Men declared it impossible, but it is done.

It need not be said that numerous applications of the highest importance will immediately arise from the transmission of speech by electricity. Any one who is not deaf and dumb may use this mode of transmission, which would require no apparatus except an electric battery, two vibrating disks and a wire. In many cases, as, for example, in large establishments, orders might be transmitted in this way, although transmission in this way will not be used while it is necessary to transmit letter by letter, and to make use of telegraphs which require use and apprenticeship. However this may be, it is certain that in a more or less distant future, speech will be transmitted by electricity. I have made some experiments in this direction. They are delicate, and demand time and patience; but the approximations obtained promise a favorable result.

Charles Bourseul
Paris, August 18, 1854

So there you have it: the fax machine preceded the telephone—by a good 20 years or more. This is somewhat of a paradox, considering the electromechanical complexity of a facsimile-machine to the basic simplicity of a telephone. Bourseul pointed out, however, that those first fax machines left much to be desired; they were crude devices, painfully slow and frustratingly cantankerous. Transmitter-receiver synchronization was a major problem. It wasn't until the mid-1880s, when Patrick Delany introduced his improved machine, that a reasonably practical fax machine appeared. But even this was soon forgotten; fax transmission was just another idea ahead of its time and the available technology. Elisha Gray was the only pioneer to make a commercial success of facsimile transmission with his invention of the telautograph (see chap. 1).

However, Bourseul's article seems to be the first one claiming that electrical transmission of speech was technically possible. Bourseul's method anticipated that of Germany's Philipp Reis, which brings up an interesting question: did Reis know of Bourseul's article and experiments? There is nothing to indicate that Reis did know of it, and nothing to indicate the contrary. It makes little difference even if Reis did know; he proved that Bourseul was correct in his prediction. However, the final vindication of Bourseul is found in Emile Berliner's "submarine" patent, No. 463,669, finally issued on November 17, 1891, after moldering in the Patent Office for 14 years (see chap. 15). It is almost identical to Bourseul's proposed design.

APPENDIX G

George Brown's Copy of Bell's Patent Application (ca. 1876)

This is a verbatim copy (from *U.S. Reports* [126 US 88] October term 1887) of Bell's patent application (U.S. No. Patent 174,465), which George Brown of Toronto took to England to secure a British patent. The exact date on which he received this copy has never been determined, but we do know that it was before he sailed for England on January 26, 1876.

This copy was retrieved from George Brown on November 12, 1878, by Thomas Watson, supposedly for use in the upcoming Dowd case. Although it was found among the Dowd documents, it was never introduced into that case and never mentioned during any of the other court cases that followed. It did not reappear again until 1887, when it was introduced in a brief filed by Lysander Hill, counsel for the People's Telephone Company, at the Supreme Court. Hill was attempting to prove that Bell's application had been fraudulently altered after it was filed at the Patent Office.

That this was a prior copy of the finished application that Bell gave to his attorneys on January 20 is quite apparent. In that era before copying machines, making exact copies of a document was a laborious operation, entailing the painstaking rewriting of the original document. Persons who could write with a good hand found steady employment as copyists (amanuenses). Therefore, to save both time and money, Bell would have used for Brown's copy a previous, but accurate, version of the final document. However, regardless of the nature of Brown's copy, it would have had to be recopied in England to meet British requirements. Since both Bell and Brown were well aware of this, there would have been little need for a letter-perfect version.

To preserve the original flavor of this document, in the form that it was offered into evidence at the Supreme Court, the following conventions have been used. Words that were marked for deletion (crossed out) are shown in square brackets [ ]. Words or phrases that were added (interlined) are shown in SMALL CAPS. These conventions will make it easy to compare this document with the final version of the issued patent No. 174,465 as shown in Appendix D, the version supposedly given to Bell's attorneys on January 20, 1876. The figures referred to in this copy are the same as those depicted in Appendix D.

The reader will note that, at the end of this document, Bell offers two versions of his claims. Both versions are essentially the same, differing only in detail. The important point to observe, however, is that in both versions there are only four claims, none of which mention the concept of variable resistance. The mysterious fourth claim that appears in the American patent, embracing variable resistance, was inserted between claims three and four of Brown's copy. Claim four of Brown's copy became claim five of the American patent.

Not only is there no mention in Brown's copy of using variable resistance to produce undulatory current, but Bell states midway through this document that "there are many ways of producing undulatory currents of electricity, but all of them depend for effect upon the vibration or motion of bodies capable of inductive action." In other words, in Bell's opinion at the time he wrote this, electromagnetic induction was the only method of producing undulatory currents. Other than the puzzling omission of the variable resistance clause and the fourth claim, Brown's copy and U.S. Patent No. 174,465 are essentially the same.

United States Patent Office

[Alexander Graham Bell of Salem, Assignor to Himself and Thomas Sanders of Haverhill, and Gardiner G. Hubbard of Cambridge, Massachusetts.]

To all whom it may concern, be it known, that I, Alexander Graham Bell of Salem, Massachusetts, have invented certain new and useful improvements in Telegraphy, of which the following is a specification:

In [another application for] Letters Patent granted to me [in] April 6th, 1875 (161,739), I have described a method of and apparatus for transmitting two or more telegraphic signals simultaneously along a single wire by the employment of *Transmitting Instruments*, each of which occasions a succession of electrical impulses differing in rate from the others; and of *Receiving Instruments* each tuned to a pitch at which it will be put in vibration to produce its fundamental tone by one only of the Transmitting Instruments; and of *Vibratory Circuit Breakers*, operating to convert the vibratory movement of the Receiving Instruments into a permanent make or break (as the case may be) of a local circuit in which is placed a Morse Sounder Register, or other telegraphic apparatus. I have also therein described a form of Autographic Telegraph based upon the action of the above mentioned instruments.

In illustration of my method of Multiple Telegraphy I have shown in the [application] PATENT aforesaid, as one form of Transmitting Instrument an electro-magnet having a steel spring armature which is kept in vibration by the action of a local battery. This armature in vibrating makes and breaks the main circuit, producing an intermittent current upon the line-wire. I have found, however, that upon this plan the limit to the number of signals that can be sent simultaneously over the same circuit is very speedily reached; for when a number of Transmitting Instruments, having different rates of vibration, are simultaneously making and breaking the same circuit, the effect upon the main line is practically equivalent to *one continuous current.*

My present invention consists in the employment of a vibratory or undulat[ing]ORY current of electricity in place of a merely intermittent one; and of a method of, and apparatus for, producing electrical undulations upon the line-wire. The advantages [claimed for the undulatory current over the] I CLAIM TO DERIVE FROM THE USE OF AN UNDULATORY CURRENT IN PLACE OF A merely intermittent one, are,

1. That a very much larger number of signals can be transmitted simultaneously over the same circuit.
2. That a closed circuit and a single main battery may be employed.
3. That communication in both directions is established without the necessity of using special induction coils.
4. And that—as the circuit is never broken—a spark arrester becomes unnecessary.

It has long been known that when a permanent magnet is caused to approach the pole of an electro-magnet a current of electricity is induced in the coils of the latter, and that when it is made to recede, a current of opposite polarity to the first appears upon the wire. When, therefore, a permanent magnet is caused to *vibrate* in front of the pole of an electro-magnet, an undulatory current of electricity is induced in the coils of the electro-magnet, the undulations of which correspond in rate of succession to the vibration of the magnets, in polarity to the direction of its motion, and in intensity to the amplitude of its vibration. That the difference between an undulatory and intermittent current may be more clearly understood, I shall describe the condition of the electrical current when THE ATTEMPT IS MADE TO TRANSMIT two musical notes [of different pitch are] simultaneously [transmitted along the same wire] FIRST UPON THE ONE PLAN AND THEN UPON THE OTHER. Let the interval between the two sounds be a major third. Then their rates of vibration are in the ratio of 4:5.

Now, when the intermittent current is used the circuit is made and broken four times by one TRANSMITTING instrument in the same time that five makes and breaks are caused by the other [instrument].

A and B (Figs. I., II. and III.) represent the intermittent currents produced; four impulses of A being made in the same time as five impulses of B. *c, c, c,* &c., show where and for how long a time the circuit is made, and *d, d, d,* &c., indicate the duration of the makes and breaks of the circuit.

The line A + B shows the total effect upon the current when the transmitting instruments for A and B are caused [to] simultaneously to make and break the same circuit. The resultant effect depends very much upon the duration of the make relative to the break. In Fig. I. the rate is 1:4; in Fig. II. as 1:2; and in Fig. III. the makes and breaks are of equal duration.

The combined effect of A + B (Fig. III.) is very nearly equivalent to a continuous current.

When many transmitting instruments of different [pitch] RATES OF VIBRATION are simultaneously making and breaking the same circuit, the current upon the main line [loses altogether its intermittent character and] becomes for all practical purposes continuous.

[But now] Next consider the effect when an undulatory current is employed.

Electrical undulations induced by the vibration of a body capable of inductive action can be represented graphically without error by the same sinusoidal curve which expresses the vibration of the inducing body itself, and the effect of its vibration upon the air.

For, as stated above, the rate of oscillation in the electrical current corresponds to the rate of vibration of the inducing body, that is, to the pitch of the sound produced; the intensity of the current varies with the amplitude of the vibration, that is, with the loudness of the sound; and the polarity of the current corresponds to the direction of the motion of the vibrating body, that is to the condensations and rarefactions of the air produced by the vibration. Hence the sinusoidal curve A or B (Fig. IV.) represents graphically the electrical undulations induced in a circuit by the vibration of a body capable of inductive action.

The horizontal line (*a, d, b, f*) represents the zero of current; the elevation (*c, c, c*) indicates impulses of positive electricity; the depressions (*e, e, e*) show impulses of negative electricity; the vertical distance (*cd* or *ef*) of any [point on] PORTION OF the curve from the zero line expresses the intensity of the positive and negative impulse at the part OBSERVED; and the horizontal distance (*a, a*) indicates the duration of the electrical oscillation.

The vibrations represented by the sinusoidal curves A and B (Fig. IV.) are in the ratio aforesaid, of 4:5,—that is, four oscillations of A are made in the same time as five oscillations of B.

The combined effect of A and B, when induced simultaneously on the same circuit, is expressed by the curve A + B (Fig. IV.), which is the algebraic sum of the sinusoidal curves A and B. This curve (A + B) also indicates the actual motion of the air when the two musical notes considered are sounded simultaneously.

Thus, when electrical undulations of different rates are simultaneously induced in the same circuit, an effect is produced exactly analogous to that occasioned in the air by the vibration of the inducing bodies.

Hence the coexistence [of] UPON a telegraphic circuit of electrical vibrations of different pitch is manifest,—not by the obliteration of the vibratory character of the current, but by peculiarities in the shapes of the electrical undulations; or, in other words, by the peculiarities in the shapes of the curves which represent those undulations.

[Undulatory currents of electricity may be produced in many other ways than that described above, but all the methods depend for effect upon the vibration or motion of bodies capable of inductive action.]

THERE ARE MANY [other] WAYS OF PRODUCING UNDULATORY CURRENTS OF ELECTRICITY, BUT ALL OF THEM DEPEND FOR EFFECT UPON THE VIBRATION OR MOTION OF BODIES CAPABLE OF INDUCTIVE ACTION. A FEW OF THE METHODS THAT MAY BE EMPLOYED I SHALL HERE SPECIFY.

[I shall specify a few of the methods that may be used to produce the effect.]

When a wire through which a continuous current of electricity is passing is caused to vibrate in the neighborhood of another wire, an undulatory current of electricity is induced in the latter.

When a cylinder upon which are arranged bar-magnets is made to rotate in front of the pole of an electro-magnet an undulatory current is induced in the coils of the electro-magnet.

Undulations may also be caused in a continuous voltaic current by the vibration or motion of bodies capable of inductive action, or by the vibration of the conducting wire itself in the neighborhood of such bodies.

[Author's Note: The variable resistance clause found in the Patent Office copy was inserted at this point.]

In illustration of the method of creating electrical undulations, I shall show and describe one form of apparatus for producing the effect.

I prefer to employ for this purpose an electro-magnet (A, Fig. 5) having a coil upon only one of its legs (6). A steel spring armature (c) is firmly clamped by one extremity to the uncovered leg (d) of the magnet, and its free end is allowed to project above the pole of the covered leg. The armature (c) can be set in vibration in a variety of ways (one of which is by wind), and in vibrating yields a musical note of a certain definite pitch.

When the instrument (A) is placed in a voltaic circuit (*g, b, e, f, g*) the armature (*c*) becomes magnetic, and the polarity of its free end is opposed to that of the magnet underneath. So long as the armature (*c*) remains at rest no effect is produced upon the voltaic current, but the moment it is set in vibration to produce its musical note a powerful inductive action takes place, and electrical undulations traverse the circuit (*g, b, e, f, g*). The vibratory current passing through the coils of the distant electro-magnet (*f*) causes vibration in its armature (*h*), when the armatures (*c, h*) of the two instruments (A, I) are normally in unison with one another; but the armature (*h*) is unaffected by the passage of the undulatory current when the pitches of the two instruments (A, I) are different [from one another].

A number of instruments may be placed upon a telegraphic circuit (as in Fig. VI.). When the armature of any one of the instruments is set in vibration all the other instruments on the circuit which are in unison with it respond, but those which have normally a different rate of vibration remain silent. Thus if A (Fig. VI.) is set in vibration, the armatures of A1 and A2 will vibrate also, but all the others on the circuit will remain still. So also if B1 is caused to emit its musical note the instruments B, B2 respond. They continue sounding so long as the mechanical vibration of B1 is continued, but become silent the moment its motion stops. The duration of the sound may be made to signify the dot or dash of the Morse alphabet, and thus a telegraphic dispatch can be transmitted by alternately interrupting and renewing the sound.

When two or more instruments of different pitch are simultaneously caused to vibrate, all the instruments of corresponding pitches upon the circuit are set in vibration, each responding to that one only of the Transmitting Instruments with which it is in unison. Thus the signals of A are repeated by A1 and A2, but by no other instruments upon the circuit; the signals of B2 by B and B1, and the signals of C1 by C and C2, whether A, B2, and C1 are successively or simultaneously set in vibration.

Hence by these instruments, two or more telegraphic signals or messages may be sent simultaneously over the same circuit without interfering with one another.

I desire here to remark that there are many other uses to which these instruments may be put, such as the simultaneous transmission of musical notes differing in *loudness* as well as in pitch, and the telegraphic transmission of noises or sounds of any kind.

When the armature *c* (Fig. V.) is mechanically set in vibration the armature *h* responds not only in pitch but in loudness. Thus when *c* vibrates with little amplitude, a very soft musical note proceeds from *h*, and when *c* vibrates forcibly the amplitude of vibration of *h* is considerably increased, and sound becomes louder. So if A and B (Fig. VI.) are sounded simultaneously (A loudly and B softly) the instruments A1, A2 repeat loudly the signals of A, and the instruments B1, B2 repeat gently those of B.

One of the ways in which the armature (*c*) Fig. VI. may be set in vibration has been stated above to be by wind. Another mode is shown [by] IN Fig. VII. [which] WHEREBY motion can be imparted to the armature by means of the human voice, or by the tones of a musical instrument.

The armature *c* (Fig. VII.) is fastened loosely by one extremity to the uncovered pole (*d*) of the electro-magnet (*b*), and its other extremity is attached to the centre of a stretched membrane (*a*). A cone A is used to converge sound vibrations upon the membrane. When a loud sound is uttered in the cone the membrane (*a*) is set in vibration; the armature *c* is forced to partake of the motion, and thus electrical undulations are caused upon the circuit E, *b*, *e*, *f*, *g*. These undulations are similar in *form* to the air vibrations caused by the sound,—that is, they [are] CAN BE represented graphically by similar curves. The undulatory current passing through the electro-magnet (*f*) influences [the] ITS armature (*h*) to copy the motions [s] of the armature (*c*). A similar sound to that uttered into A is then heard to proceed from L.

[Having described my invention, what I claim and desire to secure by Letters Patent is as follows:

1. A system of telegraphy in which the receiver is set in vibration by the employment of [vibratory or] undulatory currents of electricity.
2. The method of creating an undulatory current of electricity by the vibration of a permanent magnet or other body capable of inductive action.

3. The method of inducing undulations in a continuous voltaic circuit by the vibration or motion of bodies capable of inductive action.
4. The method of and apparatus for transmitting vocal or other sounds telegraphically by [inducing in a continuous voltaic circuit] CAUSING ELECTRICAL undulations similar in form to the vibration of the air accompanying said vocal or other sounds the whole for operation substantially as HEREIN shown and described.]

In this specification the three words "oscillation," "vibration" and "undulation" are used synonymously.

By the term "body capable of inductive action" I mean a body which, when in motion, produces dynamical electricity. I include in the category of bodies capable of inductive action, brass, copper and other metals, as well as iron and steel.

Having described my invention, what I claim and desire to secure by Letters Patent is as follows:

1. A system of telegraphy in which the receiver is set in vibration by the employment of undulatory currents of electricity.
2. The combination of a permanent magnet, or other body capable of inductive action with a closed circuit, so that the vibration of the one shall produce electrical undulations in the other or in itself.

   Thus (*a.*) The permanent magnet or other body capable of inductive action may be set in vibration in the neighborhood of the conducting wire forming the circuit.

   (*b.*) The conducting wire may be set in vibration in the neighborhood of the permanent magnet.

   (*c.*) The conducting wire and the permanent magnet may both simultaneously be set in vibration in each other's neighborhood; and in any or all of these cases electrical undulations will be produced upon the circuit.
3. The method of producing undulations in a continuous voltaic circuit by the vibration or motion of bodies capable of inductive action, or by the vibration or motion of the conducting wire itself in the neighborhood of such bodies.
4. The method of and apparatus for transmitting vocal or other sounds telegraphically, as herein described, by causing electrical undulations similar in form to the vibrations of the air accompanying the said vocal or other sounds.

Selected Bibliography

Aitken, William, *Who Invented the Telephone?* Blackie and Son, London and Glasgow, 1939.
American Bell Telephone Company, *Deposition of Alexander Graham Bell*, 1908.
American National Biography, Oxford University Press, NY, 1998.
Atkinson, E., *Elementary Treatise on Physics*, Wm. Wood & Co. New York, 1886.
Bell correspondence (AGB), Bell Collection, Library of Congress, Washington, D.C.
Bell Telephone Laboratories, *A History of Engineering and Science in the Bell System: The Early Years* (1875–1925). 1975.
Bell-Gray correspondence from the Gray Collection, Archive Center, National Museum of American History.
Brooks, John, *Telephone: The First Hundred Years*, Harper & Row, New York, 1975.
Bruce, Robert V., *Alexander Graham Bell and the Conquest of Solitude*, Cornell University Press, Ithaca and London, 1990.
Carhart, Henry S., *Primary Batteries*, Allyn and Bacon, Boston, 1891.
Casson, Herbert N., *The History of the Telephone*, A. C. McClurg, Chicago, 1910.
Coe, Lewis, *The Telegraph*, McFarland, Jefferson, N.C., 1990.
_____, *The Telephone and Its Several Inventors*, McFarland, Jefferson, N.C., 1995.
Compton's Picture Encyclopedia, F.E. Compton & Co., Chicago, 1933.
Conot, Robert, *Thomas A. Edison: A Streak of Luck*, Da Capo, New York, 1979.
Costain, Thomas B., *The Cord of Steel: The Story of the Invention of the Telephone*, Doubleday, New York, 1960.
Count Du Moncel, *The Telephone, the Microphone and the Phonograph*, Harper & Brothers, New York, 1879.
Deschanel, A. Privat *Elementary Treatise on Natural Philosophy*, D. Appleton, New York, 1878.

Dictionary of American Biography, Scribner, NY, 1961.

Dowd Case 1878–79, *Bell Telephone Co. et al. v. Peter A. Dowd*, A. Mudge, Boston, 1880.

Encyclopædia Britannica, 11th ed., The Encyclopædia Britannica Co., NY, 1910.

Encyclopædia Britannica, 14th ed., The Encyclopædia Britannica Co., NY, 1929.

Francis Jehl, *Menlo Park Reminiscences*, Edison Institute, Dearborn, Mich., 1938.

Gray, Elisha, *Nature's Miracles*, Baker & Taylor, New York, 1900.

Guide to the Practice of the Patent Office, Washington, D.C., 1853.

Harder, Warren J., *Daniel Drawbaugh: The Edison of the Cumberland Valley*, University of Pennsylvania Press, 1960.

Harlow, Alvin F., *Old Wires and New Waves*, D. Appleton-Century, New York, 1936.

Jones, Alexander, *Historical Sketch of the Electric Telegraph*, Putnam, New York, 1852.

Mackenzie, Catherine D., *Alexander Graham Bell*, Grosset & Dunlap, New York, 1928.

Patent Office internal memos and correspondence from patent folder No. 174,465 (Alexander Bell), National Archives, College Park, MD.

Petition of Elisha Gray to Re-open Interference Hearings, 1888.

Prescott, George B., *Bell's Electric Speaking Telephone,* D. Appleton, New York, 1884.

_____, *History, Theory and Practice of the Electric Telegraph*, Ticknor and Fields, Boston, 1866.

_____, *The Speaking Telephone, Electric Light,* D. Appleton, New York, 1879.

Rhodes, Frederick L., *The Beginnings of Telegraphy*, Harper, New York, 1929.

Smith, George D., *The Anatomy of a Business Strategy*, Johns Hopkins University Press, Baltimore, 1985.

The Telephone Cases (126US1–584), United States Supreme Court Records, vol. 126, 1888.

Thompson, Silvanus P., *Philipp Reis: Inventor of the Telephone*, E. & F. N. Spon, London, 1883.

Tosiello, R. J., *The Birth and Early Years of the Bell Telephone System, 1876–1880*, Boston University, 1971, Ph.D. dissertation.

Universal Standard Encyclopedia, Unicorn Publishers, Inc., NY, 1954.

Watson, Thomas A., *Exploring Life*, D. Appleton, New York, 1926.

Wilson, Mitchell, *American Science and Invention*, Bonanza, New York, 1960.

Index